David Osher   Kevin Dwyer   Stephanie Jackson

SAFE, SUPPORTIVE
AND
Successful
SCHOOLS

Step by Step

American Institutes for Research

D1511511

SOPRIS WEST EDUCATIONAL SERVICES
A CAMBIUM LEARNING COMPANY

BOSTON • NEW YORK • LONGMONT, CO

PowerPoint is a registered trademark of Microsoft Corporation. PeaceBuilders is a registered trademark of Heartsprings, Inc. ThinkTime is a registered trademark of Cyprus Group, Inc.

DISCLAIMER—This publication was prepared by the Center for Effective Collaboration and Practice (CECP) at the American Institutes for Research with support from the Substance Abuse and Mental Health Services Administration (SAMHSA), U.S. Department of Health and Human Services (HHS) under Contract No. 00M00825001D, Denise Middlebrook, Government Project Officer. The content of the publication does not necessarily reflect the views or policies of SAMHSA or HHS.

ISBN 1-57035-918-0

Copy editing by Patricia Brown
Design and layout by Sherri Rowe
Proofreading by Francelia Sevin

Cover Photo—Salinas, California elementary, middle, and high school students courtesy of the Salinas Safe Schools/Healthy Students Initiative.

07 06 05 04   6 5 4

Printed in the United States of America

Published and Distributed by

SOPRIS
WEST
EDUCATIONAL SERVICES

4093 Specialty Place ▲ Longmont, Colorado 80504 ▲ (303) 651-2829
www.**sopriswest**.com

Acknowledgments

Many individuals contributed to the development of *Safe, Supportive, and Successful Schools Step by Step*. Some provided materials, others reviewed drafts, still others provided input through participation in focus groups or workshops. Their names are listed in Appendix C. Listed here are the school communities that hosted the authors and provided the vignettes used throughout the guide:

> California's San Juan Unified School District; the Cleveland Elementary School in Tampa, Florida; the East Baltimore Mental Health Partnership School-Based Program in Baltimore, Maryland; the Jesse Keen Elementary School in Lakeland, Florida; the Lafourche Parish, Louisiana, Schools; the Los Angeles, California, Unified School District; the Fern Ridge Middle School, Elmira, Oregon; the Pinion Unified School District, Arizona; the Salinas, California, School District's Safe Schools/Healthy Students grantee; the Westside Alternative School in Hays, Kansas; and the Westerly, Rhode Island, Public School District.

Contents

List of Figures

List of Sidebars

List of Sidebars (continued)

List of Sidebars (continued)

Foreword

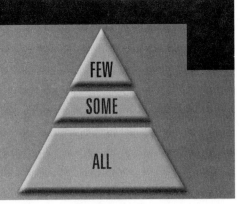

Dear Colleague:

All schools want to

▲ improve academic achievement;

▲ improve school safety and discipline;

▲ decrease referrals for special education and improve special education outcomes;

▲ increase teacher and parent satisfaction;

▲ improve attendance and graduation rates;

▲ decrease class disruptions, office referrals, suspensions, and expulsions;

▲ decrease bullying and fighting;

▲ reduce administrative burdens; and

▲ employ time, space, and financial resources efficiently.

These goals are not incompatible. Rather, research and practical experience demonstrate that they are mutually reinforcing. Improved instruction, for example, can reduce school discipline and safety issues; improved school discipline and safety can reduce administrative burdens and allow teachers to spend more time raising academic performance.

Achieving these goals requires strategic, coordinated efforts within the entire school community. Success can be achieved when a community builds on its own local assets and works (together) to overcome barriers that thwart continuous school improvement.

Safe, Supportive, and Successful Schools Step by Step is a guide with enhanced, in-depth material to help plan and fund three levels of school improvement: (1) schoolwide programs for all students; (2) early interventions for students who have behavioral problems; and (3) intensive interventions for students who experience significant emotional and behavioral disorders. It elaborates on and extends two important resources that were sent to every school in the country, in part to respond to the growing number of multiple shootings in U.S. schools: *Early Warning, Timely Response: A Guide to Safe Schools* (Dwyer, Osher, and Warger, 1998) and *Safeguarding Our Children: An Action Guide* (Dwyer and Osher, 2000). These research-based, practical guides were developed by the U.S. Departments of Education (Office of Safe and Drug-Free Schools [OSDFS] and Office of Special Education Programs [OSEP]) and Justice (Office of Juvenile Justice and Delinquency Prevention [OJJDP]), in collaboration with the U.S. Department of Health and Human Services (National Institute of Mental Health [NIMH] and the Substance Abuse and Mental Health Services Administration [SAMHSA]) and 26 national associations. The guides reflect more than three years of sustained work.

Step by Step reflects the continued collaboration of these associations along with the guidance and support of federal officials connected with the Safe Schools/Healthy Students Initiative, especially Anne Mathews-Younes and Denise Middlebrook (SAMHSA), Kellie J. Dressler and Betty Chemers (U.S. Department of Justice), Eve K. Moscicki (NIMH), and Bill Modzeleski (OSDFS). *Step by Step* also reflects the generous assistance of many of our colleagues at our two organizations as well as the guidance and support of the many researchers, developers, educators, technical assistance providers, family members, youth, and organizations listed in Appendix C.[1]

We hope the research-based, practical suggestions offered in *Step by Step* will support a caring climate within your school community to meet the academic, intellectual, social, and emotional needs of *all* students. Doing so not only makes schools safer, but also raises student achievement, enhances the value of all educational services, and strengthens our nation.

David Osher, Ph.D.
Managing Research Scientist
American Institutes for Research
Washington, DC

Susan Gorin, CAE
Executive Director
National Association of
    School Psychologists
Bethesda, Maryland

---

[1] The development of *Step by Step* and the accompanying video, *Promising Practices for Safe and Effective Schools*, was supported, in part, by the Center for Mental Health Services, Substance Abuse and Mental Health Services Administration, U.S. Department of Health and Human Services. The views and opinions reflected in this document do not necessarily represent those of CMHS, SAMSHA, or HHS.

The Resource Kit

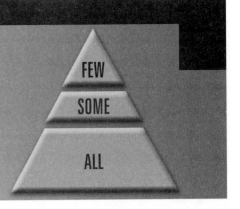

Safe, Supportive, and Successful Schools Step by Step is the fourth component of a Safe Schools/Healthy Students Resource Kit that will help you design, coordinate, and evaluate your efforts to improve your school. The type and intensity of the problems you are facing will determine how much of this Kit you use and where you should begin. Make sure that your school's approach to improvement is comprehensive and meets the needs of all students. The first three components of the Resource Kit are on the companion CD-ROM.

▲ *Early Warning, Timely Response: A Guide to Safe Schools* (*Early Warning Guide*)

This research-based guide helps you identify and reach out to troubled students. It presents a brief summary of the research on the characteristics of a responsive, caring school; the early and imminent warning signs of violence (what to look for); the foundation for schoolwide, early, and intensive interventions (what to do); and school crisis response planning. The *Early Warning Guide* should be given to policymakers and community groups to help them think of strategic responses to youth violence. This guide is available in English and Spanish.

▲ *Safeguarding Our Children: An Action Guide* (*Action Guide*)

The *Action Guide* is an elaboration of the *Early Warning Guide*. It suggests what can be done in each of the three levels of intervention (schoolwide prevention, early intervention, and intensive intervention) to address the mental health needs of students and improve school discipline and safety. It emphasizes creating and implementing a comprehensive plan. This guide is available in English and Spanish.

▲ *Promising Practices for Safe and Effective Schools* (Video)

This award-winning video, available from the Center for Mental Health Services, Substance Abuse and Mental Health Services Administration (2002), shows theory-based research put into practice in three school districts. These examples illustrate strategic planning, school-community collaboration and training, and school-based leadership with consultation support. Use this video with your team to buttress your safe and supportive proposal to policymakers and community stakeholders, including parents. This video can be viewed as a whole or in parts that are organized around the three levels of prevention.

▲ *Safe, Supportive, and Successful Schools Step by Step*

This extension of the *Action Guide* will help you build a schoolwide team, assess your school's strengths and needs, and translate your vision into a comprehensive action plan. A detailed discussion of financial resources suggests ways to build on existing assets and to explore untapped funding and technical assistance for implementing your comprehensive plan. Abstracts of more than 30 evidence-based programs can help you select the strategies you wish to use to meet your school improvement needs. Tools, such as surveys, that you can copy or adapt are included in Appendix B. Frequent references to Web sites or other publications provide additional resources and examples of what can be done. It is ringbound to facilitate copying.

Each component can stand alone and serve its specific purpose. Used together, they support comprehensive school improvement efforts that address academic achievement, student mental health, and school safety.

Introduction

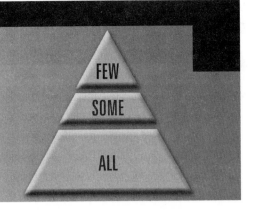

The strategies described in *Safe, Supportive, and Successful Schools Step by Step* are based on decades of research and practical experience. Examples from schools that have applied these principles and strategies, including the schools highlighted in the video *Promising Practices for Safe and Effective Schools*, show how these strategies can help you meet ambitious goals.

Research and practice suggest that sustainable school improvement requires at least 14 ingredients:

1. **Address the needs of your school and community.** Take into account school and community characteristics throughout the change process.

2. **Be strategic and comprehensive.** Develop a strategic plan for addressing the needs of all children through universal prevention, early intervention, and individualized intensive intervention.

3. **Be systemic.** Effective change aligns improvements in key areas simultaneously: curriculum, teaching and teacher training, school culture and environment, and student support systems.

4. **Don't do it alone.** Serving all students requires interagency collaboration.

5. **Involve the entire community.** Include all stakeholders—students, families, and policymakers—in program development, monitoring, and evaluation.

6. **Understand and manage change.** Change is not easy. A well-trained team, representative of and accessible to all stakeholders and skilled in cooperative problem solving, should manage change.

7. **Build a learning organization.** School staff should have the time and support to discuss, plan, and reflect on new approaches.

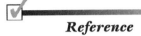

Reference

Schools that satisfy students' basic needs benefit from students' improved attitudes and behavior. In addition to helping their students learn and grow—academically, socially, emotionally, and ethically—these schools also help the students avoid problems ranging from emotional distress to drug use to violence. Promoting academic achievement is of course an essential goal for schools, but outcomes in these other areas are also critical. The mission of our public schools historically has been—and still needs to be—to prepare students to be productive citizens, to cultivate moral character, and to promote an appreciation of the arts and culture. Emphasizing the importance of learning along with other qualities that are essential to our society, such as fairness, concern for others, and responsibility, helps promote a shared commitment to the school's goals, establishes common ground, and shapes the norms that govern daily interactions.

Every Student Learning: Safe and Supportive Schools. (2001). Learning First Alliance.

8. **Value and address diversity.** Programs and practices should be sensitive to and respectful of the culturally and linguistically diverse students, families, and staff who are part of the school and community.

9. **Assess and address strengths and challenges.** Build on existing resources and leverage what is working in your school and community. Some interventions, however, may not work or may not have sufficient power to realize your goals. Others may even have harmful effects. Improve or eliminate ineffective programs; identify and eliminate harmful programs and practices.

10. **Employ evidence-based programs and practices.** Select evidence-based programs and practices that fit your school. Be an intelligent consumer. Make sure the programs and practices have produced results under conditions that suggest that they will work in your own school and community.

11. **Build capacity.** Develop and fund organizational capacity, including necessary staff and training to ensure that programs can be implemented effectively.

12. **Employ data.** Collect and assess data on an ongoing basis and use the data to refine programs and procedures. Whenever possible, employ or refine existing data sources.

13. **Evaluate outcomes.** Evaluate programs to ensure that they produce sufficiently positive outcomes.

14. **Focus on the long haul.** Change is neither easy nor cheap. Don't focus on symbolic actions and quick fixes. Develop an organizational capacity to maintain and sustain school improvement.

School improvement is challenging. Change must be more than cosmetic. For students to reap the benefits of your efforts, school-community members and other stakeholders must ensure that improvements are deep and systemic, changing both the structure and culture of the school.

Change is a journey, not a blueprint (Fullan & Miles, 1992). The group that manages change must expect and be able to deal with risk, fiscal stress, uncertainty, and other discomforts associated with adopting new practices and abandoning less effective, but familiar approaches (Annie E. Casey Foundation, 1995). Evidence from years of slow and laborious efforts to improve schools demonstrates that progress is limited by inadequate resources and value conflicts (Fullan & Miles, 1992).

The good news is that educators in states as different as California, Maryland, Oregon, Kansas, Hawaii, and Florida have applied these 14 ingredients to strengthen their schools. The results? Students learn more, feel safer and more connected to the school, and are less likely to engage in violent or destructive behavior. The payoff, according to students, families, teachers and staff, administrators, and researchers who have evaluated the changes, far outweighs the initial effort.

What made these comprehensive and evidence-based approaches and schools successful? How did these educators begin? What does it take to improve the behavior, connectedness, and academic performance of all students? What would it take to institute these valuable improvements in your school community? Effective change efforts include

- ▲ teams that create a common vision and keep that vision in focus throughout the process;
- ▲ strong administrative leaders;
- ▲ staff buy-in and understanding of, and support for, school improvement;
- ▲ a long-term perspective that provides for unanticipated challenges and delayed dividends;
- ▲ capacity-building efforts that include extensive training and support;
- ▲ the efficient use of human and material resources; and
- ▲ a culture and a structure that help all members of the school community succeed.

A Web-Based Resource on Implementing Change

Raising Student Achievement: An Internet Resource Guide for Redesigning Low-Performing Schools, American Federation of Teachers (http://www.aft.org/edissues/rsa/guide/).

This web-based guide has a useful section on implementing change, which includes a valuable checklist that you can adapt to help you plan (*AFT Suggested Checklist for Ensuring a Fair and Effective School Improvement Process*). This guide also contains information on five promising programs (including one that is described in the *Action Guide* and three that are described in Appendix A), six promising schoolwide programs, and eleven effective reading and English language programs.

The Three-Level Approach to Intervention

This triangle models the comprehensive three-level approach that is the most efficient and cost-effective way to improve school discipline, safety, and academic achievement. It was presented in *Safeguarding Our Children: An Action Guide* (Dwyer & Osher, 2000) as the framework for building a comprehensive plan. Chapters 3, 4, and 5 of this guide elaborate on what can be done at each level.

Build a Schoolwide Foundation

Support positive discipline, academic success, and mental and emotional wellness by providing a caring school environment to which all students, families, and staff feel connected; teaching appropriate behaviors and problem-solving skills; and offering positive behavioral support and appropriate academic instruction.

Provide Intensive Interventions for a Few Children

Intervene Early for Some Children

Build a Schoolwide Foundation for All Children

Intervene Early

Create services and supports that eliminate or address risk factors and build or strengthen protective factors for students at risk for severe academic or behavioral difficulties.

Provide Intensive Interventions

Provide coordinated, comprehensive, intensive, sustained, culturally appropriate, child- and family-focused services and supports.

Definitions

Although this book employs language that most audiences understand, the following words and phrases may be new to you or may have new connotations when used here.

▲ *School community* refers to all the members of a school, including families.

▲ *School improvement* refers to change efforts that link safe and supportive schools with school reform efforts that focus on academic achievement.

▲ *Behavioral skills* refer to the numerous behaviors required for developmental learning and social adjustment.

▲ *Social-emotional development and learning* include social skills and competencies, problem solving and reflective thinking, and coping skills (Elias et al., 1997).

▲ *Strategies and interventions* refer to specific activities that address a skill or problem. Strategies and interventions include curriculum, management, therapeutic techniques, and other techniques that may serve a specific student or group of students.

▲ *Program* refers to a set of strategies and interventions that are integrated in a planned fashion for implementation. Effective programs address the development of the whole child with an emphasis on learning and behavior.

▲ *Cultural competence* is a set of congruent behaviors, attitudes, and policies that come together in a system, in a school or an agency, or among professionals to enable that system, school, or agency or those professionals to work effectively in cross-cultural situations (Cross, Bazron, Dennis, & Isaacs, 1989; Isaacs & Benjamin, 1991). Operationally defined, cultural competence is the integration and transformation of knowledge about individuals and groups of people into specific standards, policies, practices, and attitudes. Cultural competence increases the quality of services, thereby producing better outcomes (Sims, King, & Osher, 1998).

▲ *Universal interventions* are districtwide, schoolwide, and classroomwide interventions for every child in the district, school, or class. Universal interventions prevent risk factors from developing or intensifying and build a foundation that supports the efficiency and effectiveness of early and intensive interventions.

▲ *Early intervention* refers to services and supports that eliminate or address risk factors and build or strengthen protective factors for students who are at risk for severe academic or behavioral difficulties.

▲ *Intensive interventions* provide coordinated, comprehensive, intensive, sustained, culturally appropriate, child- and family-focused services and supports for students with intense levels of need.

Getting Started

CHAPTER

1

FEW
SOME
ALL

School improvement begins with

▲ building a schoolwide team;

▲ translating a vision into action through planning; and

▲ evaluating and monitoring results.

Building the Schoolwide Team

Significant school improvement cannot be started by one person, nor does such change begin out of the blue. A core group of leaders usually begins the change, which is designed to address or expand on the existing school system mission or vision statements. The *Action Guide* recommends that "schools employ two teams: one that addresses overall school performance [the **schoolwide team**] and another that addresses individual student problems [the **student support team**]. These teams are integral to creating and implementing a comprehensive plan for safe and effective schools. A minimum of three people—the principal, a teacher, and a mental health specialist—should serve on both teams" (*Action Guide*, p. 5).

This section describes how to secure support, form a schoolwide team, and allocate team member functions. (Chapter 4 provides information on the student support team and how to link it with the schoolwide team.) The Schoolwide Team Checklist (see Appendix B) can guide your development of the schoolwide team.

Securing Approval and Administrative Buy-In

Your team will not be effective unless you have both the authority to act and the support of your school community. Authority comes from the district central office and principal and must be formally granted. Support comes from the school community and must be earned by the way your team acts and the way it involves the members of the school community.

Cross Reference

This chapter expands on Chapter 5 of *Safeguarding Our Children: An Action Guide* (pp. 41–48), which outlines how to build a schoolwide team that can develop and implement a comprehensive plan.

The district mandate that authorizes your work is important. It should include a commitment to long-term planning and implementation. The district leadership should understand (1) the three-level approach to prevention and intervention; (2) the nature of the multiyear commitment; (3) the time it will take to produce outcomes; (4) the active role it must take to secure success; and (5) the resources, monitoring, and evaluation needed for change. The mandate should include central office awareness that ensuring school safety and addressing student mental health are not add-ons but are essential elements of any school improvement process. Your superintendent should publicly support the mandate.

Asking for this commitment, however, requires understanding the demands that superintendents and principals face, such as tight budgets, fiscal accountability, and the pressure to improve test scores for all students under the federal No Child Left Behind (NCLB) legislation (see the Sidebar, No Child Left Behind). This legislation, which requires that schools demonstrate adequate yearly progress for all students, places pressure on superintendents and principals (as well as on school boards, school staff, children, and parents) to improve academic outcomes as measured by test scores, attendance, grade retention, and graduation rates.

No Child Left Behind

The U.S. Department of Education summarizes the key provisions of the No Child Left Behind legislation as follows:

- States create their own standards for what a child should know and learn for all grades. Standards must be developed in math and reading immediately. Standards must also be developed for science by the 2005–06 school year.

- With standards in place, states must test every student's progress toward those standards by using tests that are aligned with the standards. Beginning in the 2002–03 school year, all schools must administer tests in each of three grade spans: grades 3–5, grades 6–9, and grades 10–12. Beginning in the 2005–06 school year, tests must be administered every year in grades 3 through 8 in math and reading. Beginning in the 2007–08 school year, science achievement must also be tested.

- Each state, school district, and school will be expected to make adequate yearly progress toward meeting state standards. This progress will be measured for all students by sorting test results for students who are economically disadvantaged, are from racial or ethnic minority groups, have disabilities, or have limited English proficiency.

- School and district performance will be publicly reported in district and state report cards. Individual school results will be on the district report cards.

- If the district or school continually fails to make adequate progress toward the standards, then it will be held accountable.

This and other information, including fact sheets, a glossary, resources, key dates, and frequently asked questions about No Child Left Behind, can be found at http://www.nclb.gov/next/overview/index.html.

The many state, federal, and national calls for school reform that link student support and academic achievement can help you secure buy-in from school administrators. You may find particularly helpful *Every Child Learning: Safe and Supportive Schools* (2001), which was produced by the Learning First Alliance, a policymaking alliance of 12 national associations that includes key stakeholders in your school (e.g., principals, teachers, and parents). This document, which identifies the link between supportive schools and improved academic performance, calls for two teams (a schoolwide team and a student support team), and employs the three-level approach to intervention (see the Introduction). Similarly, the Policymakers Partnership (PMP) at the National Association of State Directors of Special Education (NASDSE) and the National Association of State Mental Health Program Directors (NASMHPD) employed the same prevention, early intervention, and intensive intervention framework for its vision of school mental health (PMP, 2002). Along with the *Action Guide*, documents such as these may help remove any doubt about the validity of your efforts.

Gaining School Community Buy-In

For the school community, buy-in is not a one-time event. Rather, it is an ongoing process in which members of the school community increase their level of understanding and investment in school improvement. Daniel Yankelovitch (1991) suggests that an individual may be at one of eight stages of readiness to support change in a sustained manner. In regard to school improvement, members of the school community may be at the following stages:

Stage 1: Lack of Awareness. Being unaware of the importance of school safety, supportive environments, student mental health, and their links to academic improvement.

Stage 2: Awareness. Becoming aware of the importance of school safety, supportive environments, student mental health, and their links to academic improvement.

Stage 3: Urgency. Feeling a need to address these matters.

Stage 4: Looking for Answers. Searching for ways to improve school safety, student support, student mental health, and academic performance.

Stage 5: Resistance. Resisting possible solutions.

Stage 6: Weighing the Choices. Rationally weighing choices and balancing the pros and cons of different choices.

Reference

Undertaking a comprehensive reform program will involve everyone in learning new content, new skills, and new ways of thinking about education and the classroom. Therefore, each person involved in the reform must be regarded as a learner. This includes teachers, principals, administrators, parents, and students.

Voices From the Field: Success in School Reform. (2000). Hord, Sparks, Brown, Havens, & Calderon. http://www.sedl.org/csrd/voices/3.html#1

Stage 7: Intellectual Acceptance. Changing their attitude so that they are ready to support the school improvement effort.

Stage 8: Full Acceptance. Implementing comprehensive school improvement.

When providing information to school community members, take into account their different levels of readiness and help them reach greater levels of understanding and commitment regarding academic improvement, supportive environments, student mental health, and school safety. Developing a communication strategy that employs different approaches for individuals at different levels of awareness may involve making presentations or circulating newsletters that focus on aspects of school reform. PowerPoint® presentations can be obtained from the Center for Effective Collaboration and Practice Web site (www.air.org/cecp). Videos such as *Promising Practices for Safe and Effective Schools* can be used to provoke discussion. The *Early Warning Guide* and the *Action Guide* also contain information that can help secure initial buy-in.

Informal discussions and structured focus groups can identify concerns, individuals who will champion change, and those who might resist it. Although "idea champions" should be seen as allies and recruited (Sparks, 1993), it is just as important to elicit the questions and concerns of those who will not be your initial adopters. Your communication efforts and implementation strategies should be sure to address them. For example, a focus group discussion may uncover fears that must be addressed: "We did something like this before and I didn't receive any support" or "I just mastered Second Step, so why should I try something else?" You can also use focus groups to identify indicators, which, when achieved, will help secure commitment. Although some initial adopters will fully commit to change on the basis of the information that you present, other individuals will give their full commitment only when they see results. Change often takes time; therefore, it is important to identify indicators that can secure the buy-in of some individuals and sustain the commitment of others.

Forming the Schoolwide Team

Working With Existing Teams

Do not reinvent the wheel. Does an existing schoolwide improvement team already address issues such as academic performance and family involvement? Creating a parallel team could cause confusion, competition, and fragmentation. Piggybacking on and expanding the existing team could be the solution. If so, your first task may be to gain administrative authorization, as well as

---

Tips for Using Focus Groups

The following suggestions may be helpful in conducting focus groups (Bradley & West, 1994; Krueger, 1988):

– Decide whom to include (allow for viewpoints from a variety of personnel).

– Limit the number of participants (five–seven people).

– Set a time limit and adhere to it (60–90 minutes).

– Prepare questions ahead of time (approximately five questions).

– Use open-ended questions.

– Begin with a statement of purpose and rules for participation.

– Take notes and tape-record the focus groups.

– End with a summary and thank the participants.

buy-in from the existing team, for integrating student support, student mental health, and school safety into reform efforts. Emphasizing the benefits of such integration may help.

For example, ACHIEVE developers have demonstrated to existing schoolwide teams that instructional time actually increases when ACHIEVE concepts are integrated into the school's action plans. Similarly, they demonstrated to principals that ACHIEVE reduces the rate of discipline referrals. (For more about ACHIEVE, see Appendix A and the *Action Guide*, page 13.)

Expanding an existing team's mission may require time and resources. When teams already exist, they have formal and informal operational rules as well as personal interests in what they do. New roles and membership require trust and acceptance, which takes time. The principal and the mental health professional (school counselor, psychologist, social worker) may already be members of the existing schoolwide team, which may ease the integration.

If your school has several teams, each focused on different academic, behavioral, and community components, consider combining those that have overlapping functions related to student support, schoolwide management, and change. Multiple teams can cause management and coordination problems. Multiple symptom-focused teams consume valuable staff leadership resources, time, and finances.

Establishing a New Schoolwide Team

If you need to *establish* a schoolwide team where none exists, determine how to recruit members, maintain their involvement, and sustain their effectiveness. For example, will teachers and support staff elect their representatives? Will all interested community groups become members? Most important, how will the new team leadership be determined?

Selecting Team Members

Your team must have five assets—knowledge, perspective, technical skills, personal skills, and legitimacy. Team members should be knowledgeable about your school community, and at least some of them should be knowledgeable about school safety, student support, mental health, and school reform. Team members should reflect the variety of stakeholder perspectives that make up your school community. Some team members should have the technical skills, such as data analysis, that are necessary to carry out your team's tasks. All team members should possess the interpersonal skills important for smooth functioning. Finally, they should be individuals who are respected by the school community for who they are and how they were selected.

Team Selection Criteria

Remember that your work should help streamline existing school improvement efforts. When determining the makeup of the schoolwide team, consider members of existing school improvement teams as well as other members of the school community whose participation will consolidate the team's authority and extend buy-in. Use the following questions as selection criteria:

▲ **Political.** Some team members should give you access to political support among important constituencies. Who are the sanctioned leaders, the power brokers, the persuaders, the dealmakers, the peacemakers, and the gatekeepers for support and resources? These individuals can be parents, professionals, teachers, staff (their organizational representatives), students, administrators, clergy, and so on. Are there power brokers who can serve as "guardian angels" to help you get needed political or financial support?

▲ **Administrative.** Some team members should provide access to administrative support. Who is fully in charge? Who controls the resources? Whose job is it to see that the school performs well? Who is on the line if the change fails? Who officially gets recognized for the positive results of the change? Who pushes the paper? What red tape should be applied? Who develops policies that facilitate or block the change?

▲ **Symbolic.** Some team members should help legitimate the team in the eyes of school and community members. Who is important, given the culture, history, and traditions of your school and community? Who is most likely to garner support for your team and the plan?

▲ **Functional.** Some team members should be selected to provide specialized knowledge and skill. Who understands prevention, behavior, and psychosocial development? Who has skills in teaming, facilitation, and evaluation? Who is an effective communicator?

Representatives of the Broader Community

Ensure that your team includes community representatives. To find them, look first at the individuals and organizations that already partner with your school, but do not stop there. Identify those organizations or agencies (e.g., community mental health agencies) whose involvement will be necessary to implement part or all of the prevention or intervention plan. In larger schools, existing partnerships may not be obvious, so you may need to survey staff to identify all organizations that work with the school. Examples of organizations that may have links with the school are the following:

- ▲ Youth centers (e.g., Boys and Girls Clubs)
- ▲ Community-based organizations
- ▲ County recreation programs
- ▲ Universities and colleges
- ▲ Businesses
- ▲ Religious leaders and organizations
- ▲ Community mental health and health agencies
- ▲ Social service agencies
- ▲ Community police, juvenile justice, and the courts
- ▲ Parent groups, including PTAs, PTOs, and other groups
- ▲ Civil rights and advocacy organizations
- ▲ Foundations

The Community Linkages Assessment Form (see Appendix B) frames questions that can help schools identify and solidify community linkages.

Linking Schools and Law Enforcement

Relationships between schools and law enforcement agencies have existed for many years. Some urban school districts have had their own school police forces for decades (e.g., Los Angeles). However, assigning officers to schools on a full- or part-time basis is still new in many parts of the country. Police officers linked to schools frequently work closely with pupil services and mental health personnel. The training and responsibilities of officers vary. Some districts fill the role of security guard with individuals who lack certified law enforcement training and have no arrest authority. Other districts employ trained and certified law officers who have complete arrest powers and who perform broad roles in planning and implementing school safety.

A School Resource Officer (SRO) is a certified law enforcement officer who is permanently assigned to a school or a set of schools. An SRO is specifically trained to perform the roles of law enforcement officer and law-related counselor and teacher. SROs should be incorporated into the schoolwide planning process to ensure that services are coordinated.

SROs are not certified or licensed counselors, however, and do not carry out the functions of counselors or other school mental health professionals. As law-related counselors, SROs inform students about the juvenile court system and give advice and guidance on its processes and services. SROs can suggest programs that are available, refer students to the Student Support Team, and help students access the school's counseling services. When necessary, and in coordination with school staff, they can help students and parents negotiate the justice system by pointing out options and connecting students to appropriate law-related services in the community. SROs can also enhance teachers' efforts to educate students about laws, rights, and responsibilities. Further, like any adult member of the school staff, they are available to mentor students and to build a caring and supportive school climate.

When student safety is a concern, SROs (or other law enforcement personnel assigned or related to the school) should be involved in team problem solving to plan effective interventions for individual students as well as schoolwide prevention interventions. At times, police may be required to assist in determining the imminent danger of a student threat or suspected violation of school safety laws. SROs and police are experts in examining the physical aspects of school safety, in facilitating gang abatement, and in assessing community-related safety data, including such issues as illicit alcohol and drug trafficking. As team members, they can help assess needs and secure data for evaluating individualized and schoolwide interventions.

For resources about SROs, go to the Web site of the Center for the Prevention of School Violence (http://www.ncsu.edu/cpsv/index.htm).

Underrepresented Persons and Groups

It is essential to include people who will be affected by the comprehensive plan, such as underrepresented community groups who are all too frequently left out (e.g., families of students with emotional and behavioral problems, individuals with disabilities, and members of ethnic communities). Examine your community's characteristics and make sure that these groups are included—and that their effective participation is supported. Support may include scheduling meetings at convenient times, providing transportation, and addressing child-care needs.

Determining Team Size and Delineating Team Member Functions

Team size can be critical—neither too small nor too large. A team of five or fewer members may make each member's tasks overwhelming. Further, its "inclusiveness" may be challenged. A team of 20 or more may be cumbersome, and it may spend more time on process and information sharing than on action.

Team members can have multiple and changeable functions and responsibilities. The team responsibilities included in the following sidebar are suggested functions that team members may take on.

Attending to Logistics, Roles, and Responsibilities

Logistics matter. Team operations are neither smooth nor automatic. Your team's division of labor should attend to the day-to-day assignments that keep the team working efficiently. Ensure that key roles are performed and that logistical tasks are addressed. For example, does everyone know who schedules the meetings, secures the resources for the team, records and disseminates the minutes, and makes progress reports to the superintendent?

An effective schoolwide team has a minimum of eight roles and responsibilities as defined as follows. In some cases, individuals may take on multiple roles. In other cases, multiple individuals may share the same role. In still other cases, school administrative staff (e.g., a secretary) may be assigned to perform support tasks for the team. In all cases, team members should be clear about who has (or shares) responsibility for particular tasks.

Formal Leadership. Teams require leadership. The principal may function (or sanction someone to serve) as the team leader to ensure authority for planning, budgeting, and delegating responsibilities.

Operational Leadership. Day-to-day scheduling of meetings and planning are necessary and may be delegated to an assistant

Team Responsibilities

The District Administrator

- Gives authorization to proceed and the long-term commitment to resources for the team.
- Applies existing policies, secures waivers to facilitate planning and implementation, and develops needed policies and interagency agreements for program implementation.
- Advocates and champions the planning, vision, goals, and implementation process.

The Principal

- Sanctions the makeup of the team.
- Sanctions the selection of a team coordinator responsible for developing and managing the schoolwide team.
- Facilitates resource support for team logistics.
- Actively participates as a member of the team.
- Reinforces the integration of school safety and psychosocial wellness into the mission of school reform.
- Helps secure school-community buy-in for the necessary changes.
- Models commitment to the four components of a schoolwide foundation.
- Supports staff development, engagement, and problem solving regarding prevention and intervention.

School Mental Health and Other Pupil Personnel Staff

- Provide expert information about mental health as it relates to learning, motivation, and psychosocial development.
- Provide information about the comprehensive model of prevention and early and intensive intervention.
- Help identify effective strategies and interventions that address behavior.
- Actively participate in and facilitate the team process.
- Seek and support the inclusion of agency partners.
- Assist in designing the school-community assessment of risk and protective factors and in identifying strategies and interventions.
- Assist in designing the evaluation process.

Teachers

- Actively participate in identifying problems and strengths and in developing realistic objectives for school improvement.
- Help identify academic and other instructional strategies for all children.
- Facilitate support for the vision statement and its implementation among school peers.
- Support the development (or expansion) of teacher dialogue and collaboration.

Families

- Actively participate in assessing problems and strengths and in identifying meaningful goals and objectives.
- Provide expert information about family perspectives and family involvement.
- Provide assistance in ensuring that approaches are culturally competent.
- Facilitate support for school improvement among families and community.

Community Members

- Participate fully in the team planning.
- Identify community resources and provide information about the links between school and community problems.
- Secure community buy-in for goals and objectives.
- Assist in developing and securing cooperative agreements and coordinated services required to implement the plan.
- Help ensure the cultural competence of the plan.

Assessing Mental Health Support

Schools frequently have limited resources. Every school does not have a full-time, on-site mental health service professional. However, most have access to certified professional school counselors, psychologists, and social workers who can support the planning effort. School counselors, psychologists, and social workers maintain professional standards for practice that include skills in system organization, systems consultation, and teaming as well as prevention and behavioral and mental health intervention. Although desirable, these professionals do not need to be school-based to provide their expertise to the team. For details on skills and standards, see http://www.nasponline.org, http://www.naswdc.org, and http://www.schoolcounselor.org and the *Handbook of School Mental Health* (Weist, Evans, & Lever, 2003).

leader. That individual or someone else should maintain an accurate list of team members, including their names, contact information (phone, e-mail), and defined roles or responsibilities.

Facilitation. Someone should facilitate meetings. Facilitation requires specific skills and knowledge of team decision making. Sometimes a second person may work with the facilitator to observe the group processes and recommend adjustments or process changes to ensure that everybody is participating comfortably.

Data Analysis. At least one team member should be comfortable with analyzing data and helping others understand the meaning of the data collected.

Recording. A team secretary or recorder should keep a record of all decisions.

Archiving. Either the secretary or another person should be responsible for collecting and archiving the team's materials.

Work Groups. Ways should be established for members to work together or with other members of the school community between formal meetings to prepare or follow up on agenda items.

Communication and Liaison. One or more team members should serve as the ongoing liaison with the administration, teachers, support staff, paraprofessionals, and community groups to report frequently on progress. This will maintain authority and buy-in.

Translating a Vision Into Action Through Planning

Developing a comprehensive plan creates another opportunity to involve the school community, solidify buy-in, and publicize the change effort. This is also an opportunity to further link the goals of safe, supportive, and successful schools with the other goals of school reform. The plan should

▲ be well thought out;

▲ be comprehensive;

▲ be flexible, but with clear direction for school improvement that can guide the schoolwide team as well as all other participants in the school improvement effort;

▲ contain goals, objectives, benchmarks, indicators, standards for interpreting the indicators, and a time frame;

▲ be based on an objective assessment of needs and assets;

▲ build on the school's past accomplishments and align with other school planning efforts;

▲ specify the actions steps that will be taken to realize each goal;

Note

For an excellent resource for team development, see *Implementing School-wide Programs: An Idea Book on Planning, Volume 1.* (1998). Washington, DC: U.S. Department of Education. Available at http://www.ed.gov/pubs/Idea_Planning/index.html. For a free copy, call 877-4ED-PUBS.

Note

For federal and state planning resources, see "Federal Resources That Can Support Safe School Planning" (p. 39) and "State-Supported Safe School Programs and Related Activities That Can Support School Improvement" (p. 40).

- ▲ address logistics;
- ▲ identify and allocate resources;
- ▲ provide for staff development and support;
- ▲ define monitoring and evaluation processes; and
- ▲ allow for revision that is based on the experience of the school community as well as on monitoring and evaluation data.

Definitions of Planning Terms

The planning process is most efficient and effective when all members of the team understand and agree on what the following terms mean:

- Goals are the meaningful outcomes that you seek through school improvement. Goals can include better reading or math scores, greater parent satisfaction, or fewer suspensions. Goals should be realistic and stated in a clear manner. They should be relatively few in number (e.g., five to ten), stated unambiguously, and measurable.

- Objectives are the steps that will lead to each goal. Objectives, for example, could include new teaching approaches to improve test results (e.g., classwide peer tutoring), strategies for engaging parents to improve parent satisfaction, and positive behavioral supports to reduce the number of suspensions.

- Benchmarks are milestones that you will employ to track your progress (e.g., all third-grade teachers will be trained in classwide peer tutoring by March 15).

- Indicators are the measures you will employ to identify needs as well as demonstrate success (e.g., reading scores on a statewide test).

- Standards are the level of success that you will employ to measure progress (e.g., students will read at grade level).

- Time frame specifies the time line for accomplishing the goals, indicating how much progress you hope to achieve at specified benchmarks (e.g., after one, two, and three years).

The planning process has three phases: *developing a vision, conducting a needs assessment,* and *developing a comprehensive action plan.* Visions drive planning; they provide a picture of what the change process should accomplish. Needs assessment prioritizes school improvement, grounds planning in needs and resources, and identifies solutions for addressing the needs. Action planning constructs a foundation for implementing solutions in a coordinated manner that can be monitored, evaluated, and sustained.

Six Resources for Comprehensive Planning

Many organizations and centers can help you implement a comprehensive approach to safe, supportive, and successful schools. You will find the following six resources particularly useful in planning and implementing a three-level approach.

The **Center for Substance Abuse Prevention** (CSAP) of the Substance Abuse and Mental Health Services Administration has produced an efficient web-based resource for prevention planning. This Decision Support System follows a logic model that is consistent with the planning process described in this resource kit. It has seven elements: assess your needs, develop capacity, select programs, implement programs, evaluate programs, write reports, and get training and support. The CSAP Decision Support System can be found at http://www.preventiondss.org.

The **Center for School Mental Health** (http://smhp.psych.ucla.edu) produces a newsletter, *Addressing Barriers to Learning*. Its Web site offers many useful tools, reports, and guides, such as a gateway to web-based resources on a set of surveys to map what a school has and what it needs; a policymaker's guide to restructuring; a guide to the enabling component (supports that address barriers to learning); a report on how to restructure student services; a guide to policies that can address barriers to learning; and guides on school-community partnerships. The Web site also includes a gateway to web-based resources in five areas: a comprehensive focus on mental health in schools; barriers to learning and development; positive social/emotional development and prevention of psychosocial/mental health problems; children's psychosocial problems; and severe mental disorders in children.

The **Center for Effective Collaboration and Practice** (www.air.org/cecp) has a Web site that includes resources for implementing the *Early Warning* and *Action Guides* (including Spanish and reference-based versions of the guide) and briefs for families on evidenced-based practices. It offers more than 20 monographs on the areas covered by the guide, including cultural competency, functional behavioral assessment, collaboration with families, wrap-around planning, and systems of care. Users have access to a web-based conference that features interviews with experts and presentations on prevention, early intervention, intensive treatments, collabo-

ration with families, and cultural competency. This Web site, which also has a search engine, provides links to resources in education, mental health, juvenile justice, child welfare, youth development, and violence prevention.

The **Learning First Alliance** is a permanent partnership of 12 leading educational associations that have come together to improve student learning in America's public elementary and secondary schools.

– American Association of Colleges for Teacher Education
– American Association of School Administrators
– American Federation of Teachers
– Association for Supervision and Curriculum Development
– Council of Chief State School Officers
– Education Commission of the States
– National Association of Elementary School Principals
– National Association of Secondary School Principals
– National Association of State Boards of Education
– National School Boards Association
– National Education Association
– The National PTA

The Alliance has three major goals:

1. Ensure that high academic expectations are held for all students

2. Ensure a safe and supportive place of learning for all students

3. Engage parents and other community members in helping students achieve high academic expectations

The Learning First Alliance Web site (http://www.learningfirst.org) provides links to these organizations as well as access to documents that the Alliance has produced: *Ensuring the Success of Children & Youth in American Communities*; *Every Child Learning: Safe and Supportive Schools*; *Every Child Reading: A Professional Development Guide*; *Every Child Mathematically Proficient: An Action Plan*; and *Every Child Reading: An Action Plan*. In addition, the Web site includes a summary of resources related to the implementation of the No Child Left Behind legislation, such as links to relevant parts of its members' Web sites as well as to other Web sites that provide resources that can be employed to implement the legislation.

→

(continued) *Six Resources for Comprehensive Planning*

The U.S. Department of Education's Safe and Drug-Free Schools Program (SDFS) has undertaken several initiatives to enhance schools' understanding of what works and to expand the inventory of effective programs. Among these initiatives is the **National Coordinator Training and Technical Assistance Center for Drug Prevention and School Safety Program Coordinators** (http://www.k12coordinator.org). This initiative was reauthorized in 2002 to recruit, hire, and train individuals to serve as drug prevention and school safety coordinators in elementary, middle, and high schools with significant drug and school safety problems.

The Center provides training and ongoing support to help coordinators fulfill the responsibilities of their new jobs. These responsibilities include the following:

– Assessing drug- and violence-related problems among students

– Identifying research-based drug- and violence-prevention strategies appropriate for K–12 schools

– Working with parents and students to obtain information about effective programs and strategies and encouraging their participation in development and implementation

– Developing and implementing programs that are developmentally appropriate

– Assisting schools to adopt the most successful strategies, including training teachers and staff, in accordance with the No Child Left Behind Act of 2001

– Assisting schools in developing and improving school safety plans that address responses to and recovery from large-scale disasters

– Facilitating evaluation of prevention activities and use of findings to modify programs, as needed

– Identifying additional funding sources for prevention activities

– Providing feedback to state education agencies on programs and activities that have proven to be successful in reducing drug use and violent behavior

– Coordinating with student and employee assistance programs

– Linking to other educational resources, such as Title I Compensatory Education Funds, to deliver programs and strategies that serve to create safer, more orderly schools

– Developing measurable goals and objectives and reporting annually on progress toward meeting those goals and objectives

The following archived events are currently available:

– Promoting Prevention through School-Community Partnerships

– Using Existing Data in Your Needs Assessment

– Identifying Prevention Priorities and Strategies for Success

– Selecting Research-Based Prevention Programs for Your School

– Implementing Research-Based Prevention Programs in Schools

– Sustaining Your Prevention Initiative

– Linking Violence and Substance Abuse Prevention to Academic Success

– Crisis Response: Creating Safe Schools

– Middle School Coordinators as Change Agents

The **Northwest Regional Educational Laboratory** has developed Safe and Secure: Guides to Creating Safer Schools. These eight guides are available on the Center for Effective Collaboration and Practice Web site (www.air.org/cecp).

Guide 1: Creating Schoolwide Prevention and Intervention Strategies by Jeffrey Sprague and Hill Walker

Guide 2: School Policies and Legal Issues Supporting Safe Schools by Kirk Bailey

Guide 3: Implementing Ongoing Staff Development to Enhance Safe Schools by Steve Kimberling and Cyril Wantland

Guide 4: Ensuring Quality School Facilities and Security Technologies by Tod Schneider

Guide 5: Fostering School-Law Enforcement Partnerships by Anne Atkinson

Guide 6: Instituting School-Based Links With Mental Health and Social Service Agencies by David Osher and Sandra Keenan

Guide 7: Fostering School, Family, and Community Involvement by Howard Adelman and Linda Taylor

Guide 8: Acquiring and Utilizing Resources to Enhance and Sustain a Safe Learning Environment by Mary Grenz Jalloh and Kathleen Schmalz

Note

A vision statement is symbolic and functional. Functionality can be realized through the use of "by" statements. For example, if one line of the vision statement reads, "Our school will be a safe learning environment for all learners," it should also include, *"by using effective academic instruction and positive strategies to support appropriate school behavior."* A vision statement must be part of the overall change process. Vision statements can be expansive and definitive or narrow and provisional. For example, the vision statement may specifically reflect what the school hopes to achieve through the adoption of research-based practices, and the principles that will guide their efforts. Alternatively, the vision statement may be broad as well as provisional during the early stages so that it can be refined as members of the school community experience the school improvement effort.

Change Forces: Probing the Depth of Educational Reform. (1993). Fullan.

Developing a Vision for School Improvement

For change efforts to be successful, every member of the school community should share the same image of change. The school-wide team should work with the school community to develop a common vision of how to respond to problems. A common vision focuses your planning and evaluation efforts. The vision should build on the existing school mission—particularly if it has been developed recently—or the team can initiate a process for creating and sharing a vision of what the school and classrooms will look like once the school improvement is implemented.

Your team should identify the best ways to get input from all stakeholders—teachers, staff, administrators, parents, students, and community members. Holding focus groups and creating a task force to solicit written or oral feedback are effective approaches. It is important to ensure the participation of staff with diverse points of view and culturally and linguistically diverse community members.

Once the vision is developed, you should publicize it. Schoolwide team communications and school newsletters should continually refer to the vision. The vision statement should be displayed prominently throughout the school building. Teams working on a school improvement program can use the Vision Statement Checklist (see Appendix B) to craft a meaningful vision statement.

Conducting a Needs Assessment

Usually, you will need several months to identify your school's needs and level of readiness for school improvement. Ideally, the schoolwide team will conduct its assessment over one school term. The team will want to schedule routine meetings to review findings and discuss results.

There is no one way to work through the assessment. However, you should develop a working plan for each component that fits your team members' preferred styles. Read through this guide first, then determine a work plan for gathering the needed information. You can use the Needs Assessment Checklist (see Appendix B) to coordinate the needs assessment. In some cases, team members should interview other members of the school community; in other cases, they need to review documents or conduct studies.

The assessment should involve three steps:

1. **Identify the problem and available resources.** Define the problem as you and other schoolwide team members perceive it, agree on the scope and severity of the problem, and identify resources available to address the problem. Example: The number of office referrals for inappropriate behavior is increasing.

2. **Analyze the problem. Dissect the possible causes and effects of the problem.** Who, what, where, when, and why questions should be answered at this point. Example: No schoolwide discipline plan is in place, and teachers have inconsistent expectations for behavior.

3. **Identify the solutions.** Look at your needs, look at your resources (e.g., current activities that support your goals), and develop solutions to address key needs. Example: Convene a group that includes school staff and family members to design a discipline plan for the entire school.

A good place to start in implementing a needs assessment are the 13 "Characteristics of a School That Is Safe and Responsive to All Children" from the *Early Warning Guide* (pp. 3–5). Framed as operational questions, the needs assessment should determine whether your school

▲ focuses on academic achievement;

▲ involves families in meaningful ways;

▲ has effective links to the community;

▲ emphasizes and develops positive relationships among and between students and staff;

▲ discusses safety issues openly;

The Importance of a Needs Assessment

Conducting a needs assessment helps planners focus better on school-wide issues and link goals with hard data. Central Elementary School in Henderson County, Kentucky, rose from among the state's lowest ranking schools to become an institution repeatedly recognized and rewarded for its academic progress. Principal Diane Embry reported that during the needs assessment, "We planned ahead and used data to make our decisions. We were no longer acting only on our perceptions of how the students were doing."

Implementing Schoolwide Programs: An Idea Book on Planning, Volume 1. (1998). U.S. Department of Education.

Reference

Indicator data on safety and the school's social environment should be gathered from teachers, other school staff, students, and parents. These same stakeholders should be involved in analyzing the data and in the decisionmaking that follows. Schools routinely keep some types of data, such as the number of discipline referrals per unit time. Other information (for example, levels of school connectedness) may need to be gathered through periodic surveys of students, teachers, and others. Gathered data should then be systematically reported and used to identify and guide needed improvements.

Every Child Learning: Safe and Supportive Schools. (2001). Learning First Alliance.

Tips for Using Questionnaires

The National Resource Center for Safe Schools, www.safetyzone.org, has developed school and community variables to consider when assessing your school-community needs:

– Inform respondents of the purpose of the questionnaire.

– Provide incentives to encourage respondents to complete the questionnaire (pens, stickers, tea bags, or candy).

– Tell respondents approximately how long it will take to complete the questionnaire.

– Be brief.

– Use questions that may be answered by circling a number on a four-point scale.

– List topics for communication and ask respondents to number them in order of their need for information.

– Allow anonymous responses.

– Thank respondents individually or as a group.

(See the Needs Assessment Checklist in Appendix B for an adapted example of these variables.)

▲ treats all students with equal respect;

▲ has created ways for students to share their concerns;

▲ helps students feel safe expressing their feelings;

▲ has in place a system for referring children who are suspected of being abused or neglected;

▲ offers extended day programs for children;

▲ promotes good citizenship and character and socially responsible behavior;

▲ identifies problems and assesses progress toward solutions; and

▲ supports students in making transitions, including the transition to adult life and the workplace.

Some schools assess these characteristics by categorizing each as a strength or a weakness. Other schools use four categories: exemplary practices in place; adequate practices in place; needs improvement; none.

It is important to determine what types of evidence to use. You can assess some characteristics by reviewing existing data. For example, academic achievement can be measured by reviewing schoolwide test scores or other assessment data. Other characteristics, however, may be more difficult to measure with existing data (e.g., "treating each child with equal respect"). Questionnaires and focus groups can be used. Instruments to anonymously survey climate and safety are available (e.g., see California School Climate and Safety Survey in Appendix B).

Assessing characteristics without substantial objective data may overlook some problems and focus the school's or district's resources on inadequate interventions. Data can illuminate unidentified challenges and resources. For example, you may use a questionnaire to determine how safe children feel; similarly, you may interview teachers to determine their training needs.

The schoolwide team may do this work itself, or it may create a workgroup or workgroups, perhaps led by team members. Workgroups spread the work and involve other members of the school community. How you proceed depends on how much time team members have as well as on the availability of other school-community members.

Sometimes in-depth analyses are needed for some or all of the characteristics. For an example of an in-depth analysis, see the following sidebar, Assessing Family Involvement.

Assessing Family Involvement

(1) Assess Strengths and Needs

- **Inclusiveness.** What are the existing programs and outreach efforts? Do all families feel welcome? Are families included in planning and developing school goals and objectives? Are all parents made to feel welcome when they enter the school? Do activities respect and address the language, culture, and background of families? Have specific outreach strategies been developed to increase participation? Does the school have a parent information center?

- **Positive Focus.** Do families have opportunities to contribute in positive ways—not just in problem or crisis situations? Do activities encourage families to contribute their expertise, strengths, and talents to the school?

- **Communication.** Are parents getting the message (in their native languages) that their involvement is important to the school community and to their individual children? Is staff systematically encouraging family involvement through positive communication?

- **Training.** What training is provided to staff for facilitating family involvement? Have faculty and staff received training in how to best understand and work with family members? Does the school seek out parents to support staff training and cultural competence activities?

- **Support.** Are family support systems in place? Are supports and resources available for family and staff involvement? Do families have easy access to information that meets their children's individual needs?

(2) Analyze the Problem

Using your data from the strengths and needs discussion, determine what aspects of the school require improvement. Identify the barriers to realizing your goals as well as the assets that will help you reach them.

(3) Develop Solutions

- **Involve families** in school activities that **respect their cultures**, languages, and needs. Write invitations, announcements, and programs that all parents understand. Encourage families and teachers to work together to translate correspondence. Use nontechnical, jargon-free language in all communication with families. Try a variety of outreach strategies to contact parents, and let them know that their participation is important. Provide translators when necessary—do not use children in this role.

- **Expand your concept of families** to include grandparents, aunts and uncles, foster parents, and other kinship care providers.

- **Involve families in decision making.** Actively seek the advice of family members when making decisions that affect the school and their children. Actively involve parents in identifying appropriate school behaviors and setting school rules. Involve families in designing the school discipline code. Include norms and values that reinforce positive school behaviors, which families can reinforce at home.

- **Make sure to schedule activities at a convenient time for families.** Help families with transportation, and set up a place for childcare while parents attend meetings or programs.

- **Provide families with respectful training and support** to help them address the social, behavioral, and developmental needs of their children. Implement programs such as the Strengthening Families Program (see Appendix A).

- **Teach families** how they can help their children learn at home. Help families set up a "homework center" or let them know whom to call if their children are having problems. When necessary, provide families with additional support so they can help their children succeed.

- **Train faculty** to communicate with families and to increase family involvement.

- **Provide meaningful opportunities for parents to become involved.** Brainstorm with families ways for parents to contribute to the learning community. Recognize that families have many strengths and talents they can share. Encourage parents from different cultural backgrounds to discuss their customs with a class. Look for parents who may be able to tutor a child or organize a field trip. Be mindful of parents who may not be able to visit the school regularly and offer them opportunities to be involved from home (e.g., making tracking materials, making phone calls). Recognize that as children get older, they may no longer feel comfortable having their parents volunteer in their classrooms. Seek out parents to be ambassadors to your school's interventions and programs. Let parents know that when they volunteer anywhere in the school, they are making a valuable contribution to the school community.

References

The decade-long effort to improve student performance has rightly focused on setting academic standards, measuring progress toward meeting those standards, and providing the resources and supports to make attainment of high standards possible. The same approach, which has been effective in advancing academic achievement, should be used to foster safe and supportive school communities that enable students to thrive socially, psychologically, ethically, and academically.

Every Child Learning: Safe and Supportive Schools. (2001). Learning First Alliance.

For a continuous improvement process to be effective, districts and schools should ensure that teams are adequately trained in data analysis, including basic techniques for summarizing and interpreting data and identifying trends. The training should be provided to teams before they set goals, select indicators and measures, and collect data relevant to achievement, climate, and safety standards.

Every Child Learning: Safe and Supportive Schools. (2001). Learning First Alliance.

Collecting and Using Data

Every school collects data that can be used to identify strengths and to determine problems. Many of these data sets are computerized, within each school and across the school system. Information about students' grades, attendance, mobility, reading and math achievement scores, discipline data, class size, faculty qualifications, and staff satisfaction or turnover should be available. Vandalism data are frequently available, as are the number of grade retentions and the rates and patterns of special education referral. Identify what data your school and district collect. Determine which data will contribute to your needs assessment, planning, monitoring, and evaluation efforts.

Look at community data also. Community mapping is one technique that schools have found helpful. Consider the number of children in poverty, the number who are uninsured, the rates of mental health referrals, the number of students on probation, and community crime statistics. These data can be gathered through interagency cooperation.

At Oregon's Fern Ridge Elementary, staff collected data about behavior incidents: where and when they occur, types of behavior, and victims. Using these data as part of a Positive Behavioral Interventions and Supports (PBIS), intervention (see Appendix A), they gained a clear picture of the extent of their school safety problems and were able to prioritize and address their concerns. Ongoing data collection and analysis keep the school staff informed about whether their interventions are working.

Obtaining some information may require surveys or questionnaires. Sometimes you may focus on problems, for example, bullying rates, student drug use, and gang activity. In other cases, you may want to focus on assets, for example, examining the number of children participating in extracurricular activities, community service, and peer mentoring. Other matters worthy of study are the number and type of community services available, the level of available technology and its use, and the numbers of business partnerships.

Developing a Comprehensive Action Plan

Once the team (or workgroup) has developed a vision and conducted the needs assessment, it is time to identify and prioritize areas for improvement, establish goals for these priority areas, determine measurable objectives that will lead to the realization of the goals, identify solutions, and develop a plan for implementing the solutions. For each area, the team (or a workgroup) should

▲   develop goals and objectives;

- ▲ select the type of data that will be used as indicators of improvement;
- ▲ ratify solutions identified during the needs assessment;
- ▲ identify what is needed to implement the solutions;
- ▲ specify a time line for implementing solutions;
- ▲ determine benchmarks to mark progress in implementing solutions;
- ▲ determine the standards that will be employed to evaluate efforts and measure success; and
- ▲ develop a plan for implementing each solution and coordinating the implementation of all solutions.

Using Indicators

Indicators are identifiable evidence of something you want to measure (e.g., academic achievement). Indicators are often employed in school and district planning. For example, Illinois' learning standards employ indicators (Illinois State Board of Education, 1997). Figure 1 (next page) provides an example of an indicator that relates to school behavior. If your school or district has already identified indicators and collects them on a school- or districtwide basis, start with them and determine whether they provide information that is sufficient, useful, and credible to stakeholders. If they are satisfactory, employ them. If you find a gap in some area because they are not useful, credible, or sufficient, determine what other data you can collect to improve their utility and credibility.

Identifying Solutions

All solutions are not the same. Some can be brainstormed, planned out, and implemented—if the planning group has the appropriate skills. For example, teaching positive behavior can be addressed when the team includes a mental health specialist or special educator who understands positive behavioral support or when useful information is easily available (e.g., the *Addressing Student Problem Behavior* series and videos from the Center for Effective Collaboration and Practice). Other solutions may require more research. The team or workgroup will want to explore alternative programs and the evidence of their effectiveness. The Program Evaluation Criteria (*Action Guide*, p. 8), the Program Briefs in Appendix A, and the electronic links to the programs that can be found in the web-based versions of the *Action Guide* http://www.air.org/cecp/guide/actionguide.htm are good places to begin this research.

The process of identifying a solution may be as important as the solution itself. The process should build on, as well as align with and strengthen, existing resources. For example, your school may already have one or more groups that are studying a particular

The Danger of Impatience and Superficial Solutions

Reforms . . . fail because our attempts to solve problems are frequently superficial. Superficial solutions, introduced quickly in an atmosphere of crisis, normally make matters worse.

Getting Reform Right: What Works and What Doesn't. (1992). Fullan & Miles.

(This important and influential work is available online at http://www.enc.org/professional/learn/change/resources/readings/document.shtm?input=A.)

area. These may vary from formal whole-faculty study groups supported by districts to informal study groups that individuals have set up. Whenever possible, use these resources. If they do not exist, build them and support them by granting released time, using substitute teachers, and reorganizing the school schedule to support planning (see the sidebar Creating an Atmosphere and Context for Change).

FIGURE 1: *Example of State-Defined Indicators*

– Promote and enhance health and well-being through the use of effective communication and decision-making skills.

– Learning Standard 24A: Demonstrate procedures for communicating in positive ways, resolving differences and preventing conflict.

Skill	Sample Indicators
24.A.1a Differentiate between positive and negative behaviors (e.g., waiting your turn vs. pushing in line, honesty vs. lying, informing for safety vs. tattling).	Practice positive behavior (e.g., waiting your turn). Identify negative behavior (e.g., pushing in line).
24.A.1b Identify positive verbal and nonverbal communication skills (e.g., body language, manners, listening).	Identify basic communication skills. Practice listening skills. Identify when to ask for adult help.

From Illinois Learning Standards. Illinois State Board of Education. http://www.isbe.state.il.us/ils/

Creating an Atmosphere and a Context for Change

Because the very basis of school reform involves changing the way the school and its staff approach their work, it is vital to create an environment where change is encouraged. A safe and collaborative atmosphere that promotes a sense of trust is essential as school staff must be comfortable learning new skills and taking the risks necessary to put these new skills into practice.

Undertaking a comprehensive reform program involves everyone in learning new content, new skills, and new ways of thinking about education and the classroom. Therefore, each person involved in the reform must be regarded as a learner. This includes teachers, principals, administrators, parents, and students.

By sharing responsibility and re-casting everyone involved as learners, you help create a critically important context for change. As this new learning environment is created and nurtured, new instructional practices, organizational structures, and content will be introduced. It is important to reflect on each change and note which practices are working well and which are not meeting with success.

Voices from the Field: Successes in School Reform. (2000).
Hord, Sparks, Brown, Havens, & Calderon.

Comprehensive Plan to Reduce Classroom Disruptions

Using indicators, a team selects and identifies action interventions and the resources necessary to implement those interventions. The team then directs both the implementation of the intervention and the monitoring and evaluation of the results.

Indicator. During the school year, your 440-student elementary school had 233 student referrals to the principal for classroom disruptions and inappropriate behaviors, from refusal to follow rules to in-class fighting.

Goal. (Included in the School Improvement Program) Increase instructional time 20 minutes a day by reducing classroom disruptions by 80 percent within three years.

Analysis

Year 1 Objective. Reduce classroom disruptions by 30 percent.

Action Intervention 1. School psychologists (trained in "stop-and-think" and positive behavioral classroom supports) provide weeklong training to *all* staff on these interventions, followed by modeling and coaching and ongoing teacher consultation within classrooms at all grade levels.

Action Intervention 2. The school counselor develops, manages, and monitors a school conflict resolution program for students whose disruption involves student-to-student conflicts.

Action Intervention 3. Pupil services and mental health agency staff give teachers a range of individually focused functional behavior plans as well as student support team evaluations, and they support or provide selected and intensive interventions to students with moderate to severe emotional, academic, or conduct problems.

Implementation. The principal appoints a workgroup to incorporate the school behavioral program into instruction and classroom procedures beginning in September. The principal ensures that teachers and staff are supported with resources and professional consultation. Program fidelity measures are determined and communicated.

Time Frame, Benchmarks, and Evaluation

- Office referrals for classroom disruptions will be monitored monthly and evaluated each semester, using the previous year's monthly and semester data.

- Length of instructional time/day (pre/post) will be sampled monthly.

- Process data will be recorded to determine resource use and level of adoption of intervention.

- Fidelity measures will be evaluated.

- In a comprehensive plan, it is essential to address those situations that require early and intensive interventions to ensure that the total student population, including students having problems, is included. Some situations may require specific classroom modifications, staff interventions, and treatment resulting in multiple action interventions and evaluations to accomplish the goal of an 80 percent reduction in classroom disruptions.

Workgroups or teams may identify individual solutions; it is important to avoid quick and symbolic fixes. The team should select theoretically sound, evidence-based solutions that have been evaluated in real-world settings. The team should anticipate and plan to address any negative consequences of introducing the proposed solution (e.g., anticipate how students will initially react to a new approach to discipline).

Planning for Implementation

Develop a strategic plan that builds on your school's resources and aligns your strategies and interventions to achieve your goals and objectives. School improvement efforts are often limited by diffuse objectives, lack of technical skills, or insufficient resources. Effective implementation requires

▲ clear objectives;

▲ specific action steps to implement these objectives;

▲ realistic time lines;

▲ effective communication with the school community;

▲ staff development and support; and

▲ attention to logistics.

See Goals and Objectives Checklist (in Appendix B).

The action planning process should ensure that *objectives* are sufficiently clear. Once they are, the team should develop clear *action steps* and *realistic time lines* for implementing each solution (e.g., train all staff in classwide peer tutoring, roll out peer tutoring one grade per term starting with first grade, coach teachers and students in peer tutoring). See the preceding sidebar Comprehensive Plan to Reduce Classroom Disruptions for an example of how to use indicators as a basis for planning action interventions.

Effective communication is needed to address the concerns that individuals have during the stages of implementing school improvements. The Concerns-Based Adoption Model (CBAM; Loucks-Horsley, 2002), which aligns with Yankelovitch's stages of readiness (Yankelovitch, 1991), distinguishes the different information needs and concerns that individuals have when initiating, implementing, or institutionalizing an innovation. Figure 2 applies the CBAM Stages of Concern to the evidence-based academic solution classwide peer tutoring (described in the *Action Guide*, p. 15). Communication strategies should be sensitive to these stages of concern. For example, during initiation, many teachers will want to know what workshops, released time, and other support they will receive to help implement an intervention. They will want to know what the intervention is and how it works; what it looks like in classrooms; and what materials, rearrangements, and time the intervention will require.

FIGURE 2: *Stages of Concern Applied to Classwide Peer Tutoring*

Stages of Concern	Expressions of Concern
Awareness	I am not concerned about classwide peer tutoring.
Informational	I would like to know more about classwide peer tutoring.
Personal	How will classwide peer tutoring affect me?
Management	I seem to be spending too much time changing my lesson plans.
Consequence	How is my use of classwide peer tutoring affecting my students?
Collaboration	I am concerned about relating what I am doing with what other instructors are doing.
Refocusing	I have an idea about something that will improve the way we implement peer tutoring.

Adapted from Hall, G. E. & Loucks, S. F. (1978). Teacher concerns as a basis for facilitating staff development. *Teachers College Record, 80* (1), 36-53.

School improvement requires staff to develop new skills, knowledge, strategies, and, in many cases, attitudes. Staff will need time for learning, trying out, and mastering new skills and strategies. Therefore, *staff development* must be more than one-shot training. Effective implementation requires coaching from someone who has mastered the new practice or strategy, collaborative learning and problem solving among colleagues who are also implementing the solution, and booster sessions to renew skills and address new problems. Some schools, districts, and regional organizations employ professional development staff to do this coaching; other schools train individuals with appropriate expertise (e.g., school social workers or special educators) and release their time to perform this function. Everybody who will employ the intervention—teachers, staff, administrators, and, in many cases, family members—should be trained.

Staff development should also take into account the CBAM levels of concern. For example, at the start, teachers are likely to be concerned with how to implement the solutions, keep the class in order, and get the rest of their work done. At this stage, teachers require hands-on experience with the materials and strategies they will use and opportunities to practice in a safe, supportive environment. Once they start using the new approaches with their students, teachers require coaching as well as discussions with other teachers to support problem solving and let them know that their concerns are not unique. Teacher self-help is a powerful tool for implementing new practices and counters the isolation and alienation many teachers experience. Coaching and staff discussion bolsters a problem-solving rather than a problem-avoiding mentality and helps teachers focus on the new practice and expand their capacity to implement it (Quinn, Osher, Hoffman, & Hanley, 1998).

No matter how powerful an intervention is or how well staff members are trained, the nuts and bolts of implementing an intervention are important to its success. *Logistics* includes procuring time, space, equipment, technology, and materials. Essential needs that are often overlooked are storage space, instruction in operating technology, and the physical infrastructure necessary to use equipment and materials, such as floor space and power outlets.

Rolling Out the Plan

Before the plan is finalized, the schoolwide team should examine it as a comprehensive whole; communicate the plan to the school and community for feedback; review feedback; and determine how to deal with resistance. The team should also develop an evaluation plan (see the Evaluating section) and ensure that the necessary resources are available to fund the plan (see Chapter 2).

The planning process initially focused on specific solutions for specific problems. The schoolwide team should now identify the links between specific solutions and align them so that they build on, and do not undercut, each other. The team should also stagger the rollout of specific solutions so that the community is not overwhelmed by change.

Once the team has aligned the components of the comprehensive plan, it is important to present it to all the relevant stakeholders for their understanding and feedback. This provides you an opportunity to persuade them to accept the logic of the overall plan. It also gives them the opportunity to ask questions, raise concerns, and endorse the plan. The feedback that you solicit has two functions. First, it produces information that you can use in finalizing the plan. Second, it secures buy-in and investment in the plan.

No matter how effective your efforts are, you will likely encounter some resistance. Resistance should not be misunderstood. Many individuals have experienced ill-conceived reform initiatives, a lack of logistical support for change, "innovations of the month or year," and silver bullets that did not work. Still others are burnt out. Cynicism and resistance are understandable and, in most cases, can be addressed. As Fullan and Miles (1992) suggest, "Reframing the legitimate basis of most forms of resistance will allow us to get a more productive start and to isolate the real problems of improvement." (See the following sidebar, 10 Things to Do About Resistance.)

10 Things to Do About Resistance

1. **Acknowledge change as a process.** Change is not an isolated event, but a series of stages that requires time. Remember that the process of educational change is lengthy and may take years from goal-setting to stable establishment. Missteps and setbacks are common. Conflict and resistance are natural products of change, not automatic signs of failure.

2. **Empower stakeholders.** As critical components of innovation, stakeholders must be included as decision makers. If change means that individual needs are met, negative behavior and resistance are less likely. Empowering people means creating mechanisms that provide them with genuine authority and responsibility; otherwise, change efforts become incoherent. Remember, however, that real or perceived shifts in power can spark resistance by colleagues, administrators, or board members. To minimize discord, negotiation should guide the change process.

3. **Encourage all stakeholders.** Stakeholders must be active, invested participants throughout the change process. Often it is beneficial to focus directly on helping participants understand the innovation being tried. Providing a variety of opportunities (for both individuals and groups) to vent concerns also can be particularly effective. Being "heard" is fundamental in establishing understanding and consensus.

4. **Set concrete goals.** Agreed-upon goals should form a shared agenda reached by consensus, thus creating a broad sense of ownership and strengthening communication among stakeholders. This step is critically important because if anything goes awry later in the change process, the stakeholders will be able to return to a shared agenda and refocus their intent and efforts.

5. **Show sensitivity.** Managing conflict means being aware of differences among individuals. Each stakeholder must genuinely feel that he or she is an equal and valued party throughout the change process, not just in the initial trust-building stage. All persons need to be treated with respect, sensitivity, and support as they struggle to redefine their roles and master new concepts.

6. **Model process skills.** Teaching through modeling the appropriate process skills and actions is fundamental to successful staff development initiatives. Staff developers may find, for example, that reflecting publicly and straightforwardly on their own doubts and resistance to change may help others. At the very least, honesty goes a long way toward building credibility. When staff developers model desirable behaviors, they give other stakeholders a chance to identify with someone going through the difficult process of change.

7. **Develop strategies for dealing with emotions.** All too often, educators concentrate on outcomes and neglect the emotional experiences—anxiety, fear, loss, and grief—of change. Effective staff development programs include activities and strategies to address those emotions. Focus on such questions: How will our lives be different with the changes? How do we feel about the changes? Is there anything that can or should be done to honor the past before we move on?

8. **Manage conflict.** Ideally, change is a negotiated process. Stakeholders should be invited to negotiate on issues that provoke their resistance. For example, an assistant principal may need to negotiate the needs of the whole school with faculty members who rank their departmental priorities higher.

9. **Communicate.** Openness in communication is a necessary component of collaborative problem solving. Communication that focuses on differences can move issues of concern out of the shadows. Another technique that increases communication is reflective questioning: The questioner tries to help stakeholders explore their thinking, feelings, needs, or attitudes. Questions can include: Where are we in the change process? What has changed so far? Where are we headed?

10. **Monitor process dynamics.** The constant interplay between the various tensions within the change process must be monitored, and appropriate adjustments must be made. Evaluation begins with the original assessment of the need and readiness to change and remains a key factor throughout systemic reform. Reflection forms the scaffolding of the evaluation process and ongoing assessments of progress serve as checkpoints on the reform journey.

Shhhhh, the dragon is asleep and its name is resistance. (1998). *Journal of Staff Development.*

Monitoring Efforts and Evaluating Results

The schoolwide team must monitor implementation and evaluate results. Although some of the same indicators are relevant for both activities, the difference between the two is that monitoring is ongoing, whereas evaluating takes place at particular points in time. Monitoring uses data to continuously improve implementation.

School Improvement Is a Problem-Rich Process

Change threatens existing interests and routines, heightens uncertainty, and increases complexity. . . . Problems arise naturally from the demands of the change process itself, from the people involved, and from the structure and procedures of schools and districts. Some are easily solved; others are almost intractable. . . . Problems are our friends because only through immersing ourselves in problems can we come up with creative solutions. Problems are the route to deeper change and deeper satisfaction. In this sense, effective organizations "embrace problems" rather than avoid them. Too often, change-related problems are ignored, denied, or treated as an occasion for blame and defense. Success in school reform efforts is much more likely when problems are treated as natural, expected phenomena. Only by tracking problems can we understand what we need to do next to get what we want. Problems must be taken seriously, not attributed to "resistance" or to the ignorance and wrong-headedness of others.

Getting Reform Right: What Works and What Doesn't. (1992). Fullan & Miles.

Reference

We monitor discipline referrals by student, time of day, type of infraction, location, and type of consequence. This has been helpful in monitoring students who are frequently in trouble. It is also helpful in monitoring program effectiveness so that adjustments can be made to address concerns.

Larry Michael, school psychologist in Anchorage, Alaska, Project ACHIEVE School.

Monitoring

Effective practitioners monitor their work regularly. Teachers, for example, look at what students are doing regularly through some form of curriculum-based measurement. Individual interventions as well as the comprehensive schoolwide effort should be similarly monitored. Every intervention and every school improvement effort will encounter problems. Monitoring helps you address problems as they arise—quickly and effectively. Monitoring can be both ongoing or intermittent, measuring benchmarks specified in the plan. Monitoring can employ quantitative indicators (e.g., tests and surveys) and qualitative indicators (e.g., focus groups, structured observations, and anecdotal reports).

Monitoring should be built into the comprehensive plan. It should be as routine and easy as possible in order to ensure that it is carried out with fidelity. Monitoring is easier in schools that have adopted a problem-solving approach, a commitment to build a learning community, or a commitment to continuous improvement.

Service Planning and Monitoring in Hays, Kansas

For many years, school psychologists in Hays, Kansas, have, with formal parental consent, met monthly with clinical therapists and case managers from High Plains Mental Health Center to coordinate treatment services and to enhance communication.

Service planning is a collaborative effort that is a critical component for successful treatment. The mental health center staff are kept apprised of academic performance, social functioning, and the success or failure of behavioral plans; the school psychologists receive information they need to reinforce clinical treatment objectives in the school setting.

For example, if a therapist recommends a particular strategy for the child to use to decrease feelings of anxiety or to defuse anger, the school psychologist can instruct the child's teacher to employ prompts or cues when needed. Similarly, information from the mental health center staff can increase the school's understanding of the child's psychiatric issues, medication status, family dynamics, substance abuse, and home issues.

This coordination enhances Hays' Safe Schools/Healthy Students initiatives and improves outcomes for the child and family because treatment efforts are reinforced in the school setting, where the child spends a significant amount of time. These meetings increase the mental health center staff's awareness of the school's culture and increase the quality of recommendations that they make.

Evaluating

Accountability for many schools means state-mandated, standardized, high-stakes academic achievement tests, which do not measure student behavior and wellness. The schoolwide team should ensure that the behavioral goals and objectives addressed by interventions are also measured for effects. Comparing pre- and post-intervention data on selected indicators on a semester or yearly basis is a possible evaluation activity. The relationship between behavior and academic achievement should be examined.

Measuring results is essential. It provides feedback to the implementers (the school staff), and it helps stakeholders understand the improvement process. Appropriate behaviors do not replace inappropriate behaviors overnight, but incremental positive changes are measurable. Frequent periodic measurement also enables your school to modify interventions that are ineffective or to determine whether the interventions are being implemented with reasonable fidelity.

Effective evaluations require a knowledge of research and statistics. Some schools have employed an independent (local university) evaluator; others have used their central or school staff expertise. The data sets used in your needs assessment and connected to the goals and objectives you developed in the planning phase should inform your evaluation.

Project Evaluations

Three Oregon Safe Schools/Healthy Students sites, in Springfield, Gresham, and Deschutes Counties, have joined with the University of Oregon to conduct their project evaluations. All three sites are gathering data on attendance, grades, and behavioral referrals as well as on the effects on school culture of the implementation of *First Step to Success*, which is described on page 26 of *Safeguarding Our Children: An Action Guide*. School culture and interventions to increase individual protective factors and decrease individual risk factors are also part of the evaluation.

A Resource for Evaluating Violence Prevention

The ERIC Clearinghouse on Urban Education has produced *Evaluating School Violence Programs* (Flaxman, 2001). This guide includes chapters on:

- challenges to evaluating school and community-based violence prevention programs, needs assessment, outcome evaluation, process evaluation, and cost-benefit analysis;

- assessing conflict resolution programs; and

- evaluating school and community-based violence prevention resource guides.

Tools and Resources for Involving Practitioners and Families in Evaluation

A useful resource for planning and evaluation is *Getting to Outcomes: Methods and Tools for Planning, Self-Evaluation, and Accountability* (GTO), which was developed as an approach to help practitioners plan, implement, and evaluate substance abuse prevention programs to achieve results (Wandersman, Imm, Chinman, & Kaftarian, 1999). *GTO* is a manual that leads you through an empowerment evaluation model by asking ten questions that incorporate the basic elements of program planning, implementation, evaluation, and sustainability. By answering the ten accountability questions well, program developers increase the probability of achieving outcomes and demonstrate their accountability to stakeholders. Here are the ten questions:

1. What are the needs and resources in my organization/school/community/state?

2. What are the goals, target population, and desired outcomes (objectives) for my school/community/state?

3. How does this program incorporate knowledge of science and best practice in this area?

4. How does this program fit with other programs already being offered?

5. What capacities do I need in order to put this program into place with quality?

6. How will this program be carried out?

7. How will the quality of program implementation be assessed?

8. How well did the program work?

9. How will continuous quality improvement strategies be incorporated?

10. If the program (or components of the program) is successful, how will the program be sustained?

For free PDFs of this guide and instruments, go to http://www.stanford.edu/~davidf/empowermentevaluation.html and click *GTO I* and *GTO II*.

The Federation of Families for Children's Mental Health (www.ffcmh.org) has developed a curriculum to train families to understand and use research and evaluation findings and participate as equal partners on evaluation and research teams. For information, contact the Federation of Families for Children's Mental Health at (703) 684-7710.

Federal Resources That Can Support Safe School Planning

Many federal agencies have created or supported the development of resources that you can use to help in the planning process. The following list may prove useful.

Centers for the Application of Prevention Technologies
http://www.captus.org

Center for Effective Collaboration and Practice
http://www.air.org/cecp/

Center for Mental Health in Schools
http://smhp.psych.ucla.edu/smhptoc.htm

Center for Mental Health Services
http://www.mentalhealth.org/cmhs/

Center for School Mental Health Assistance
http://csmha.umaryland.edu

Center for the Study and Prevention of Violence
http://www.colorado.edu/cspv/blueprints

Center for Substance Abuse Prevention's Decision Support System
http://www.samhsa.gov/centers/csap/csap.html

CSAP Decision Support System
http://www.preventiondss.org

Making Health Academic
http://www2.edc.org/MakingHealthAcademic

National Center on Education, Disability, and Juvenile Justice
http://www.edjj.org

National Center for Mental Health Promotion and Youth Violence Prevention
http://www.promoteprevent.org

National Clearinghouse for Alcohol and Drug Information
http://www.health.org/features/multicultural/asian/

National Clearinghouse on Child Abuse and Neglect Information
http://www.calib.com/nccanch/

National Coordinator Training and Technical Assistance Center
http://www.k12coordinator.org

National Evaluation and Technical Assistance Center for the Education of Children Who are Neglected, Delinquent, or At Risk
http://www.neglected-delinquent.org

National Injury and Violence Prevention Resource Center
http://www.childrenssafetynetwork.org

National Mental Health and Education Center
www.naspcenter.org

National Resource Center for Safe Schools
http://www.nwrel.org/safe/

National School Safety Center
http://www.nssc1.org

National Youth Violence Prevention Resource Center
http://www.safeyouth.org/home.htm

OSEP Technical Assistance Center on Positive Behavioral Interventions and Supports
http://pbis.org

Partnerships Against Violence Network
http://www.pavnet.org

Safe Schools/Healthy Students Action Center
http://www.sshsac.org/

Technical Assistance Partnership for Child and Family Mental Health
www.air.org/tapartnership

State-Supported Safe School Programs and Related Activities That Can Support School Improvement

Many states have created centers to support safe school planning. These centers are listed below. Note that some Web sites are restricted to in-state access and use.

California Safe Schools and Violence Prevention Office
http://www.cde.ca.gov/spbranch/safety/

Colorado Safe Communities—Safe Schools
http://www.colorado.edu/cspv/safeschools/mainpage.htm

Connecticut Safe Schools & Communities Coalition (SSCC)
http://www.drugsdontwork.org

Florida Safe, Disciplined, and Drug-Free Schools (SDDFS)
http://www.unf.edu/dept/fie/sdfs

Georgia Emergency Management Agency
http://www2.state.ga.us/GEMA

Illinois State Board of Education School Safety
http://www.isbe.state.il.us/safeschools/default.htm

Indiana School Safety Specialist Academy
http://ideanet.doe.state.in.us/isssa/

Iowa Department of Education Success4
http://www.state.ia.us/educate/programs/success4/

Kentucky Center for School Safety (KCSS)
http://www.kysafeschools.org

Mississippi Department of Education, Division of Safe and Orderly Schools
http://www.mde.k12.ms.us/lead/osos/

Missouri Center for Safe Schools
http://www.umkc.edu/safe-school/

Montana Behavioral Initiative
http://www.metnet.state.mt.us/SpecialEdu/MBI/HTM/

New York State Center for School Safety
http://int11.mhrcc.org/scss

North Carolina Center for the Prevention of School Violence
http://www.ncsu.edu/cpsv/

Ohio Safe Schools Center
http://www.uc.edu/safeschools

Pennsylvania Center for Safe Schools
http://www.center-school.org/viol_prev/css/css-s-about.html

South Carolina Center for Safe Schools
http://sde.state.sc.us/sde/educator/safedrug/sccss.htm

Tennessee School Safety Center
http://www.state.tn.us/education/tssc.htm

Texas School Safety Center
http://www.txssc.swt.edu

Utah Behavioral and Educational Strategies for Teachers (BEST)
http://cecp.air.org/resources/success/best.htm

Vermont Department of Education
Action Planning Guide
http://www.state.vt.us/educ/new/html/pubs/action_planning_guide.html

Vermont Department of Education
BEST: Building Effective Support for Teaching Students with Behavioral Challenges
http://www.uvm.edu/~cdci/programs/best.html

Vermont Department of Education
School Improvement Support Guide
http://data.ed.state.vt.us/apg/index.html

Virginia Center for School Safety
http://www.virginiaschoolsafety.com

Washington State School Safety Center
http://www.k12.wa.us/safetycenter/

Funding School Improvement

FEW
SOME
ALL

Like school improvement itself, funding has no one-size-fits-all formula. Schools have limited resources and limited control over some resources. Districts and states also have limited resources. Approaching school change as an add-on to existing school programs is likely to be more expensive and less effective than an integrated approach that blends, braids, or otherwise aligns existing resources and new funding. This chapter explains how you can:

▲ Redeploy resources to support comprehensive approaches to improving school safety and academic achievement.

▲ Combine funding to maximize services.

▲ Garner additional funding to purchase goods and services that will support comprehensive approaches to improving school safety and academic achievement.

The following sidebar, Organizational Capacity, provides examples of how schools can accomplish these three tasks.

Note

In seeking new funding for schoolwide improvement projects, schools should determine whether (1) the district already receives funds that could support new or expanded initiatives; (2) the district is eligible for such funds; (3) the district makes allocations to schools; and (4) the school is free to pursue additional funding independently.

Health Is Academic, A Guide to Coordinated School Health Programs. (1998). Marx & Wooley.

Organizational Capacity

In School A, the principal identifies 20 children who do not meet district reading standards. She taps district resources and increases class size for the successful students to fund a computerized reading curriculum that (on review) differs significantly from the system's existing reading curriculum. She hires two teacher aides and purchases several computers to implement this curriculum to serve the 20 low-performing students. The new curriculum, computers, and staff positions cost $90,000 a year, including salary and benefits.

In School B, the principal identifies 20 children who do not meet district reading standards. Looking further at her students' test scores, she sees that many other students are at risk of failing math. By tapping the same district resources as Principal A and using additional resources from her community and state and federal programs, Principal B can fund a solidly researched reading and math professional development program for all teachers. By shifting staff instructional responsibilities and developing a community-supported after-school "study/activity center," she is also able to increase instructional time for those who have fallen behind. The cost of this approach is likely to exceed $90,000, but not by much. As a result of taking a comprehensive approach to the diverse challenges facing her school, Principal B will see improved math and reading scores among a much larger student population. Improved safety and greater community-school collaboration are incidental outcomes of this effort. Improved reading and math achievement for the original 20 children is the payoff.

The ability of a school to address the challenges it faces is called *organizational capacity.* Capacity includes the number of staff, the capabilities and training of the staff, funding, leadership, and all other tangible and intangible assets. School A is focused on increasing a narrow band of capacity—the ability to raise reading scores for a few children. Increasing school capacity on a broader scale requires more effort up front, but pays greater dividends because it leads to many more dimensions of school improvement.

Before you can redeploy, combine, or identify new funding, however, you need to understand where funds come from—funding streams.

Funding Streams

Funds for school improvement come from many sources, both public and private, and from many levels—federal, state, and local (county, city, town, or school district). Some funds are allocated to smaller units in block grants. Other funds are provided to schools, districts, or children that meet specific eligibility requirements. Figure 3 summarizes the types and uses of federal, state, and local funding. Funding sources vary from district to district and, in many cases, from school to school. It is important to know your federal, state, and local funding formula and the rules governing the use of funds. You should also be familiar with the resources that your local philanthropic organizations (e.g., corporate foundations, community-based organizations, and other local volunteer organizations) can provide.

FIGURE 3: *Types of Funds and Their Uses*

Funding Stream	Range of Total Funding*	Typical Use or Function of Funds
Local (Public)	40%–80%	Basic operating funds for schools
State	15%–50%	Equalization, special initiatives, assessment, curriculum development, key programs
Federal	7%–15%	Categorical programs for specific groups (based on disability, poverty, risk factors, etc.)
Private	1%	Varies by community

The percentages are hypothetical. The range varies from state to state and district to district within states. Statewide funding exists in Hawaii and the District of Columbia, which are single-district school systems.

Federal Funds

Federal funds are granted to states, local public and private agencies, and individuals in one of four forms:

▲ Block (or formula) grants

▲ Project (or discretionary) grants

▲ Legislative earmarks

▲ Direct payments

Block grants include such programs as Temporary Assistance to Needy Families (TANF), Maternal and Child Health Services Block Grants, Community Mental Health Services Block Grants, Substance Abuse Treatment Block Grants, Social Services Block Grants, and Part B of the Individuals with Disabilities Education Act (IDEA). These grants distribute a fixed amount of funding to states or localities; the amount is based on established formulas that vary from grant to grant. Formula grants are usually based on population, unemployment levels, census data, or other demographic indicators. Most formula grants go directly to state agencies for ongoing services through block grants or categorical programs. Most block grants must be used to meet a range of specified objectives.

Project grants (sometimes referred to as discretionary grants) typically support highly specific purposes and are awarded on the basis of competitive applications. The applicant may be a state or local, public or private, entity, depending on the program. The funding is for fixed or known periods and for specific projects or the delivery of specific services or products. Project grants include fellowships, scholarships, research grants, training grants, traineeships, experimental and demonstration grants, evaluation grants, planning grants, technical assistance grants, survey grants, construction grants, and unsolicited contractual agreements.

Legislative earmarks are funds set aside for specific organizations by legislative directives in appropriations laws (as distinct from authorization acts). These directives dictate how to spend certain portions of funds appropriated within larger funding programs. Earmarks can be "hard" or "soft." Hard earmarks are written into legislation, usually with specific amounts to be spent and the specific recipient of the funding identified. Soft earmarks are based on conference reports. Earmarks are awarded noncompetitively and occur in a specific fiscal year and may not be continued to the next fiscal year. Both public organizations and private agencies can receive earmarks.

Direct payments provide financial assistance directly to individuals who satisfy federal eligibility requirements. These programs may, however, be administered by an intermediate state agency.

School-Based Mental Health Services Under Medicaid Managed Care

School-based mental health programs traditionally have a mix of funding sources, with heavy reliance on state general funds, private foundations, and federal grants. Thirty-seven states and the District of Columbia helped to fund at least some of the centers. Funding from third-party insurance reimbursement is increasing. Medicaid fee-for-service, Medicaid managed care, commercial insurance revenues, and State Child Health Insurance Program (SCHIP) outreach were reported by schools as sources of revenue (Center for Health and Health Care in Schools, 1998). Fifteen states reported Medicaid fee-for-service revenue, five reported Medicaid managed care revenue, and seven reported commercial insurance revenue.

School-Based Mental Health Services Under Medicaid Managed Care. (2000). Robinson, Barrett, Tunkelrott, and Kim.

In some key entitlement programs, such as Medicaid (Title XIX) and the State Children's Health Insurance Program (SCHIP) (Title XXI), the federal government matches state expenditures, and the matched rate is indexed by state poverty rates.

Common sources of federal funds are described in Figure 4. Although your school may be accessing these funds in a traditional manner—as stand-alone projects focused on specific students—the U.S. Department of Education encourages schools and districts to combine funds to more efficiently raise the achievement of the whole school community, thus increasing the capacity of the school as a whole instead of targeting specific children. Many schools and districts successfully combine funding streams. For example, some schools and districts are funding prevention and intervention initiatives by combining local regular and special education funds, state grants, Medicaid, SCHIP and other health insurance, and Title I funds, among others (Nastasi, Vargas, & Bernstein, 1998; Quinn et al., 1998).

Information about combining federal funds is widely available from the U.S. Department of Education and through the program administrative offices in your state education department. For example, IDEA funds can help pay for a campus learning center that provides specialized services for all students. In some cases, categorical programs, such as Title I (for schools serving students in poverty) and IDEA, may be combined to support your change efforts. *Implementing Schoolwide Programs: An Idea Book on Planning*, published by the U.S. Department of Education (1998) and available free, is an excellent resource about federal support for school reform.

Figure 4 identifies federal grant programs, which may provide existing resources that you can leverage (because they already exist in your school, district, or community), and new resources, which you may want to apply for. Some of these programs are relevant to universal interventions (see Chapter 3), others, to early interventions (Chapter 4), and still others, to intensive interventions (Chapter 5). Some programs fund school safety initiatives, others fund student support, and still others fund academic improvements. Every program may not be funded every year, and some may be eliminated. In addition, some programs may be added, and some are not included here. Hence it is important to check the Web sites of particular programs or departments to identify current or anticipated grant opportunities.

FIGURE 4: *Sources of Federal Funding*

Funding Source	Eligibility Criteria	Legislative/Regulatory Requirements
Individuals with Disabilities Education Act (IDEA)	Children ages 3–21 within one of the 13 specific categories (including mental retardation and serious emotional disturbance) of disability who need special education and related services.	– Development of an Individualized Education Program (IEP). – Comprehensive evaluation every three years. – Appropriate related services, including counseling, psychological, and social work services, must be provided when part of the IEP at no cost to the family.
Title V: Maternal and Child Health (MCH) Services Block Grant	Children, adolescents, pregnant women. Emphasizes, but does not require, serving low-income children and pregnant women.	– At least 30 percent for preventative and primary care for children. – At least 30 percent for community-based care for children with special needs.
Community Services Block Grant	Low-income individuals and families living at 125 percent or less of the national poverty level.	– Funds must be sub-granted to "eligible entities" (a not-for-profit organization with a tripartite board that provides services in a specific area of a state) to provide services that address the causes of poverty.
Community Mental Health Services (CMHS) Block Grant	The Block Grant covers all ages. Some states do not target children and youth. If they are served, children must have serious emotional disturbance to be eligible. Serious emotional disturbance is defined in regulations.	– For children, a mental health services plan must be created to provide an integrated system of services linked to a defined geographic area that includes education, substance abuse, health, juvenile and social services, and mental health care. – CMHS funds can be spent only on the community-based mental health services portion of the plan. – Funds are available only to community mental health centers, child mental health programs, psychosocial rehabilitation programs, mental health peer-support programs, and mental health primary consumer-directed programs.
Comprehensive Community Mental Health Services for Children with Serious Emotional Disturbances	Children with serious emotional disturbances and their families.	– Funding can be used to support a public community-based system of care for children and adolescents suffering from serious emotional disturbances and their families.
Medicaid (Title XIX)	Each state determines eligibility in accordance with Federal regulations. Low-income members of families with dependent children; low-income children and pregnant women; persons who are over age 65, blind, or disabled; and certain Medicare beneficiaries will benefit. Most states permit Medicaid reimbursement for school mental health services provided by school psychologists and school social workers, as well as licensed clinical providers.	– Required services include in-patient and out-patient hospital services; rural health clinic services; federally qualified health center services; physician's services; pediatric or family nurse practitioner services; early and periodic screening, diagnosis, and treatment (EPSDT) services.

Funding Source	Eligibility Criteria	Legislative/Regulatory Requirements
Early and Periodic Screening, Diagnosis, and Treatment (EPSDT)	Medicaid-eligible individuals under the age of 21. Schools can be reimbursed for EPSDT services.	– Certain types of services are specifically prohibited under Federal Medicaid rules. Medicaid funds may not be used to pay for education or vocational services, including job training. Medicaid also does not pay for recreational or social services with no therapeutic value. – Establishment of medically reasonable periodic schedules to determine when screening should occur.
State Children's Health Insurance Program (SCHIP)	CHIP provides Federal funds to ensure health care coverage for uninsured children in families with incomes up to 200 percent of the Federal poverty level (in a very few states, up to 250 percent of poverty).	– Funds must be used to initiate and expand child health coverage to uninsured, low-income children. – Up to 10 percent of funds may be spent on nonbenefit activities that include outreach, administration, health services initiatives, and other child health assistance.
Temporary Assistance to Needy Families (TANF)	Needy families with children as determined eligible by the applicant state, territory, or tribe in the plan.	– Funds may be used for cash grants and work opportunities and in any other way to meet the purpose of the program.
Title I Grants to Local Education Agencies	Children (preschool and K–12) who are failing or who are most at-risk of failing to meet state academic standards will benefit.	– The use of funds can vary broadly to address student needs. – If a participating school has at least 50 percent of its student population at the poverty level, the school may choose to operate a schoolwide program that allows Title I funds to be blended with other Federal, state, and local funds to upgrade the school's instructional program.
Safe and Drug-Free Schools and Communities Act Title IV of IASA, 1994	Provides state education agencies with funding for grants to local education agencies. Provides funds through the governor for community-based organizations.	– Funds for school drug and violence prevention, early intervention, rehabilitation, and preventive education.
Education for Homeless Children and Youth	Homeless children and youth in elementary and secondary schools, preschool children, and the parents of these children.	– Funds may be used for a variety of activities to ensure educational success for homeless children.
Even Start—American Indian Tribes and Tribal Organizations	Participants are parents and their children. Parents must meet eligibility requirements under the Adult Education Act. Children must be age seven or younger. Families must demonstrate a need for services by way of a low-income level and a low level of adult literacy or proficiency in English, or other need-related factor.	– Funding may be used for early childhood education, adult literacy, adult basic education, and parenting education. Grants may also be used to recruit and screen children and parents, design programs, train staff, do evaluations, and coordinate with other programs.

⟶

Funding Source	Eligibility Criteria	Legislative/Regulatory Requirements
Even Start—State Education Agencies	Only State education agencies are eligible to apply for funding. Participants are parents and their children. (See above for eligibility.)	– Funding may be used for early childhood education, adult literacy, adult basic education, and parenting education. Grants may also be used to recruit and screen children and parents, design programs, train staff, do evaluations, and coordinate with other programs.
Family Support Model Demonstration Projects	Families of children with disabilities and professionals working with children with disabilities.	– Some of the areas eligible for funds are ensuring the active involvement of parents in developing, implementing, and evaluating the system; establishing a state policy council for families; or establishing training and technical assistance for families.
Healthy Schools, Healthy Communities	Public and private nonprofit community-based health care entities are eligible to apply for funding. Beneficiaries are students attending the schools where a health center is established and their families.	– Funds must be used to establish school-based health centers that provide comprehensive primary and preventive health care services. – A two percent set-aside is required for technical assistance and activities to improve collaborative performance.
Migrant Education—Basic State Grant Program	This grant is open to state education agencies or other appropriate entities. This grant supports services to children ages 0–21 whose parents are migratory agricultural workers or fishers who have moved across school district lines during the previous 36 months to obtain seasonal employment in various food-processing activities.	– Funds may address the needs of migrant children by supporting high-quality and comprehensive education programs. – Programs are intended to ensure that migrant children receive educational services to compete with peers in stable settings.
Safe Schools/Healthy Students Initiative	Students, schools, and families in the geographic areas served by grants. Local education agencies may apply for funding.	– Plans must address safe school environment, youth alcohol and drug prevention, school and community mental health programs, early childhood psychosocial and emotional development services, educational reform, and safe school policies.
Twenty-First Century Community Learning Centers	Eligibility is limited to rural or inner-city public elementary or secondary schools, a consortium of such schools, or local education agencies that apply on behalf of the schools.	– Funding may be used for early childhood education, adult literacy, adult basic education, and parenting education. Grants may also be used to recruit and screen children and parents, design programs, train staff, do evaluations, and coordinate with other programs.

State Funds

States make important contributions to funding education. Some states have made school reform funding more available in order to promote higher standards and accountability. These funds may or may not be flexible at the school or district level. However, because local goals are likely to be consistent with state goals, state funds can often be used to support local school improvement efforts.

Local Funds

Local funds vary from district to district both in quantity and flexibility. Many districts have school improvement programs that could support your change efforts. However, local resources are frequently limited because they are generally designed to support just the basic school components. Often, the best strategy for applying these funds to school change is to realign them at the school site. As you go through the planning process, you will identify your school's key goals and objectives. Once you have developed these goals and objectives, examine your current school organization and determine whether your basic school resources (teachers, administrators, counselors, and other staff) align with them. Make sure to use your resources in a manner consistent with your stated goals and objectives.

Private Funds

National and state foundations (public and corporate) and organizations sometimes fund local efforts. Frequently local organizations play an important role. PTAs and PTOs have long been sources of revenue and other resources. Private corpora-

Los Angeles Unified School District— Partnering With the Department of Mental Health

For years, the Los Angeles Unified School District had been spending its general funds and state and locally generated funds on mandated mental health services to children, without accessing Medicaid funding through EPSDT.

In 1992, the school system was approached by the Los Angeles County Department of Mental Health, whose interest was in increasing services in the community. By becoming a contract agency through a partnership with the Department of Mental Health, the school system became a certified Medicaid provider.

The school district can now claim Medicaid reimbursement for many of the services to children for which it previously used its general funds. In turn, the school district now uses its general fund dollars to pay for services to children who are not Medicaid-eligible. The Los Angeles County Department of Mental Health is able to extend its services to this needy but underserved population.

The result: a win-win situation for both organizations, with expanded resources to provide a larger number of children with increased services.

tions, professional organizations, and faith-based institutions are increasingly visible school partners. The World Wide Web is an excellent tool for tapping into these organizations. Most large companies, for example, have an office for community relations and can provide details about how school communities can access company resources, such as financial donations, volunteers, and computer equipment. For example, in Hays, Kansas, the school district was awarded a Safe Schools/Healthy Students grant and sought other bundled funding for its schoolwide prevention program from the district, Wal-Mart, AmeriCorps, The Bullying Prevention Project, and YouthFriends.

Using Public Funds Efficiently

Public funds provide important opportunities for schools looking to build or expand services for children. Understanding how to take advantage of these funds is essential to finding the right funding source for your program and maximizing the dollars that may be allocated. Two sets of strategies can help you make the best use of public funds. The first does not involve securing more resources. Rather, it involves *redeploying* existing public funds to support program objectives. The second involves securing additional funding, usually by *maximizing* the use of Medicaid, particularly EPSDT.

Redeploying Existing Public Funds

Here are some ways to make the best use of existing public funds:

▲ Free existing funds by eliminating or downsizing redundant, ineffective programs or by implementing prevention initiatives that will enable you to shift funds from expensive intensive treatments to early interventions after your prevention efforts succeed.

▲ Collaborate to combine resources in ways that enhance efficiency without a loss (and possibly with an increase) in effectiveness (e.g., interagency collaboration, public-private partnerships, blended funding). Collaboration may include:

– *aligning and coordinating* the use of categorical funds to enhance their efficiency;

– *pooling* funds across agency or program lines to create a less restrictive source of funding for local programs;

– *braiding* funds so that each agency can track and retain its identity and requirements for its funding while the monies from different agencies are "braided" together to fund one Integrated Service Plan; and

> ### Combining Resources to Fund Children's Services
>
> Early and Periodic Screening, Diagnosis, and Treatment (EPSDT) dollars are generally not sufficient to support freestanding mental health services to children; however, if they are combined with general education funds to support the hiring of a school psychologist (if within the scope of your state Medicaid plan), the position can become self-sustaining. Costs can be defrayed by billable hours for EPSDT services, relying less on local school budgets.

Children who are eligible for Medicaid are entitled to any federally authorized Medicaid service. Under the Early and Periodic Screening, Diagnosis, and Treatment (EPSDT) mandate, all states must screen eligible children, diagnose any conditions found through a screen, and then furnish appropriate medically necessary treatment to "correct or ameliorate defects and physical and mental illness and conditions discovered by the screening services." The services must be provided to children even if the state otherwise limits access to certain services to the rest of the population covered by Medicaid. A screen can be a formal checkup, covering both physical and mental health issues, or it can be any contact with a health care professional for assessment of a potential problem. Thus, children who need mental health care can be assessed by a community [or school] mental health provider and this assessment then entitles the child to any services necessary to treat the diagnosed condition.

Children have a broader entitlement than adults who qualify for Medicaid. For adults, some services are mandatory, but some need only be provided at a state's option. A state will list its "optional" services in its Medicaid plan, but must make available to children all services listed in the federal Medicaid law "whether or not such services are covered under the state plan." However, a child is eligible only for services determined medically necessary.

Making Sense of Medicaid for Children with Serious Emotional Disturbance. (1999). Bazelon Center for Mental Health Law, Washington, DC.

– *capturing and reinvesting* funds saved through programs that appropriately reduce costs (e.g., when fewer referrals for costly services are made).

Maximizing Public Funding

The second strategy for using public funds is to maximize resources by finding new ways to access public funds. You can use three strategies to maximize one major source: Medicaid. Medicaid (as well as SCHIP) is a federal and state health program that is state administered, so regulations vary for each state. Check with your state education, mental health, and Medicaid agencies to determine how your school can use these sources. School-based planning, direct services, and psychological services are some of the possible uses.

▲ **Fee-for-Service Claiming.** Under fee-for-service claiming, Medicaid payments are available as reimbursements for services provided. If you are in a state that reimburses on a fee-for-service basis, your school may be able to be reimbursed for some or all services that are eligible for Medicaid reimbursement. If your school does not yet provide Medicaid-eligible services, Medicaid reimbursement may make it possible. Claims for the cost of services are submitted to the state Medicaid agency. (To find out how to contact your state agency, use the list of State Medicaid Directors found at the Web site of the American Public Human Services Association, http://medicaid.aphsa.org/members.htm.)

▲ **Administrative Claiming.** Another form of Medicaid reimbursement available to schools is administrative claiming. Its advantage is that it requires less detailed documentation of the costs for large amounts of work done by local agency staff. By using a formula to arrive at the amount of time spent and the number of individuals involved, administrative claiming makes it possible to calculate costs quickly.

▲ **Leveraged Funds.** Yet another strategy to maximize Medicaid funding is for two or more agencies to create a formal partnership to leverage new or additional Medicaid funding. These funds are generated through an agreement between two or more agencies, at least one of which has access to Medicaid reimbursement funds and at least one of which has access to non-Medicaid funds and resources. Alone, neither the Medicaid-certified agency nor the ineligible agency can generate new revenue; together, they can.

You can find more information about maximizing public funding and creating more flexibility in using public funds on the Finance Project Web site, at http://www.financeproject.org.

Accessing and Coordinating Funds for School Improvement

Identifying and coordinating your school's or district's school improvement funds requires an individual to coordinate the effort and the assistance of interested team members. For example, the funding coordinator could assign one team member to monitor each funding stream. Federal resources generally have similar reporting and accountability requirements, but other sources might have specific rules that require separate monitoring. Having "specialists" track different funding sources will help ensure efficient support of your schoolwide efforts. The Financial Planning Checklist (see Appendix B) can help you organize the financial planning process.

Mobilizing Support

Fund-raising requires support. No matter which specific program or plan you adopt, you should allot resources to secure support. This is important because schools face competing priorities. The school community will rally behind a plan that supports its improvement or reform goals, and you must demonstrate that your plan does this.

Funding Preventive Mental Health Services in the Lafourche Parish Schools

Lafourche Parish Schools in Louisiana uses Medicaid's Early and Periodic Screening, Diagnosis, and Treatment (EPSDT) funds to provide services to children at risk for mental health problems. The schools use both school system staff and psychiatric residents from the University Medical School. Since most children in the schools are Medicaid-eligible, preventive services are made available across the school.

Pages 44–47 of the *Action Guide* provide details about the process of bringing the school community together behind your efforts.

State universities and colleges often want to collaborate with school districts for research, training, and technical assistance projects. State associations and organizations also offer grant opportunities.

Allotting Time and Resources

The Education Quality Institute identified the following books as being useful to support comprehensive reform efforts (http://www.eqireports.org/Resources/resources_on_allotting_time_and_.htm):

– Hawley-Miles, K., & Darling-Hammond, L. (1998). *Rethinking the allocation of teaching resources: Some lessons from high-performing schools*. Philadelphia: Consortium for Policy Research in Education. Available at http://nces.ed.gov/pubs98/dev97/98212e.html

– Keltner, B. (1998). *Funding comprehensive school reform*. Santa Monica, CA: RAND. Available at http://www.rand.org/publications/IP/IP175/

– Odden, A. (1997). *How to rethink school budgets to support school transformation*. Arlington, VA: New American Schools. Available at http://www.naschools.org/uploadedfiles/HowtoRethinkSchoolBudgetstoSupportSchoolTransformation.pdf

– Odden, A. (1998). *Creating school finance policies that facilitate new goals* (CPRE Policy Brief). Philadelphia: Consortium for Policy Research in Education. Available at http://www.edsource.org/edu_fin_res_odden2.cfm

Always include parents and community groups when seeking support. Although working with resources outside of the school can be labor-intensive, it has several benefits: bringing the community together around your school; providing access to expertise, experience, and financial support; and connecting parents, students, and school employees.

Spread out this effort—each team member can make some community contacts. Tell potential partners about your effort and ask them to contribute to school improvement. At least one member of the schoolwide team should be in charge of seeking assistance from local, state, and federal government resources; foundations; religious organizations; and civic groups. Remember to seek the assistance of school district staff whose jobs focus on the problems you are addressing.

Although nearly every school campus feels strapped for financial and other resources, you should not neglect school improvement for this reason alone. Use the Financial Planning Checklist in Appendix B to explore potential resources and ways to realign existing resources to support your reform efforts.

Funding Ponds: Identifying Funding Sources

A funding stream can be identified at its national or state source and traced to a local endpoint where districts or schools access it. However, funding streams often are redirected at the state and local (county, district, municipal, or community) level. For example, Medicaid starts out as a federal program, but once it reaches the state, it takes on a state identity and is implemented through state regulations and procedures. At the local level, federal and state funds mix with local sources to create funding ponds, which you can draw on to fund school improvement. The pond can be used to fund improvements as diverse as under-writing professional development, hiring subject matter specialists, implementing drug prevention programs, and reducing class size. Funding ponds differ somewhat from locality to locality. Figure 5, Funding Pond for Salinas, California, provides an example of a funding pond used by a Safe Schools/Healthy Students (SS/HS) grantee.

FIGURE 5: *The Funding Pond of Salinas, California*

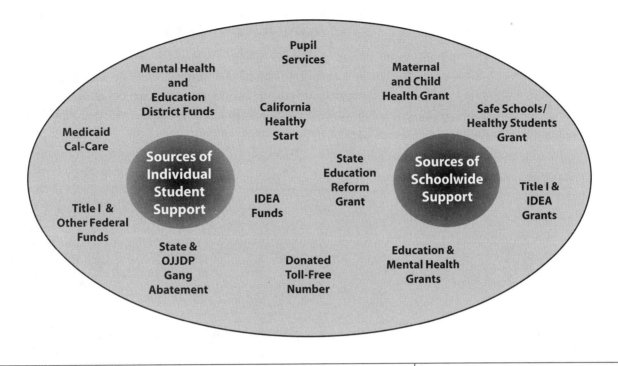

Tools for Tracking Potential Education Funding

The U.S. Department of Education Web site contains a *Guide to Education Programs* (http://web99.ed.gov/GTEP/Program2.nsf), which includes a database that is searchable by topical heading (e.g., safe and drug-free schools), by Catalog of Federal Domestic Assistance number (CFDA #), by administering office (e.g., Office of Special Education and Rehabilitative Services), by who may apply (e.g., school districts), by subject index (e.g., educationally disadvantaged), by educational level (e.g., middle school), and by assistance (e.g., formula grants).

The Web site also includes the annual *Forecast of Funding Opportunities Under the Department of Education Discretionary Grant Programs* (http://www.ed.gov/offices/OCFO/grants/forecast.html#Chart%201). This document lists all programs and competitions under which the Department has invited or expects to invite applications for new awards and provides actual or estimated deadline dates for the transmittal of applications under these programs. The lists are in the form of charts—organized according to the Department's principal program offices—and include previously announced programs and competitions, as well as those that the Department plans to announce at a later date.

Directory of Resources on Funding for Schoolwide Improvement[1]

Catalog of Federal Domestic Assistance
www.cfda.gov

The *Catalog of Federal Domestic Assistance* is a governmentwide compendium of federal programs, projects, services, and activities that provide assistance or benefits to the American public. It details every federal grant, including description, eligibility, deadlines, and award procedures. It contains financial and nonfinancial assistance programs administered by departments and establishments of the federal government. To do an online search directly, go to www.cfda.gov/public/faprs.htm. The catalog can be ordered from the Superintendent of Documents, U.S. Government Printing Office, Washington, DC 20402, 202-512-1800.

The Center for Health and Health Care in Schools
(formerly *Making the Grade*)
http://www.gwu.edu/~mtg/sbhcs/financing.htm

This Web site focuses on financing issues related to school-based health centers. You can access the following papers:

- ▲ *Issues in Financing School-Based Health Centers: A Guide for State Officials*

- ▲ *Medicaid, Managed Care, and School-Based Health Centers: Proceedings of a Meeting With Policy Makers and Providers*

- ▲ *The New Child Health Insurance Expansions: How Will School-Based Health Centers Fit In?*

- ▲ *Nine State Strategies to Support SBHCs—Executive Summary*

The Centers for Medicare & Medicaid Services (CMS)
http://cms.hhs.gov

This resource provides general information on service funding related to Medicaid/EPSDT and the State Children's Health Insurance Program (SCHIP). Specific information can be found on each state's Web site, which can be accessed through the U.S. State and Local Government Gateway (www.statelocal.gov/).

[1] Some of this information is adapted from the Center for Mental Health in Schools. (2000). *Financial Strategies to Aid in Addressing Barriers to Learning.* http://smhp.psych.ucla.edu/pdfdocs/Financial/Fund2000.pdf

Federal Register
http://www.access.gpo.gov/su_docs/aces/aces140.html

The *Federal Register* is the main resource for federal funding opportunities. It is published Monday through Friday, except federal holidays. The current year's *Federal Register* database is updated daily by 6 A.M.

The Finance Project
http://www.financeproject.org

The Finance Project is a national initiative to create knowledge and share information that will lead to the improved well-being of children, families, and communities. The Finance Project develops working papers and other tools and products; convenes meetings, roundtables, and forums; and conducts technical assistance activities. Its Web site lists new initiatives, project descriptions, publications, and resources such as *Federal Financing Issues and Options*; *State and Local Financing Issues and Options*; *Financing Comprehensive, Community-Based Supports and Services*; *Results-Based Planning, Budgeting, Management, and Accountability Issues*; *Financing Early Childhood Supports and Services*; and *School Finance Issues*. The Finance Project also hosts the Welfare Information Network, a valuable source of information about welfare, income security, and welfare-to-work programs (http://www.welfareinfo.org/). Among the many useful guides are the following:

▲ *Juvenile Accountability Incentive Block Grants: Strategic Planning Guide* by Anna E. Danegger, Carol E. Cohen, Cheryl D. Hayes, and Gwen A. Holden

▲ *Towards an "Economics of Prevention": Illustrations From Vermont's Experience* by Cornelius Hogan and David Murphey (December 2000)

▲ *Developing Cost Accounting and Decision Support Software for Comprehensive Community-Based Support Systems: Integrated Feasibility Analysis* by Robert Harrington and Peter Jenkins with Carolyn Marzke and Carol Cohen (February 1999)

▲ *Financing Strategies to Support Comprehensive, Community-Based Services for Children and Families* by Mary M. O'Brien, National Child Welfare Resource Center for Organizational Improvement (March 1997)

▲ *Financing Family Resource Centers: A Guide to Funding Sources and Strategies* by Sara Watson and Miriam Westheimer (April 2000)

▲ *Creating Dedicated Local Revenue Sources for Early Care and Educational Initiatives* by Barbara Hanson Langford (April 2000)

- *Cost Framework for Teacher Preparation and Professional Development* by Jennifer King Rice (June 2001)

- *Issues and Challenges in Financing Professional Development in Education* by Carol Cohen (June 2001)

- *Catalog and Guide to Federal Funding Sources for Professional Development in Education* by Carol Cohen and Anya Freiman (June 2001)

- *Money Matters: A Guide to Financing Quality Education and Other Children's Services* (January 1997)

- *Finding Funding: A Guide to Federal Sources for Out-of-School Time and Community School Initiatives* by Nancy D. Reder (April 2000)

- *Using CCDF to Finance Out-of-School Time and Community School Initiatives* by Sharon Deich with Erika Bryant and Elisabeth Wright (August 2001)

- *Maximizing Medicaid Funding to Support Health and Mental Health Services for School-Age Children and Youth* by Andrew Bundy with Victoria Wegener (October 2000)

- *Using TANF to Finance Out-of-School Time and Community School Initiatives* by Margaret Flynn (October 1999)

- *A Guide to Successful Public-Private Partnerships for Out-of-School Time and Community School Initiatives* by Sharon Deich (January 2001)

- *Using Title I to Finance Out-of-School Time and Community School Initiatives* by Sharon Deich, Victoria Wegener, and Elisabeth Wright (December 2001)

- *Financing Transportation Services for Out-of-School Time and Community School Programs* by Barbara Hanson Langford and Michele Gilbert (November 2001)

- *Using the Community Development Block Grant to Support Out-of-School Time and Community School Initiatives*

- *Adapting to Changing Conditions: Accessing Tobacco Settlement Revenues for Out-of-School Time and Community School Initiatives* by Carol Cohen and Victoria Wegener (December 2000)

- *Maximizing Medicaid Funding to Support Health and Mental Health Services for School-Age Children and Youth* by Andrew Bundy with Victoria Wegener (October 2000)

- *Maximizing Federal Food and Nutrition Funds for Out-of-School Time and Community School Initiatives* by Barbara Hanson Langford (February 2000)

- *Resources for Improving Mental Health Services for Low-Income Children* by Kelly O'Dell (October 2001)
- *Financing Broad-Based Community Collaboratives* by S. Cates (September 1998)

First Government
http://firstgov.gov/index.shtml

First Government is the U.S. government's official portal. It provides access to a great array of federal resources. First Government provides a generic search engine; topical, searchable links to federal, state, and tribal agencies; and searchable contact information.

The Foundation Center
http://fdncenter.org/

The mission of the Foundation Center is to foster public understanding of the foundation field by collecting, organizing, analyzing, and disseminating information on foundations, corporate giving, and related subjects. It publishes the *Philanthropy News Digest*, a weekly listing of requests for proposals (RFPs) from U.S. grant makers (http://fdncenter.org/pnd/current/index.html).

Many foundations have a focus on health, mental health, and schools: Annie E. Casey Foundation, Robert Wood Johnson Foundation, W. K. Kellogg Foundation, Charles Stewart Mott Foundation, Commonwealth Fund, Pew Charitable Trusts, DeWitt Wallace–Readers Digest Foundation, William T. Grant Foundation, Rockefeller Foundation, Harris Foundation, Public Welfare Foundation, R. G. Hemingway Foundation, and the Carnegie Corporation, among others. You can, of course, go directly to the foundation Web sites and find information about what they currently fund. Contacting organizations directly to discuss your proposal is often a good strategy.

The Future of Children
http://www.futureofchildren.org/

Financing Schools was the topic of the Winter 1997 edition of *The Future of Children* (Vol. 7, No. 3). It is available in PDF form. The articles include:

- Financing Schools: Analysis and Recommendations
- School Finance: Fifty Years of Expansion
- Sources of Funding for Schools
- How and Where the Education Dollar Is Spent
- Equity and Adequacy in School Funding

▲ School Finance Policy and Students' Opportunities to Learn: Kentucky's Experience

▲ Considering Nontraditional Alternatives: Charters, Private Contracts, and Vouchers

GrantsWeb
http://www.research.sunysb.edu/research/kirby.html#index

GrantsWeb is a starting point for accessing grants-related information and resources on the Internet. GrantsWeb offers links to grants-related Web sites and resources, including funding opportunities, grants databases, policy developments, and professional activities.

Office of Juvenile Justice and Delinquency Prevention (OJJDP),
Department of Justice
http://ojjdp.ncjrs.org

Examples of relevant grant opportunities in which the Department of Justice is or has been involved follow:

▲ **State Challenge Activities Grants Program.** The State Challenge Activities Grants Program provides incentives for states to improve their juvenile justice systems by developing, adopting, or improving policies and programs in one or more of ten specified Challenge areas.

▲ **Title II, Part B Formula Grants Program.** The Formula Grants Program is designed to support state and local delinquency prevention and intervention efforts and juvenile justice system improvements. Funds are allocated annually among the states on the basis of relative population of youth under age 18.

▲ **Weed and Seed.** Communities work with their United States Attorneys; local, state, and federal officials; community agencies; and community residents to develop and implement a Weed and Seed strategy to prevent, control, and reduce violent crime, drug abuse, and gang activity in targeted high-crime neighborhoods.

This site also offers a gateway to other Department of Justice and federal agency funding opportunities (i.e., education, health and human services, housing and urban development, and interior, labor, transportation) at http://ojjdp.ncjrs.org/grants/otherag.html.

School Grants
http://www.schoolgrants.org/grant_opps.htm

This Web site posts all types of grants for schools, teachers, and students and provides links to federal and state agencies and foundations. This site also provides online tips on fund raising and grant writing (http://www.schoolgrants.org).

School Health Finance Project of the National Conference of State Legislatures **(funded by DASH, CDC)**
http://www.ncsl.org/programs/health/pp/schlfund.htm

This summary of surveys of states and territories provides information on block grant and state support for school health programs. From the data, sources for school health funding and the procedures to access funds in each state can be identified. Information about how states and territories use federal and state funds for school health programs can be used by others who are developing and improving school health programs.

The block grant survey collects information about how states use six specific federal block grants to fund school health programs: the Community Mental Health Services Block Grant, Community Prevention Grants, Community Services Block Grant, Maternal and Child Health Services Block Grant, Preventive Health and Services Block Grant, Substance Abuse Prevention and Treatment Block Grant, Safe and Drug-Free Schools and Communities Block Grant. The state revenue survey collects information about which states appropriate state general revenue for school health programs (structured around the eight components of the CDC Coordinated School Health Program model).

School Health Program Finance Project Database
http://www2.cdc.gov/nccdphp/shpfp/index.asp

The School Health Program Finance Project searchable database contains information on federal, foundation, and state-specific funding sources for school health programs (including eligibility and application requirements) and practical information on how to acquire funds for developing and improving various components of school health programs. Project staff also publish reports about the evolving availability and nature of the diverse funding sources.

U.S. Department of Education
http://www.ed.gov/GrantApps

The simplest way to check for grants in the various units of the Department of Education is to go to the site listed above, to www.ed.gov/funding.html, or to the Catalog of Federal Domestic Assistance (www.cfda.gov/).

U.S. Department of Education Federal Register Announcements
http://www.ed.gov/legislation/FedRegister/announcements/

Another quick option for the most recent application notices is this Web site. It includes the types of relevant grant opportunities the Department of Education may fund, including:

- ▲ Alternative Strategies: Grants to Reduce Student Suspensions and Expulsions, and Ensure Educational Progress of Suspended and Expelled Students

- ▲ Neglected and Delinquent/High Risk Youth Program

- ▲ Even Start Statewide Family Literacy Initiative Grants

- ▲ 21st Century Community Learning Centers Program

- ▲ Parental Responsibility/Early Intervention Resource Centers

- ▲ Teacher Quality Enhancement Grants

- ▲ Character Education

- ▲ Emergency Immigrant Education Program

- ▲ Goals 2000 Comprehensive Local Reform Assistance Program

- ▲ Developing Hispanic Serving Institutions Program

- ▲ Linking Policy and Practice Audiences to the 1997 Amendments of IDEA

- ▲ State and Federal Policy Forum for Program Improvement

- ▲ Center on Achieving Results in Education for Students with Disabilities (Special Education)

- ▲ Rehabilitation Short-Term Training (Special Education)

- ▲ Centers for Independent Living (Special Education)

- ▲ Special Demonstration Programs (Special Education)

- ▲ Community Parent Resource Centers (Special Education)

- ▲ Elementary School Counseling Demonstration

- ▲ Middle School Drug Prevention and School Safety Program Coordinators

- ▲ State Grants for Incarcerated Youth Offenders

- ▲ Civic Education

- ▲ Systems-Change Projects to Expand Employment Opportunities for Individuals With Mental or Physical Disabilities, or Both, Who Receive Public Support

- ▲ Safe and Drug-Free Schools

- ▲ Interagency—with Departments of Justice and HHS—(www.ed.gov/offices/OESE/SDFS):

  - – Safe Schools/Healthy Students Initiative

  - – School Violence Prevention and Early Childhood Development Activities

Note: Opportunities exist to transfer a percentage of various federal grants to enable better outcomes related to the intent of the grant. For example, Title XI of the Improving America's Schools Act of 1994 allows school districts, schools, and consortia of schools to use up to five percent of their Elementary and Secondary Education Act (ESEA) funds to develop, implement, or expand efforts to coordinate services. A similar provision was included in the reauthorization of IDEA. Social services block grants have a provision that allows each state to transfer up to ten percent of its allotment for any fiscal year to preventive health and health services, alcohol and drug abuse services, mental health services, maternal and child health services, and low-income energy assistance block grants to enable the state to furnish social services best suited to the needs of individuals residing in the state.

U.S. Department of Health and Human Services
http://www.hhs.gov

The simplest way to check for grants in the various agencies of this Department is to go to the *Catalog of Federal Domestic Assistance* (www.cfda.gov/). Alternatively, go to the Department's Web address and click the agency you want to check out (e.g., Administration for Children and Families—ACF, Centers for Disease Control and Prevention—CDC, Health Resources and Services Administration—HRSA; National Institutes for Health—NIH; Substance Abuse and Mental Health Services Administration—SAMHSA). Once at the site, go to the grants pages to find out about agency grants, including what the various units are offering. For example:

▲ On SAMHSA's grant page (www.samhsa.gov/grants/grants.html), you will find information on grants from the Center for Mental Health Services, the Center for Substance Abuse Prevention, and the Center for Substance Abuse Treatment.

▲ On HRSA's grant page (www.hrsa.gov/grants.htm), you will find information on grants from the Bureau of Primary Health Care, the Bureau of Health Professions, the Bureau of Maternal and Child Health and the HIV/AIDS Bureau.

▲ On NIMH's grant page (www.nimh.nih.gov/grants/grants.cfm), you will find program announcements and requests for application.

▲ On NIDA's funding page (http://165.112.78.61/Funding.html), you will find announcements.

▲ On NIAAA's grant page (http://www.niaaa.nih.gov/extramural/grants.htm#contracts), you will find program announcements, requests for applications, and other relevant information.

Here are some examples of relevant grants the Department of Health and Human Services has funded recently:

- ▲ Comprehensive Community Mental Health Services for Children with SED
- ▲ Conference Grants Program
- ▲ Homeless Families Program
- ▲ Community Action Grants for Service Systems Change
- ▲ National Training and Technical Assistance Center for Children
- ▲ Violence Prevention/Resilience Development—School and Community Action Grants
- ▲ Violence Prevention Coordinating Center
- ▲ Community-Initiated Prevention Interventions
- ▲ Family Strengthening
- ▲ Substance Abuse Prevention/HIV Care
- ▲ Adolescent Treatment Models
- ▲ Targeted Capacity Expansion Program
- ▲ Community Action Grants
- ▲ Practice/Research Collaboratives
- ▲ Comprehensive Community Treatment Program for the Development of New and Useful Knowledge
- ▲ National Training Institute for Child Care Health Consultants
- ▲ National Resource Center for Health and Safety in Child Care
- ▲ Adolescent Health Center for State Maternal and Child Health Personnel
- ▲ Maternal and Child Health Provider Partnerships
- ▲ Community Organization Grants (COG) Program
- ▲ Interagency—with Departments of Justice and Education

Developing Schoolwide Interventions for All Students

FEW

SOME

ALL

The three-level approach to securing your school and improving academic performance, depicted by the triangle in the Introduction, is cost-effective. The three levels help you allocate precious human and fiscal resources to a schoolwide foundation for all students, early interventions for some students who require extra support, and intensive interventions for the small number of students who require even more support. This chapter explains in depth how to implement the first level by employing universal interventions to create a caring and supportive school community that lays the foundation for improved behavior and academic outcomes. The Schoolwide Prevention Program Checklist (see Appendix B) suggests what you need to create a schoolwide foundation.

We begin with a discussion of two concepts that underlie the interventions described by the *Early Warning Guide*, the *Action Guide*, and this book: **risk** and **protection**. Then we apply the planning process described in Chapter 1 to the four key elements of a comprehensive schoolwide plan (from the *Action Guide*, Chapter 2):

▲ Creating a caring school community in which all members feel connected, safe, and supported

▲ Teaching appropriate behaviors and social problem-solving skills

▲ Implementing positive behavior support systems

▲ Providing appropriate academic instruction

As Figure 6 suggests, these four elements are interdependent. For example, when students, staff, and families feel connected to their school, student behavior and grades improve and promotion rates and graduation rates increase. Similarly, when students are taught appropriate behaviors, positive behavior systems are more effective and teachers can devote more time to academic instruction. Finally, when students benefit from appropriate academic instruction, both their commitment to the school and their willingness to behave appropriately increase.

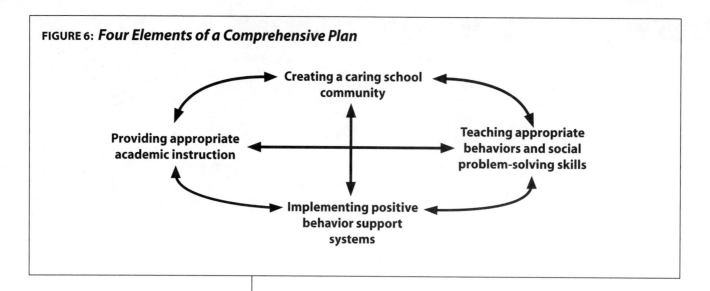

FIGURE 6: *Four Elements of a Comprehensive Plan*

Creating a caring school community

Providing appropriate academic instruction

Teaching appropriate behaviors and social problem-solving skills

Implementing positive behavior support systems

Reference

The central theme of this action plan is that every school must make the creation of a safe and supportive learning community one of its highest priorities. Each component of this phrase—safe, supportive, learning, community—is critical. Schools may be safe and orderly, but if they fail to build a supportive community and press for high academic expectations, students learn little. Similarly, schools may be warm and supportive, but if they have low expectations for their students, little learning takes place.

Every Child Learning: Safe and Supportive Schools. (2001). Learning First Alliance.

These four elements are also central to meeting both school improvement and school safety goals (Osterman, 2000). Students who are not connected to the school community are more likely to waste their academic potential. Students who cannot manage their own behavior are more likely to miss opportunities to learn as teachers attend to other students or focus only on managing student behavior. Teachers in schools lacking positive behavioral support systems frequently spend an undue amount of time on discipline issues. Many students in these classes are deprived of learning opportunities because of this. Students in schools with weak academic support are more likely to be bored or frustrated and to create discipline problems.

Reducing Risk Factors and Building Protective Factors

The concepts of risk and protection are central to the *Early Warning Guide* and *Action Guide* as well as to the interventions described in Appendix A. A *risk factor* is any factor that increases the probability that a person will suffer harm. A *protective factor* is any factor that decreases (buffers) the potential harmful effect of a risk factor. These factors can be inherent in an individual (e.g., a cognitive deficit) or in an environment (e.g., a large school). Risk and protective factors have different effects at different stages of a person's development. Risk and protective factors often cluster (e.g., a student who cannot read may also have a behavioral problem and associate with antisocial peers). Risk and protective factors often are relevant to multiple social outcomes (e.g., school dropout, delinquency, violence, and substance abuse). More risk factors place a child or children at greater risk of poor social and academic outcomes; more protective factors increase the likelihood of improved outcomes.

Understanding the limitations of what we know about, and how we can use, risk factors is important. *Youth Violence: A Report of the Surgeon General* (2001), available at http://www.surgeongeneral.gov/library/youthviolence/report.html, lists these limitations:

▲ No single risk factor or set of risk factors is powerful enough to predict with certainty that a particular youth will become violent.

▲ Because public health research is based on observations and statistical probabilities in large populations, risk factors can be used to predict violence in groups with particular characteristics or environmental conditions but not in individuals.

Given the two limitations, assessments designed to target individual youth for intervention programs must be used with great care. Most individual youth identified by existing risk factors for violence, even youth facing accumulated risks, never become violent.

Although there are many child, family, and community risk and protective factors, there are also many school-based risk and protective factors. A healthy schoolwide foundation helps all students. It may be a sufficiently strong protective factor for most students. Some students, who are exposed to more intense risk factors, may require and benefit from early interventions that target risk factors or build protective factors, but these students also benefit from a healthy schoolwide foundation because it builds protective factors (e.g., connection with adults) and reduces school-based factors that place them at risk. (Many people call this building resilience.) Still other students may require even more intense interventions that address more risk factors and build protective factors across multiple environments. Nonetheless, these students are particularly susceptible to the lack of a schoolwide foundation; therefore, intensive interventions for these students work best in schools that have a solid schoolwide foundations.

Because risk and protective factors interact and accumulate, effective interventions that target one type of risk factor may reduce risk factors in other areas. Substance abuse, which can be an early warning sign (Chapter 4) and can co-occur with intense mental health problems (Chapter 5), is an example. The Center for Substance Abuse Prevention (CSAP) has identified model programs that have been demonstrated to prevent or decrease substance abuse (see CSAP Model Programs, http://modelprograms.samhsa.gov/). Many of these programs are also identified in the *Action Guide* or in Appendix A (ACHIEVE, The Child Development Project, The Good Behavior Game, Life Skills Training, Multisystemic Therapy, Bullying Prevention Program,

What You Need to Know About Youth Violence Prevention

The Substance Abuse and Mental Health Services Administration (SAMHSA) has produced a simple guide that distills what is known about youth violence prevention. The guide, *What You Need to Know About Youth Violence Prevention*, discusses the pathways to violence, effective and ineffective approaches to prevention, and what can be done to prevent violence. The guide is available at www.samhsa.gov and through SAMHSA's National Mental Health Information Clearing Houses at (800) 789-2647.

Promoting Alternative Thinking Strategies (PATHS), Project ALERT, Project Northland, Second Step, and the Strengthening Families Program).

The Importance of Connection and Trust

Research indicates that connection plays an important role in making schools safe and successful. For example, analyses of a survey of 72,000 junior and senior high students indicate that when students feel cared for and connected at school, negative behaviors decrease and academic performance increases. This research identified school climate as a key to school connectedness, emphasizing the importance of well-managed schools and classrooms where expectations for individual responsibility are clear, teachers consistently acknowledge all students, and students are actively involved in classroom management.

Improving the Odds: The Untapped Power of Schools to Improve the Health of Teens. (2002). Blum, McNeely, and Rinehart.

Similarly, a study of school improvement in Chicago found that relational trust among teachers, administrators, parents, and students affect student attendance, academic persistence, and improved test scores. "We have learned, based on our research on school reform in Chicago, that a broad base of trust across a school community lubricates much of a school's day-to-day functioning and is a critical resource as local leaders embark on ambitious improvement plans."

Trust in Schools: A Core Resource for Improvement. (2002). Bryk and Schneider.

For a synthesis of these two studies, see Clea A. McNeely, James M. Nonnemaker, & Robert W. Blum, Promoting school connectedness: Evidence from the National Longitudinal Study of Adolescent Health, *Journal of School Health*, April 2002, 72:4, 138–146, and Anthony S. Bryk and Barbara Schneider, Trust in schools: A core resource for school reform, *Educational Leadership*, May 2003, 60:6, 40–45.

Creating a Caring, Safe, and Supportive School Community

In the video *Promising Practices for Safe and Effective Schools*, when the principal of Tampa's Cleveland Elementary School stands outside the school to welcome the students and their parents, she is getting to know them and letting them get to know her. Her staff, who are part of her team, reinforce her actions when they connect with individual children and their parents. Giving the school a human face does not happen magically. Principals need time to stand outside the school each day. Staff must have training, and the ratio of staff to students must create the opportunity for individual contacts. The actions of the principal and staff must be responsive to the needs of students and their families. Students and parents are then more likely to support the academic and behavioral goals of the school.

Assess Your School Community

Determine how students, families, and staff experience the school community.

Trust and connection are often keys to improving student and school outcomes. It is important to determine how strong the trust and connections are between and among students, families, and staff. The team can speak with *key informants*, conduct *surveys*, or hold *focus groups* to gather this information. Some schools will choose to do all three because each approach has limitations. Key informants (e.g., school counselors) can help identify issues, but their knowledge is limited to their individual experience, supplemented by what others have told them. Anonymous surveys can reach many people and solicit information that individuals will not share in public. However, it may be difficult to determine what lies beneath the surface of the responses. Face-to-face focus groups clarify the meaning of survey findings, but are limited by the experience of the participants and their willingness to share information in public. The data you collect from these sources will frame your planning efforts and provide baseline data for the future evaluation of your interventions.

Choose key informants on the basis of their access to the particular information that you need. For example, counselors can provide information on discipline-related activities; social workers are familiar with the challenges that some families confront when trying to access school services.

If you choose to do a survey, include demographic questions to find out whether some group members feel more connected to the school than others do (e.g., parents of color or students in particular grades). Surveys can include both selected-response (e.g., yes-no) questions, which are easy to compile, and open-ended questions, which solicit more specific information (e.g., How can we improve communication between the school and families?). You can survey all members of the school community or a representative sample of each group. (If you choose to sample, consult with a researcher to ensure that the sample includes a sufficient number from each group.) The *California School Climate and Safety Survey* (Furlong & Morrison, 2001), which was developed by the School Climate and Safety Partnership (University of California, Santa Barbara) is an excellent developmentally appropriate tool for surveying whole-school student populations from primary grades through high school (see Appendix B). Four sample questions are provided in Figure 7.

Working With Families in Salinas

Salinas, California, has 144,000 people; 61 percent are Latino and 45% are under 25. Approximately 35 percent of the population speak Spanish only, and about an equal percentage are involved in agriculture (20 percent are agricultural laborers and 15 percent work in food processing, packing, and shipping). The Safe Schools/Healthy Students Initiative in this predominantly young Latino community has encouraged schools to listen to families and community groups in order to find ways to actively involve all families in school-related activities. The following two Initiative activities exemplify the culturally competent approach that Salinas takes in working with families.

To help Spanish-speaking families new to Salinas understand how to deal with the culture of the school and of the community, the Initiative wanted two bilingual, bicultural individuals as Community Resource Agents. To identify these staff, the Initiative solicited advice from the Center for Community Advocacy, a community-based organization run by a board of directors that included both monolingual English-speaking employers and monolingual Spanish-speaking farm workers. The Center recommended the two people who were hired.

To encourage parents to participate in their children's instruction and in parent education, the Initiative created a *Pasaporte Hacia La Educacion* (a Parent Passport). Parents use the *Pasaporte* to record activities that they do to support their children, and they receive incentives to participate in these activities.

Because the *Pasaporte* was not working, the Initiative convened three focus groups with families to improve the incentives. The parents in the focus groups felt valued by being asked to participate. In the words of one administrator, they "took off with the thing" and "their insight and wisdom made the process easy and smooth." Focus group participants identified effective incentives, such as two-for-one meals at affordable local restaurants and discount coupons on meat, eggs, flour, and milk. Now more parents are participating.

(Salinas students are pictured on the front cover.)

A Comprehensive and Decentralized Three-Level, Districtwide Approach

California's San Juan Unified School District (see also the sidebar Building a Psychologically Safe Schoolwide Foundation in Chapter 3) covers 75 square miles and includes several well-defined communities. Different communities have different strengths and needs. The goal of the district's Safe Schools/ Healthy Students initiative, Building Bridges to Student Success (BBI), is to increase the capacity of each community to support children and families. It is implementing the comprehensive three-level approach to prevention.

The first level (for all students) includes sponsoring special events and campaigns, developing youth assets, mentoring, strengthening connections between families and the schools, providing community services, and implementing the Second Step Violence Prevention Program. The second level (early intervention for students viewed to be at risk) includes student assistance programs, more intensive staff mentoring, after-school interventions, and referrals for additional support. The third level (intensive services) includes school attendance review teams; student, family, and school consultations; family success plans; family development; home visitations; and access to community services when necessary.

BBI has replaced a district-centered approach with four regional centers to enhance accessibility and responsiveness to local site and community needs. Each center includes a multidisciplinary team that comprises a regional supervisor; a prevention specialist; an intervention specialist who works with student assistance programs (early intervention); and a student attendance review team that includes counselors, nurses, social workers, law enforcement officers, AmeriCorps volunteers, and social work and criminal justice interns who provide family-focused intensive individual services.

BBI's strategy is to reach out to community groups and agencies through regional oversight councils (ROCs). The ROCs, designed to facilitate networking and collaboration, include school staff and community service providers as well as families and students who receive BBI services. ROCs, which typically meet monthly (with workgroups meeting more frequently), provide advice and guidance to the staff of the four centers and share information about regional problems, concerns, programs, and services. The ROCs focus on six elements:

- Student and school safety

- Alcohol, tobacco, and other drug/violence prevention and intervention efforts

- School and community mental health prevention, intervention, and treatment

- Early childhood psychosocial and emotional development programs

- Education reform and alternative programs

- Safe school policies and positive school attendance

The ROCs review evaluation and other reports on regional program needs and effectiveness and (to quote their Purpose Statement) publicize and promote good work that is being done on behalf of children and families "to promote safe schools, healthy children, and strong collaboration in a region where all people live and work in harmony and are supported with resources to achieve their full potential."

During the 2000–2001 school year, more than 770 community members participated and 214 school-community partnerships were established.

The BBI evaluation surveyed 150 ROC members and determined the following:

- Eighty-seven percent indicated increased services made available to families.

- Eighty-three percent indicated improved quality of service.

- Ninety-six percent indicated greater agency and participant awareness of resources available.

FIGURE 7: *Sample Questions: California School Climate Survey, Secondary Version*

Sample Question	Strongly Disagree			Strongly Agree
I feel very safe at this school.	1	2	3	4
When students break the rules, they are treated firmly and fairly.	1	2	3	4
Rules at school are stupid.	1	2	3	4
Verbal abuse of teachers is a problem at this school.	1	2	3	4

Four of the 95 questions for grades 7–12 of the *School Safety Survey,* ©UCSB School Climate & Safety Partnership, Furlong & Morrison (2001).

Focus groups give stakeholders an opportunity to share information within a group where individuals stimulate and contextualize one another's responses. Focus groups can be homogenous (e.g., families of students with disabilities) or mixed (e.g., all families). Homogenous groups can provide rich information about particular experiences, whereas mixed groups can shed light on the diversity of experiences. Many useful guides to focus-group techniques are available. (See also the sidebar Tips for Using Focus Groups in Chapter 1.)

Assess the challenges to creating a caring community.

For example, do families have opportunities to connect with the school in a manner that makes them feel comfortable? Do staff attitudes interfere with the ability of staff to connect with students or families? Does the organization of the school interfere with the ability of staff to connect with students? Ask all the questions under the topics below.

▲ **Training.** Do staff members understand the needs of all the students? Have they received appropriate training in how to work with diverse learners, including students with challenging behavior? Are they trained to interact with parents in a culturally respectful manner?

▲ **Supports.** Are there support systems for families to participate in school activities? Are there supports for teachers to work with students and families whom they find challenging? Do the school principal and the district administration actively support these efforts? Do particular groups of students require additional support (e.g., students transitioning to a new school)?

▲ **Consultation.** Do staff have access to ongoing consultation? Do consultants have appropriate expertise for behavioral issues that affect the ability of students to connect with one another and with the school staff? Is the expertise of pupil service personnel used effectively?

Listening to Students to Prevent School Violence: Creating a Warm Line to Break the "Code of Silence"

Salinas, California's Safe School/Healthy Students Initiative is governed by a 16-person school team (called a leadership council). Members of the team include three assistant superintendents; the directors of county human services departments, including children's mental health; a representative of the police department; two teachers; two parent representatives; and two high school students. The Leadership Council meets monthly on the second Thursday of each month.

One regularly scheduled meeting took place two days after two students were killed at a high school in San Diego County, California, by a young man whom others had seen as needing help and who had communicated his deadly intent to some of his friends. When the meeting began, the student representatives asked what the school system in Salinas could do to prevent such an incident from occurring. The Council members changed the agenda to focus on the students' concerns.

They asked the students what they thought should be done. The two juniors stated that their peers wanted to break the "code of silence," but they needed a responsive and trustworthy resource that they and others could call to share their concerns, fears, and knowledge about students who might need help or who might be planning something deadly. The students said it would be nice to have a phone line that was staffed "24/7." The Council discussed the suggestion, agreed to create a "warm line," and decided that it should be bilingual in order to serve both Spanish- and English-speaking families.

Because financial resources were limited, the Council formed a workgroup of six members, including both students, to survey existing community resources. This workgroup found an 800 number that could be accessed by children and youth at no cost to the school system. The Council was able to implement the warm line and publicize it through newsletters and bilingual bookmarks.

Reducing Stress

The ability of school staff members to respond to student needs is affected by their own levels of stress, which can be exacerbated by school or national crises. *Violence in Communities and Schools: A Stress Reduction Guide for Teachers and Other School Staff* is a 41-page guide produced by the National Education Association Health Information Network (2001) in collaboration with the Center for Mental Health Services, Substance Abuse and Mental Health Services Administration at the U.S. Department of Health and Human Services. It also features a link to five practical tips for tackling the psychological impact of terrorism.

http://www.neahin.org/mentalhealth/stressguide.htm

A Resource for Working with Emotional and Behavioral Challenges

The U.S. Department of Education worked with teachers and paraprofessionals to prepare a book to help educators understand and work with students who have emotional and behavioral challenges and their families.

Teaching and Working With Children Who Have Emotional and Behavioral Challenges. (2000). Quinn, Osher, Warger, Hanley, Bader, & Hoffman.

▲ **School Organization.** Do staffing patterns and ratios enable teachers to connect with individual students? Do school routines support or discourage effective contact between teachers and families? Do schedules and routines support or inhibit collaboration among school staff and between school staff and families? Do school schedules allow time for planning or meeting with parents? Does the grouping of students (e.g., tracking) contribute to or discourage the building of a student community? Do the school's curricular and extracurricular activities reinforce cooperation or competition?

Promoting Positive Youth Development

In developing a schoolwide foundation, you may find it helpful to build on what has been learned from individuals concerned with positive youth development. In March 1998, the National Collaboration for Youth Members defined youth development as "a process which prepares youth to meet the challenges of adolescence and adulthood through a coordinated, progressive series of activities and experiences which help them to become socially, morally, emotionally, physically, and cognitively competent. Positive youth development addresses the broader developmental needs of youth, in contrast to deficit-based models which focus solely on youth problems" (National Youth Development Information Center, 2002). Rather than seeing young people as problems, positive youth development workers view youth as resources and build on their strengths and capabilities. They support activities that help youth develop social, emotional, ethical, physical, cognitive, and vocational competencies.

Youth development programs employ a structured series of activities and experiences to help youth develop social, emotional, ethical, physical, and cognitive competencies. They address the broader developmental assets that all children and youth need (such as caring relationships, safe places and activities, health and mental health, marketable skills, and opportunities for service and civic participation), in contrast to deficit-based approaches that focus solely on youth problems (National Youth Development Information Center, 2002). For a summary of the evidence on positive youth develop-

ment, see *Positive Youth Development in the United States: Research Findings on Evaluations of Positive Youth Development Programs* (Catalano et al., 1998) (http://aspe.hhs.gov/hsp/PositiveYouthDev99/) and the National Research Council's Commission on Behavioral and Social Science and Education's *Community Programs to Promote Youth Development* (2002) (Committee on Community-Level Programs for Youth, 2002).

Many other resources on youth development are available on the Internet:

– The American Youth Policy Forum's Section on Youth and Community Development (http://www.aypf.org/subcats/ycd.htm)

– The Carnegie Foundation's Focus on Youth Development (http://www.cyfernet.org/youthdev.html)

– The Forum for Youth Investment (http://www.forumforyouthinvestment.org/respapers.htm)

– The Institute for Youth Development (http://www.youthdevelopment.org)

– National Youth Development Information Center (http://www.nydic.org/nydic/)

– Public/Private Ventures resources on youth development (http://www.ppv.org/content/reports/ydv_pdf.html)

– The Search Institute (http://www.search-institute.org/)

– 4-H Centers at many Land Grant Universities, such as the University of Minnesota's Center for 4-H Youth Development (http://www.fourh.umn.edu/educators/publications.html)

▲ **School Environment.** Does the size of the school support or discourage the ability of adults to know all the students and of students to connect with one another? Is the size of the school particularly daunting for certain groups of students, such as students transitioning from smaller schools? Do elements of the physical environment (e.g., wall displays) include all students and families?

Develop a plan to improve the school community.

If your data and analysis suggest that some members of your school community do not feel connected and supported, develop a plan that builds on your school's strengths and addresses its needs. Examples of what may be done in four areas follow.

▲ **Training and Consultation.** Provide staff with training that helps them understand the strengths and needs of all the students who attend the school so that they do not misinterpret the students' behavior or respond inappropriately. Give staff the skills that help them connect and maintain relationships with students and families. A good resource for these purposes is *Teaching and Working With Children Who Have Emotional and Behavioral Challenges* (Quinn et al., 2000). This book was developed with ongoing input from 40 teachers and paraprofessionals who wanted to work more effectively with students who have emotional and behavioral challenges and their families.

Train staff to create and sustain what the Child Development Project (see Appendix A) calls "a caring community of learners" in their classrooms by building on such values as kindness, respect, and concern for others. Involve families in planning activities that enhance bonds between families and school staff. Provide ongoing support, including mentoring, coaching, and consulting, to help staff sustain these skills.

▲ **School Organization.** Modify staffing ratios and models to enable teachers to connect with individual students (e.g., employ instructional aides differently). Create daily or weekly advisory periods at which students can discuss school or relationship issues and staff can keep in touch with the academic and social concerns of students. Consider de-tracking the school and creating more noncompetitive opportunities for students to work with one another.

▲ **Block Scheduling.** Scheduling is a major challenge for teachers and administrators. Adjust the school schedule to provide planning times for teachers and opportunities for dialogue between and among students and teachers.

Consider doing this in a manner that builds on other goals (e.g., supporting the transition to adult life). New York City's Central Park East Secondary School schedules a half day of teacher planning time while students attend an internship program outside the school.

One strategy that has proved effective is block scheduling, which employs larger chunks of time to align with the learning needs of different students and content areas. Block scheduling can support teaching approaches that engage students and faculty in dialogue, harness student interest, and provide opportunities for staff planning. One resource to consult is the National Commission on Time and Learning's *Prisoners of Time* (1994) (http://www.ed.gov/pubs/PrisonersofTime/).

▲ **School Environment.** Consider creating freestanding smaller schools or scatterplex schools—two or more small schools at different sites that share a principal. Districts and schools can create schools within schools (with their own administrators) or academies (or houses) within schools where groups of students share the same staff. Middle schools, for example, could be broken up into houses where teams of teachers spend the whole day with the same students. Schools can create programs to support the transition of new students into the school community (e.g., a small school within the high school for ninth graders). Schools can consult with culturally and linguistically diverse students, families, and staff to make sure that the school surroundings convey a sense of inclusion for everybody.

Crisis Plans for Troubling Times

Although schools are generally the safest environments for children and youth, crises do occur: natural disasters, horrendous accidents, suicides and other tragic deaths, and deliberate acts of violence, including terrorist attacks and other acts of war. Preparing for these realities is part of ensuring and maintaining a caring school environment. Section 6, "What to Do: Responding to Crisis" in *Early Warning, Timely Response: A Guide to Safe Schools* (pp. 27–30) provides a foundation for schools to consider when developing crisis plans. Schools and school systems that have current and comprehensive crisis plans for today's potential crises are safe and caring.

What is a crisis? A crisis is any psychologically or physically threatening event that is rare, unpredictable, and sudden and that leaves individuals in a stressed state, so previously effective coping skills are less than effective in reducing the stress and threat of the event.

In today's world, we must ensure that we have community-coordinated plans to address the crisis resulting not only from the potential of a tornado or an enraged, dangerous student or intruder but also from a biological, chemical, or nuclear attack.

→

Three elements are critical to any plan: (1) preparation, (2) interventions during a crisis, and (3) responses to the aftermath of the crisis. Today, schools must have not only clear lock-down and evacuation procedures but also adequate food, medicines, and survival supplies on hand to sustain staff and students for long-term or community-wide crises. Communication systems must be in place to reduce confusion and reassure staff, students, and families.

A monumental task? No. Schools do not need to prepare a crisis plan on their own—to do so can be counterproductive to the safety of staff and children. Community-wide, cross-agency plans are the most effective. Federal, state, and local agencies and first responders have plans to follow—laws, policies, and procedures—that are already in place and should incorporate schools. Further, community-coordinated training of school staff can better ensure safety. Keeping students and families informed is critical to implementing an effective crisis plan.

Most of the effective school crisis plans have the following elements:

- Structured procedures for each type of crisis.

- Trained in-school team with the range of skills and responsibilities necessary to assist and direct staff, students, and responders.

- Effective, foolproof ways to communicate among staff and connect with needed support services and families.

- Clearly defined school staff roles and responsibilities that are communicated and aligned with other agencies.

- Inclusion of families in the planning.

- Information provided to families about the components of the plan, including what they can do at home and how the school plan aligns with the community response plan.

- Procedures to ensure that families are quickly informed of crisis responses. For example, a plan could have the following code system: Code Orange—Students are evacuated to a designated site where parents may pick them up or they remain until bused home. Code Blue—school and classrooms are locked down; police are on campus;

parents remain off school grounds. Code Red—School is sealed off; children and staff remain on-site for the term of the crisis in designated protected rooms; emergency personnel are on campus.

- Procedures that address the unique needs of children with disabilities whose medical and psychological needs in a crisis may require special plans including adequate supplies of medications and accessible, safe environments. The No Child Left Behind Act requires that crisis plans address the unique needs of children with disabilities.

- Plans for community-wide postcrisis treatment and interventions to reduce the lasting psychological and other effects of the crisis experience for students, staff, and families. These plans should be individualized and evidence-based because some well-intended interventions may be harmful for some students and staff.

For specific plans and materials to assist families and children, the following resources are useful. See "Responding to Crisis" in *Interventions for Academic and Behavior Problems II: Prevention and Remedial Approaches* (Shinn, Walker, & Stoner, 2002, pp. 200–206) and numerous chapters in *Best Practices in School Crisis Prevention and Intervention* (Brock, Lazarus, & Jimerson, 2002).

Many Web sites offer crisis-planning help to schools, including the following:

American Red Cross—www.redcross.org

This Web site provides information on national and local information and training.

Center for Mental Health Services—http://mentalhealth.samhsa.gov/cmhs/childrenanxiety/default.asp

This Web site provides resources to help individuals manage anxiety in times of crisis. It is intended to help them tend to their own mental health and emotional well-being so that they can be a better, more reliable resource for friends and family members during their times of need. It includes a mental health services locator.

Centers for Disease Control and Prevention—www.phppo. cdc.gov/PHTN/schools

This is a good Web site for suggestions on community-wide, interagency crisis planning. You can check your school's plans by using the frequently asked questions page.

Collaborative for Academic, Social, and Emotional Learning—http://www.casel.org/trauma.htm

This Web site provides current resources for handling trauma and crises. It organizes links to the top work in the field in three areas: (1) classroom lessons related to war, terrorist attacks, and violence, (2) parent resources, and (3) resources for teachers and health professionals.

Federal Emergency Management Agency—www.fema.org

This Web site contains fact sheets; resources for parents, children, and teachers; and a useful search engine.

Federation of Families for Children's Mental Health— http://www.ffcmh.org/Eng_one.htm

This Web site has a checklist for parents and teachers, *What about the Children & Youth with Mental Health Issues in the Event of War?* This checklist focuses on security alerts and threats as well as public violence.

National Association of School Psychologists— www.nasponline.org

This Web site provides excellent easy-to-read handouts and references for planning for crisis, as well as for addressing the mental health needs of children, staff, and families experiencing a crisis. Check *Best Practices in School Crisis Prevention and Intervention*. This frequently updated site offers Web links on developmentally appropriate materials and crisis information to help schools and families address childhood symptoms of psychological stress.

National Mental Health Association—www.nmha.org

This Web site provides information for dealing with family, child, and staff problems as well as problematic symptoms.

Ohio Commission on Dispute Resolution & Conflict Management—http://www.state.oh.us/cdr/schools/trauma/ helpingkidscope.htm

This Web site provides four pages of "Links to Help Kids

Cope . . . during turbulent times." The commission also has a Web page, http://www.state.oh.us/cdr/turb.htm, devoted to "Preparing to Support Youngsters During Turbulent Times," which identifies diverse children's behaviors that adults should be alert to, as well as what parents, teachers, and officials can do.

U.S. Department of Education—www.ed.gov/ emergencyplan

This Web site for general school preparation has excellent connections for specific groups, such as the roles of central office administrators, and specific issues, such as recommendations for keeping parents informed. This Web site is intended to be a one-stop shop and is updated regularly.

A number of books provide valuable references for planning, including these:

Brock, S. E., Lazarus, P. J., & Jimerson, S. R. (Eds.) (2002). *Best practices in school crisis prevention and intervention*. Bethesda, MD: National Association of School Psychologists.

Hartsough, D. M. & Mayers, D. G. (1985). *Disaster work and mental health: Prevention and control of stress among workers*. Rockville, MD: Substance Abuse and Mental Health Services Administration, Center for Mental Health Services.

Poland S. & McCormick, J. (1999). *Coping with crisis: Lessons learned. A complete and comprehensive guide to school crisis intervention*. Longmont, CO: Sopris West Educational Services.

Shinn, M. R., Walker, H. M., & Stoner, G. (Eds.) (2002). *Interventions for academic and behavior problems II: Prevention and remedial approaches*. Bethesda, MD: National Association of School Psychologists.

U.S. Secret Service & U.S. Department of Education. (2002). *The final report and findings of the safe school initiative: Implications for the prevention of school attacks in the United States*. Washington, DC: Author. Available at www.ed.gov/offices/OSDFS/preventingattacksreport.pdf

Prepared for the Unimaginable

I am thankful on a daily basis that our school has used the Child Development Project [see Appendix A] since 1996 to improve our school climate (including connections between and among students and staff) and to foster social emotional learning. I have never been more grateful, however, than on September 11, 2001. School was already in session here in suburban Chicago when news of the horrific terrorist attack in New York started to filter into the school. I quickly typed a memo to staff, outlining the information as we knew it, and asked them to hold developmentally appropriate discussions with their students prior to lunchtime. Because our teachers have had lots of training and are comfortable holding class meetings, it was natural for them to pull the classes together for a discussion. Thanks to the relationships that our work with this program has fostered, students were able to express their feelings, talk about their fears, and feel comforted during these conversations. As the week progressed, class meetings were held frequently to continue to help the children process this heretofore unimaginable situation. Students participated in planning for a Day of Remembrance, and parents joined us as we shared our grief and continued to build the sense of community that has been an essential component in the success of our school.

Mary Tavegia, Principal
Cossitt School
La Grange, Illinois

Teaching Appropriate Behaviors and Social Problem-Solving Skills

All students require social and emotional skills to succeed. For example, students need skills to help them deal effectively with challenging social situations, such as being teased, witnessing someone else being teased, or being picked last to join a team. The following sidebar, Social-Emotional Competencies, describes these personal competencies. Students require social skills to enable them to treat one another respectfully and to resolve conflicts appropriately. A recent analysis of bullying in the United States found that 29.9 percent of a large sample of sixth-to-tenth graders reported moderate or frequent involvement in bullying, with 13 percent acting like a bully, 10.6 percent like a victim, and 6.3 percent like both (Nansel, Overpeck, Pilla, Ruan, Simons-Morton, & Scheidt, 2001). The Checklist of Students' Social Problem-Solving Strengths Across Situations (see Appendix B) can be employed to assess school-related student problem-solving skills.

Social-Emotional Competencies

Knowledge of Self

- **Identifying Emotions.** Identifying and labeling one's feelings

- **Personal Responsibility.** Recognizing and understanding one's obligation to engage in ethical, safe, and legal behaviors

- **Recognizing Strengths.** Identifying and cultivating one's strengths and positive qualities

Caring for Others

- **Perspective-Taking.** Identifying and understanding the thoughts and feelings of others

- **Appreciating Diversity.** Understanding that individual and group differences complement each other and make the world more interesting

- **Respecting Others.** Believing that others deserve to be treated with kindness and compassion, and feeling motivated to contribute to the common good

Responsible Decision Making

- **Managing Emotions.** Monitoring and regulating feelings so they aid rather than impede the handling of situations

- **Analyzing Situations.** Accurately perceiving situations in which a decision is to be made and assessing factors that might influence one's response

- **Goal Setting.** Establishing and working toward the achievement of short- and long-term prosocial goals

- **Problem Solving.** Generating, implementing, and evaluating positive and informed solutions to problems

Social Effectiveness

- **Communication.** Using verbal and nonverbal skills to express oneself and promote positive and effective exchanges with others

- **Building Relationships.** Establishing and maintaining healthy and rewarding connections with individuals and groups

- **Negotiation.** Achieving mutually satisfactory resolutions to conflict by addressing the needs of all concerned

- **Refusal.** Effectively conveying and following through with one's decision not to engage in unwanted, unsafe, unethical, or unlawful conduct

- **Help Seeking.** Identifying the need for and accessing appropriate sources of help and support

Social and Emotional Learning (SEL) Competencies. The Collaborative to Advance Social and Emotional Learning (CASEL). http://www.casel.org/competencies.htm.

Fortunately, a variety of research-based curricula and programs can help students learn and practice appropriate behaviors and social skills. The Jesse Keen Elementary School in Lakeland, Florida, which has dramatically improved its schoolwide discipline, climate, and academic performance, is a 658-student school in which 88 percent of the students are eligible for free or reduced-price lunch. The school employs "Stop and Think," which is part of ACHIEVE (see Appendix A). In addition to teaching students necessary skills, this approach helps create a school in which all students feel connected. The sidebar Building a Psychologically Safe Schoolwide Foundation shows how a Safe Schools/Healthy Students grantee has implemented a social skills curriculum, *Second Step*, that was cited in the *Action Guide* (see its description in Appendix A).

Building a Psychologically Safe Schoolwide Foundation

California's San Juan Unified School District serves approximately 50,000 students. Its Safe Schools/Healthy Student initiative, Building Bridges to Student Success (BBI), sees a psychologically safe environment and youth assets as keys to creating a nurturing learning environment that improves attendance and academic performance. To create a safe environment, BBI sought a universal intervention that addresses problem behavior that begins with words and escalates to physical violence. It wanted to improve how students communicated with each other. They targeted skill development in three areas: empathy (which they saw as a critical element in prosocial skills), impulse control, and anger management.

BBI selected a research-based, universal intervention called *Second Step* (see Appendix A) for two reasons: it targeted empathy, impulse control, and anger management, and it had already been successfully implemented in some schools in the district. For example, in one San Juan elementary school, *Second Step* had reduced suspensions by 60 percent over one year. In the words of one fourth-grade teacher (quoted in a BBI brochure), "*Second Step* had a tremendous effect in my classroom. It has taught my students skills that enable them to solve their own problems and to control their anger." Data and testimonials such as these were shared with all 53 elementary principals when the BBI staff met with them to describe the elements of the program. BBI staff told the principals that BBI would provide training for teachers and support staff, booster training, a kick-off assembly, parent education related to *Second Step*, and ongoing support when required. Twelve schools signed up initially. A year later, 43 schools wanted to participate.

Second Step meets BBI's goal of creating a psychologically safe school environment. While the developers of the program, the Committee for Children, emphasize the skill development component of *Second Step*, BBI has found that *Second Step* transforms the school environment because it helps students and staff develop a common language and provides them with common strategies for dealing with anger and violence.

Most of these curricula and programs employ multiple approaches. They didactically teach skills, modeling, and role playing, offer opportunities to practice the new skills, and give feedback. These strategies, sometimes called social-cognitive or cognitive-behavioral interventions, are summarized in the Centers for Disease Control and Prevention's *Best Practices of Youth Violence Prevention* (see the following sidebar, Advice From the CDC).

In choosing interventions it is important to ensure that they

- ▲ are developmentally appropriate;
- ▲ are offered with a frequency, intensity, and duration that matches the needs of your school and its student body; and
- ▲ can be implemented with the human resources available within your school community.

Interventions must also address the characteristics of your school community. For example, schools serving students who are regularly exposed to violence in their neighborhoods may need to address different problems and with a different intensity than schools whose students are not exposed to community violence. For example, the impact of the Resolving Conflict

Advice From the CDC

The intervention selected for a given school or school system—and the activities and curriculum that comprise it—will depend largely on participants' ages and whether the goal is to change the behaviors and attitudes of all students or those of aggressive or violent students only. However, all social-cognitive interventions typically address the beliefs and attitudes that support aggressive behavior and teach the following skills:

- Negotiation, critical thinking, and decisionmaking

- Identifying, managing, and coping with feelings including anger

- Anticipating the consequences of one's aggressive verbal and nonverbal behavior

- Finding nonviolent alternatives to conflict

- Moral reasoning

When developing the curriculum and activities for your intervention, review interventions that have been tried in other schools. Assess whether the practices that made the intervention effective are applicable to your school or community.

You may need to customize some components of the intervention, but do so cautiously. Changing significant elements can alter the intervention's effectiveness.

Best Practices of Youth Violence Prevention: A Sourcebook for Community Action. (2000). Centers for Disease Control and Prevention (pp. 122–123).

Creatively Program (RCCP) (*Action Guide*, p. 9) was found to be weaker for students who lived in high-risk neighborhoods (Aber, Jones, Brown, Chaudry, & Samples, 1998), whereas the School Development Program may produce more powerful effects in poorer communities (Haynes, Comer, & Hamilton-Lee, 1988). Such information can help you select or modify programs. RCCP might work for students in high-risk neighborhoods, but only in more intensive doses or when linked to other interventions. The choice of effective social skill instruction should also address cultural and gender diversity (Cartledge & Milburn, 1996). For example, research has shown that Positive Adolescent Choice Training (PACT) is effective in reducing conflict and aggression among male youth in urban schools who are African American (*Action Guide*, p. 26).

The CDC *Sourcebook* identifies social-cognitive interventions as one of four best practices for preventing youth violence. The guide recommends that, when implementing these programs, schools do the following:

▲ Involve teachers and principals from the beginning.

▲ Use the words children use with their peers when they are angry.

▲ Include role-playing and small-group exercises to help children practice prosocial, nonviolent behaviors and develop automatic positive responses.

▲ Include training in intercultural understanding so young people can tolerate differences and see others' points of view.

A Guide to Social Skills Programs That Support Social and Emotional Learning

Safe and Sound: An Education Leader's Guide to Evidence-Based Social and Emotional Learning Programs

This is the most complete guide available on multiyear social skills programs for students in general education classrooms. Developed by CASEL (Collaborative for Academic, Social, and Emotional Learning), it provides a review of research on the benefits of social skills training, guidelines for program selection and implementation, and descriptions of 80 programs. This is a great resource for checking up on all those programs you've heard of, but don't know much about. Or to save time, you can go directly to the 22 most effective programs, which are designated CASEL Select.

Walker, Ramsey, and Gresham. Heading off disruptive behavior: How early intervention can reduce defiant behavior—and win back teaching time. *American Educator*, Winter 2003/04, 6–21, 45–46.

▲ Teach students about the risk factors or triggers that can lead to violent confrontation.

Both the *Action Guide* (pp. 8–10) and the CDC *Sourcebook* (pp. 134–140) offer specific guidance in implementing these interventions. In addition, the Collaborative for Academic, Social, and Emotional Learning (CASEL) has produced a practical and well-researched consumer's guide: *Safe and Sound: An Education Leader's Guide to Evidence-Based Social and Emotional Learning (SEL) Programs*. It is available online at www.casel.org.

Implementing Positive Behavior Support Systems

Although students need skills to manage their behavior, the school environment can help or hinder their efforts to behave appropriately. Two schoolwide factors that may become risk factors for school violence are the discipline system and the physical environment. The *Action Guide* (pp. 11–14) describes how to establish schoolwide systems for positive behavioral support and ways to create a safe physical environment. Here we discuss how to analyze data to refine your approach to schoolwide discipline and how to assess your school's physical space.

Analyzing Schoolwide Discipline Data

Effective schoolwide systems of behavioral support are built on an analysis of behavioral problems and the data that your school regularly collects, such as behavior incident reports and records of disciplinary referrals, detentions, suspensions, and expulsions. The schoolwide team can do this analysis, or it can be done by a workgroup that may include some, but not all, team members and other members of the school community. The Features for Assessing Behavioral Support in Your School (see Appendix B) can frame this analysis. In either case, the team should ensure that

▲ simple, efficient strategies for continually assessing and refining schoolwide approaches to positive behavioral support are in place;

▲ the knowledge and expertise of teachers, classified staff, families, pupil services personnel, and administrators are incorporated in assessing data and developing strategies; and

▲ the analyses and strategies align with other efforts to build a schoolwide foundation (e.g., connecting students to the school) as well as with efforts to aid students who exhibit early warning signs.

Tools That Will Help Your Analysis. Databases are available to assess schoolwide behavior. One is the Schoolwide Information System (SWIS), a commercial database available from the Center for Positive Behavioral Intervention Support. SWIS uses well-defined behaviors to document student behavior in context. The referral process becomes an important source of data for monitoring schoolwide discipline and individual student behavior. Assessing Behavioral Support in Your School: A Survey (see Appendix B) can help you assess schoolwide and classroom systems in your school.

Adapting Your Strategies to Your School Situation. It is important to adapt the strategies (or programs) you use to the unique characteristics of your school—for example, the number of students in your school; the resources available in your school (e.g., pupil services personnel); and the type of assistance available at district, regional, and state levels. You should also examine what the school has done in the past because this information can contribute to staff readiness or staff resistance. Further, you should identify and assess what other programs and policies are in place that will complement what you are doing (e.g., social-cognitive programs) or undercut your efforts (e.g., inflexible and punitive approaches to discipline). In sum, you should assess what is currently in place in your school, whether it is effective, and what needs to be added or improved.

Once you have analyzed schoolwide data on behavioral problems and assessed the relevant characteristics of your school, you are ready to adopt or modify a program that best addresses the strengths and needs of your school. The sidebar Key Principles of Practice delineates the characteristics of an effective behavioral system in a school.

Key Principles of Practice

- Safe schools develop and consistently enforce school-wide rules that are clear, broad-based, and fair.

- Effective schoolwide behavior systems are simple, proactive, and positive and are applied consistently across all school settings.

- Rules and disciplinary procedures are developed collaboratively by school staff, families, students, and community representatives. Rules for student behavior should be posted throughout the school and should be referenced and reinforced frequently by all staff.

- Schoolwide disciplinary policies include a code of conduct, specific rules, and consequences that can accommodate student differences.

- Effective schoolwide approaches ensure that the cultural values and educational goals of the community are reflected in the rules.

- Supports are provided throughout the school and within classrooms to implement the rules.

- Schoolwide programs can incorporate peer mediation and conflict resolution to promote a climate of nonviolence.

- Safe schools evaluate the physical environment to ensure that the campus is safe and secure.

- Students know and can explain expectations for behavior as well as the incentives and consequences associated with adherence to or violation of those expectations.

Schoolwide Approaches to Behavior is an OSEP *IDEAS That Work* fact sheet.

The school surroundings—not just the discipline system—can serve as a risk or a protective factor. To create a safe school environment and reduce problem behavior, the schoolwide team can apply some techniques that were developed to reduce community crime. For example, Crime Prevention Through Environmental Design (CPTED) (Fleissner & Heinzelmann, 1996) identifies physical design features that influence the incidence of crime, such as lighting and the number of exits and isolated areas, and points out that a properly designed space can effectively encourage and support the type of behavior that is desired in that area.

With CPTED in mind, the schoolwide team should examine how your school is laid out, identify potential problem areas, and think through strategies for improving the environment. The assessment should

▲ examine how the spaces are defined (What are the rules for use of the space? Who has "ownership" over the space?);

▲ determine whether the space is open to normal staff surveillance (Does a staff member have to step into the hallway, through a set of double doors, or around a corner to observe behavior?); and

▲ determine whether the physical design of the space supports the desired behavior (Do corridors encourage easy and quick passage and discourage lingering and socializing? Are corridors characterized by ongoing problems, such as graffiti, vandalism, and bullying?).

The assessment should take special care to examine common areas that tend to be most problematic at schools: school grounds, parking lots, locker rooms, corridors, and bathrooms.

Once the assessment is complete, a plan can be developed to ensure that problem areas:

▲ **Have clear boundaries and provide smooth transitions from public to private space.** Undifferentiated areas can become locations for informal gatherings that are outside school supervision. These areas can be places where students are victimized. They are also frequently used for prohibited behavior, such as drug use, sexual activity, and physical violence.

▲ **Are well lighted** and are not dark and isolated spaces (e.g., bathrooms located at the end of a corridor) that make some students feel fear, separation, and a lack of control.

- ▲ **Are well supervised.** Good supervision is more than a deterrent—it provides staff with an ability to support appropriate behavior and intervene early before a small problem becomes a big one.

- ▲ **Are not overly crowded.** Make sure that transitions between classes are timed to reduce congestion in hallways and to minimize the possibility that many students from different grade levels will be in the corridors at the same time.

Sometimes physical changes are not necessary—if you can change policy and practice. For example, if hallways are so crowded that jostling is getting out of hand, you can reduce the traffic flow by changing the schedule or by providing more supervision or positive behavior support (e.g., training students in appropriate hall behavior).

Providing Appropriate Academic Instruction

High academic standards are important. However, for students to reach these standards, schools must first address barriers to learning. Some of these barriers are social and emotional. Therefore, providing links to families, helping students manage their behavior, and reducing the amount of time that teachers spend inefficiently "controlling" behavior all contribute to improved academic outcomes.

Other barriers are specifically academic. Overcoming them depends on addressing ten academic factors:

1. Schoolwide belief that all children can achieve academically
2. Schoolwide commitment to learning
3. Strong teaching
4. Appropriate instructional strategies
5. Engaging curricula
6. Appropriate assessment
7. Availability of tutorial assistance for students
8. Availability of consultation for instructional staff
9. Ongoing training and support for instructional staff to help them address the learning needs of all students and to employ curricular and assessment effectively
10. Interventions backed with resources to ensure that all students receive the effective instruction and academic support necessary to achieve high standards

Schools that make these ten factors their standard, and commit themselves to helping all students, will reduce problem behaviors and the risk of violence.

Resources for Improving Instruction and Learning

The No Child Left Behind Act requires schools to educate all students. A number of resources can help schools and districts implement approaches that build their capacity to provide appropriate academic instruction:

- American Association of School Administrators, American Federation of Teachers, National Association of Elementary School Principals, National Association of Secondary School Principals, National Education Association, Educational Research Service. (1999). *An educators' guide to schoolwide reform.* Arlington, VA: Educational Research Service.

- American Federation of Teachers. (1998). *Six promising schoolwide programs for raising student achievement.* Washington, DC: Author. Available at http://www.aft.org/edissues/whatworks/six/index.htm

- Darling-Hammond, L. (1997). *The right to learn: A blueprint for creating schools that work.* San Francisco: Jossey-Bass.

- Education Commission of the States. (2003). Lagging achievement of disadvantaged students remains a critical problem. *The Progress of Education Reform, 4*(1). Available at http://www.ecs.org/clearinghouse/43/00/4300.pdf

- Educational Quality Institute. (2001). *Guidelines for ensuring the quality of national design-based assistance providers.* Washington, DC: Author. Available at http://www.eqireports.org/Publications/guidelines_toc.htm

- Elmore, R. F. & Rothman, R. (Eds.). (1999). *Testing, teaching, and learning: A guide for states and school districts.* Washington, DC: National Academy Press. Available at http://www.nap.edu/catalog/9609.html

- Johnson, J. F. & Asera, R. (Eds.). (1999). *Hope for urban education: A study of nine high-performing high-poverty urban elementary schools* (ERIC Document No. ED438362). Washington, DC: U.S. Department of Education. Available at http://www.ed.gov/pubs/urbanhope/

- Learning First Alliance. (2003). *Beyond islands of excellence: What districts can do to improve instruction and achievement in all schools—a leadership brief.* Washington, DC: Author.

- Lewis, A. & Paik, S. (2001). *Add it up: Using research to improve education for low-income and minority students.* Washington, DC: Poverty & Race Research Action Council.

- Losen, D. J. & Orfield, G. (Eds.). (2002). *Racial inequity in special education.* Cambridge, MA: Harvard Education Press.

- What Works Clearinghouse. (n.d.). *What Works Clearinghouse.* Available at http://w-w-c.org

---

The steps that the schoolwide team can take to develop the academic component of the comprehensive plan include assessing relevant data, analyzing strengths and needs, and sponsoring training and programs to address academic needs.

Assess Relevant Data

Review statistics. Data that the school regularly collects can help you pinpoint academic strengths and needs. These data include daily attendance records, number of students retained at grade level, scores on standardized tests, dropout rates, number of referrals to special education, and graduation rates. Examining these data will help you ascertain whether particular groups of students are having more problems than others. Attendance data provide a good measure of student engagement. Special education interventions can be assessed by looking at the number of goals and objectives listed in Individualized Education Programs

(IEPs) that are accomplished. The performance of all students, including those with IEPs, should be included in districtwide and statewide accountability measures.

Map academic resources. Assess the availability of tutorial and remediation programs for students with learning difficulties. For example, do students have opportunities to improve their basic skills and get help with coursework? Are individualized services available early in the school year to prevent costly grade retention? What additional instructional resources are available through the school library or resource center?

Identify the messages that the school gives students regarding academic success. Examine the number, frequency, and visibility of activities that recognize and acknowledge academic achievement. For example, what student materials are visibly displayed in public areas? Does the school provide multiple opportunities for students to succeed?

Analyze Academic Strengths and Needs

Ask questions about the following aspects of the school's academic program:

Training. Have teachers and staff received appropriate training in how to address the needs of all learners, including culturally and linguistically diverse students and students with disabilities? Are teachers provided with ongoing support through mentoring, coaching, and teacher study groups?

Instructional Techniques. Do teachers understand student-centered instructional techniques and evidence-based teaching strategies? Are lessons culturally appropriate? Do all children feel challenged, but not frustrated, about meeting academic expectations?

Supports. Are support systems available to help teachers and staff implement appropriate instruction (e.g., team teaching, master teachers, peer coaching, common planning times)? Are students provided with help to meet academic expectations (e.g., tutoring or accommodations)? Do the school principal and district administrators actively endorse the use of academic supports?

Materials and Tools. Are materials and tools adequate to help the children learn (e.g., textbooks, globes, science equipment, computers, and technology to support students with disabilities who cannot succeed without equipment such as pencil grips or speech synthesizers)? Are these tools available to all students who can benefit from them?

Consultation. Do staff have ongoing opportunities to consult on academic and behavioral issues that affect learning or instruction? Is the expertise of special educators and student support personnel used effectively?

Environmental Factors. Is the physical environment conducive to learning (e.g., is the noise level appropriate and is the temperature comfortable)?

Sponsor Training and Programs to Address Academic Needs

Align your academic plan with your schoolwide effort. The interventions that you select for your comprehensive plan might require that you do the following:

▲ Train teachers to use positive behavioral classroom management techniques, such as teaching behavioral expectations, recognizing students when they meet those expectations, problem solving with students who do not meet the expectations, and developing interventions to help students who are having trouble meeting the expectations—and providing ongoing support to teachers to help them sustain these skills.

▲ Train teachers to implement student-centered instruction techniques, such as classwide peer tutoring, direct instruction, and structured cooperative learning, which make the curriculum more meaningful to every child. Employ student-centered assessment techniques such as curriculum-based measurement (CBM), which monitors student performance by directly assessing performance on what is being taught (e.g., speed, fluency, and accuracy) and which enables teachers to target instruction and individualized academic support. Investigate the possibility of using master teachers, team teaching, coaching, and instructional support teams in this effort.

▲ Institute tutorial and remediation programs. These programs should help children improve their basic skills as well as make progress with their learning. They should be available early in the school year so that they can get the support they need before they begin to experience frustration or failure. The schedule for these programs should be as flexible as possible to ensure that they are available to every child who needs them. Investigate ways to make tutoring available before, during, or after school or on the weekends. Involve as many people from the school and community as you can in tutoring, including regular and special educators, paraprofessionals, administrators, peers, family members, and community volunteers.

▲ Acknowledge academic engagement and achievement, but in a noncompetitive way. Students should receive recognition not only for being the best or for making a perfect score, but also for working hard and making improvements.

▲ Ensure that all staff and volunteers are trained and supervised and appropriately matched with students' needs.

Selecting Universal Interventions

Appendix A includes descriptions of universal interventions selected by our expert panel. These are denoted by ▲. In addition, a number of resources are available to help identify early interventions (as well as, in some cases, universal and intensive interventions). The following six resources are particularly relevant:

▲ *Questions to Be Asked When Evaluating Comprehensive School Reform Models and Programs.* Produced by The Southwest Educational Development Laboratory, this tool delineates the questions to be posed when evaluating comprehensive school reform models and programs. It is available at http://www.sedl.org/csrd/questions.pdf.

▲ *An Educator's Guide to Schoolwide Reform.* This guide was produced by the American Institutes for Research for five national associations: the American Association of School Administrators, the American Federation of Teachers, the National Association of Elementary School Principals, the National Association of Secondary School Principals, and the National Education Association. This guide describes and assesses the evidence on the relative effectiveness of 24 approaches to school reform. It is available at http://www.aasa.org/issues_and_insights/district_organization/Reform/.

▲ *Safe and Sound: An Education Leader's Guide to Evidence-Based Social and Emotional Learning Programs.* Produced by The Collaborative for Academic, Social, and Emotional Learning, this guide identifies the critical elements of effective social and emotional learning (SEL) programs and assesses the effectiveness of 81 SEL curricula. *Safe and Sound* is available at http://www.casel.org/progrevfr.htm.

▲ Two resources, *Best Practices in School Crisis Prevention and Intervention,* and *Preventing School Problems—Promoting School Success* published by the National Association of School Psychologists (NASP) provide useful background and implementation resources for schoolwide prevention. For example, these two books provide information on

Note

Also see "Conclusion: Selecting Interventions."

practical ways for creating nurturing classrooms and how to connect social skill and bullying prevention programs to academics. These resources are available at the publications section of: www.naspoline.org.

▲ *Youth Violence: A Report of the Surgeon General*. This science-based report reviews evidence of the relative effectiveness of different interventions. It includes data on what does not work and what can be harmful. It is available at http://www.surgeongeneral.gov/library/youthviolence/report.html.

▲ SAMHSA Model Programs. SAMHSA defines science-based prevention programs in one of three categories:

– Model programs

– Effective programs

– Promising programs

SAMHSA Model Programs are "effective programs whose developers have the capacity and have coordinated and agreed with SAMHSA to provide quality materials, training, and technical assistance to practitioners who wish to adopt their programs." Model programs score, like effective programs, at least 4.0 on a 5-point scale on Integrity and Utility on the basis of a review by the National Registry of Effective Programs (NREP). NREP also designates programs as promising programs if they score 3.3 to 3.99 on Integrity and Utility on a 5-point scale. The Web site permits you to identify programs by content focus and to compare them with one another: modelprograms.samhsa.gov.

▲ Safe, Disciplined and Drug-Free Schools Expert Panel. The U.S. Department of Education and its Expert Panel on Safe, Disciplined, and Drug-Free Schools have identified nine exemplary and 33 promising programs. For a list of these programs, a description of the criteria employed to select them, and links to program Web sites, go to http://www.ed.gov/offices/OSDFS/exemplary01/index.html.

Note

Also see "Conclusion: Selecting Interventions."

Building a Capacity for Early Interventions

A schoolwide foundation that employs the universal intervention strategies described in Chapter 3 reduces the number of children who will succumb to risk factors, disrupt the school, and lower its achievement. Even so, the importance of interlocking universal prevention strategies with early intervention cannot be overstated. For example, schools that are making large numbers of referrals may find that their early interventions are not as successful as hoped because they lack a schoolwide foundation.

This chapter adds to the information provided in the *Early Warning Guide* and on pages 17–29 of the *Action Guide* by elaborating on what to look for as early warning signs; suggesting procedures to use with students who exhibit imminent warning signs; and describing the role of student support teams with an example of a student support team in action.

A Toolkit to Help Ensure Bright Futures

Screening for early warning signs is not just a school function. The Health Resources and Services Administration's Maternal and Child Health Bureau of the U.S. Department of Health and Human Services supported the development of *Bright Futures in Practice: Mental Health* (2002), a two-volume resource that provides practical consensus-based guidance on the mental health of children in a developmental context. It provides information on early recognition and intervention for specific mental health problems and mental disorders and offers a tool kit and hands-on tools that schools, health professionals, and families can use in screening, care management, and health education. Information on this guide, including a PDF version, can be found at http://www.brightfutures.org/mentalhealth/index.html.

Culturally Competent Assessment

Effective early interventions (as well as intensive interventions) depend on culturally competent assessments.

The National Association of School Psychologists, with support from the U.S. Department of Education, Office of Special Education Programs, has produced a useful multimedia professional development resource on culturally competent assessment for special education eligibility: *Portraits of the Children: Culturally Competent Assessment*. The video includes culturally diverse case studies; interviews with renowned psychologists and educators; and viewpoints shared by school personnel and parents regarding culturally competent assessment. The CD-ROM includes the video; discussion questions; and extensive references, handouts, and Web links.

For further information and purchase contact the National Association of School Psychologists, 4340 East West Highway, Suite 402, Bethesda, MD 20814; phone: 301-657-0270; www.nasponline.org.

Understanding Early Warning Signs and Interventions

Does your school

▲ have research-based schoolwide prevention strategies that will support early (and intensive) interventions?

▲ provide the necessary training and support to enable all staff to recognize and seek support for children exhibiting early warning signs?

▲ make evidence-based early interventions available for all students at risk of behavioral and academic problems?

Your comprehensive plan should "ensure that teachers, administrators, school support staff, parents, students, and the larger school community become familiar with the early warning signs and the principles for taking appropriate actions" (*Action Guide*, p. 17). Train staff and community members about what to look for and how to access help when they are concerned. First, determine their level of awareness by using focus groups or surveys. The Responding to Early Warning Signs Checklist (see Appendix B) can help you assess school capacity. Next, provide staff with the information about early warning signs. The *Early Warning Guide* lists behavioral indicators of risk (pp. 6–11) that all adults should know. Use the following sidebar, Early Warning Signs: Elaborated, to brief everyone who works with youth.

Early Warning Signs: Elaborated

Social Withdrawal

"In some situations, gradual and eventually complete withdrawal from social contacts can be an important indicator of a troubled child. The withdrawal often stems from feelings of depression, rejection, persecution, unworthiness, and lack of confidence."

Depression is one of the more common child mental-health disorders and may be as common as attention deficit-hyperactivity disorder. Depressive episodes are most frequent in adolescence. Withdrawal may also be a symptom of abuse (such as bullying or intimidation) or alienation because of social, cultural, or sexual orientation issues.

Isolation

"Research has shown that the vast majority of children who are isolated and appear to be friendless are not violent. In fact, these feelings are sometimes characteristic of children and youth who may be troubled, withdrawn, or have internal issues that hinder development of social affiliations. However, research also has shown that in some cases, feelings of isola-tion and not having friends are associated with children who behave aggressively and violently."

Children may be isolated by peers because they are aggressive. Aggressive children are more likely to be rejected by peers, teachers, and other adults. Children who move from school to school or are homeless may isolate themselves, having little control over their plight. They may find the culture of each new school overwhelming.

Rejection

"In the process of growing up, and in the course of adolescent development, many young people experience emotionally painful rejection. Children who are troubled often are isolated from their mentally healthy peers. Their responses to rejection will depend on many background factors. Without support, they may be at risk of expressing their emotional distress in negative ways—including violence. Some aggressive children who are rejected by nonaggressive peers seek out aggressive friends who, in turn, reinforce their violent tendencies."

Bullying among middle school children, particularly girls, may be based on the powerful threat of rejection. A child who is denied access to peer approval and acceptance often may be made to feel blame and self-doubt.

Victim of Violence

"Children who are victims of violence—including physical and sexual abuse—in the community, at school, or at home are sometimes at risk themselves of becoming violent toward themselves or others."

Harsh discipline and inconsistent monitoring are two leading correlates of aggressive behavior. Sexual abuse and physical abuse are far more frequent than we wish to acknowledge. Both girls and boys are abused. Many of these children are at greater risk of suicide attempts than of interpersonal violence.

Victim of Bullying

"The youth who feels constantly picked on, teased, bullied, singled out for ridicule, and humiliated at home or at school may initially withdraw socially. If not given adequate support in addressing these feelings, some children may vent them in inappropriate ways—including possible aggression or violence."

Bullying (including teasing) is one of the most common forms of youth aggression.

Low School Interest and Poor Academics

"Poor school achievement can be the result of many factors. It is important to consider whether there is a drastic change in performance [or chronic poor performance that is limiting the child's capacity to learn]. In some situations—such as when the low achiever feels frustrated, unworthy, chastised, and denigrated—acting out and aggressive behaviors may occur. It is important to assess the emotional and cognitive reasons for the academic performance change to determine the true nature of the problem."

Years of failure and alienation become critical in middle and high school. Abrupt, dramatic changes in academic progress can be clear indications of mental health, drug abuse, or other physical, cognitive, or family problems. School alienation and failure must be addressed early. Research shows that remediating reading problems with intensive targeted instruction can reduce later dropping out and delinquent behavior.

Expression of Violence in Pictures and Stories

"Children and youth often express their thoughts, feelings, desires, and intentions in their drawings and in stories, poetry, and other written expressive forms. Many children produce work about violent themes that for the most part is harmless when taken in context. However, an overrepresentation of violence in writings and drawings that is directed at specific individuals (family members, peers, other adults) consistently over time, may signal emotional problems and the potential for violence. Because there is a real danger in misdiagnosing such a sign, it is important to seek the guidance of a qualified professional—such as a school psychologist, counselor, or other mental health specialist—to determine its meaning."

Uncontrolled Anger

"Everyone gets angry; anger is a natural emotion. However, anger that is expressed frequently and intensely in response to minor irritants may signal potential violent behavior toward self or others."

Anger should be understood in terms of the child's level of development. Young schoolchildren who exhibit such behavior should be assessed as soon as possible because we know that interventions are most powerful in these early years. Newly manifested uncontrolled anger in a child or youth may signal a family or personal crisis.

Chronic Hitting

"Children often engage in acts of shoving and mild aggression. However, some mildly aggressive behaviors such as constant hitting and bullying of others that occur early in children's lives, if left unattended, might later escalate into more serious behaviors."

Bullies may continually hit smaller peers. Children who are subject to harsh discipline may become chronic hitters.

Discipline Problems

"Chronic behavior and disciplinary problems both in school and at home may suggest that underlying emotional needs are not being met. These unmet needs may be manifested in acting out and aggressive behaviors. These problems may set the stage for the child to violate norms and rules, defy authority, disengage from school, and engage in aggressive behaviors with other children and adults."

Children will engage in behaviors that other children and adults unknowingly reinforce. Schools that consistently teach peers to pay no attention to anyone who disrupts can help reduce the repetition of the behavior. Some repeated discipline problems need to be examined in relation to the context in which they occur, such as one particular class.

History of Aggressive Behavior

"Unless provided with support and counseling, a youth who has a history of aggressive or violent behavior is likely to repeat those behaviors. Aggressive and violent acts may be directed toward other individuals, be expressed in cruelty to animals, or include fire setting. Youth who show an early pattern of antisocial behavior frequently and across multiple settings are particularly at risk for future aggressive and antisocial behavior. Similarly, youth who engage in overt behaviors such as bullying, generalized aggression and defiance, and covert behaviors, such as stealing, vandalism, lying, cheating, and fire setting, also are at risk for more serious aggressive behavior. Research suggests that age of onset may be a key factor in interpreting early warning signs. For example, children who engage in aggression and drug abuse at an early age (before age 12) are more likely to show violence later on than are children who begin such behavior at an older age. In the presence of such signs it is important to review the child's history with behavioral experts and seek parents' observations and insights."

Intolerance for Differences and Prejudicial Attitudes

"All children have likes and dislikes. However, an intense prejudice toward others based on racial, ethnic, religious, language, gender, sexual orientation, ability, and physical appearance—when coupled with other factors—may lead to violent assaults against those who are perceived to be different. Membership in hate groups or the willingness to victimize individuals with disabilities or health problems also should be treated as early warning signs."

Drug Use

"Apart from being unhealthy behaviors, drug use and alcohol use reduce self-control and expose children and youth to violence, either as perpetrators, as victims, or both."

Some drugs, such as speed and cocaine, may cause violent reactions in some youth. Drug use is also more frequent among youth with impulsive behaviors and may be related to learning disabilities and untreated mental health needs.

Gangs and Guns

"Gangs that support antisocial values and behaviors—including extortion, intimidation, and acts of violence toward other students—cause fear and stress among students. Youth who are influenced by these groups—those who emulate and copy their behavior, as well as those who become affiliated with them—may adopt these values and act in violent or aggressive ways in certain situations. Gang-related violence and turf battles are common occurrences, tied to the use of drugs, that often result in injury and/or death."

The Surgeon General's report on youth violence noted that "guns, gangs, and drugs" are the major risk factors in youth violence. Gang affiliation is frequently the result of untreated alienated and aggressive youth affiliating with each other for acceptance and support.

Inappropriate Access to, Possession of, and Use of Firearms

"Children and youth who inappropriately possess or have access to firearms can have an increased risk for violence. Research shows that such youngsters also have a higher probability of becoming victims. Families can reduce inappropriate access and use by restricting, monitoring, and supervising children's access to firearms and other weapons. Children who have a history of aggression, impulsiveness, or other emotional problems should not have access to firearms and other weapons."

Firearms are used in 75–80 percent of homicides and most suicides involving youth.

Serious Threats of Violence

"Idle threats are a common response to frustration. Alternatively, one of the most reliable indicators that a youth is likely to commit a dangerous act toward self or others is a detailed and specific threat to use violence. Recent incidents across the country clearly indicate that threats to commit violence against oneself or others should be taken very seriously. Steps must be taken to understand the nature of these threats and to prevent them from being carried out."

Threats of violence should be considered an imminent warning sign. This warning sign should be understood in context and analyzed by a team that includes a mental health expert before it is categorized as "serious." Far too many schools have embarrassed themselves by "crying wolf" over an idle threat.

The Secret Service and the Federal Bureau of Investigation both recommend that schools use a team approach to examine verbal, written, and other threats in their context. A team approach is recommended for your school's plan.

Addressing Imminent Warning Signs

Your comprehensive plan should ensure that a student support team is trained and knows what to do about students who pose an imminent danger to themselves or others. Team members should recognize the imminent warning signs described in the *Early Warning Guide* (p. 11). Staff, parents, and students should be informed of how the school will address imminent warning signs.

Appropriate procedures for responding to a student exhibiting imminent warning signs include the following:

- ▲ Keeping the child or youth under adult supervision until a determination can be made about what immediate action will be taken
- ▲ Referring your concern to the school principal, who provides adult staff supervision of the student
- ▲ Convening the student support team, including the staff mental health person, additional community persons (school-community law officers if they are a part of the school) as necessary, and other knowledgeable student support team members; identifying and gathering the needed information; contacting the family to secure more input about concerns
- ▲ Carrying out a threat assessment using the problem-solving model (see the sidebar Threat Assessment)
- ▲ Developing an immediate intervention plan and beginning to explore necessary long-term action
- ▲ Evaluating the immediate response for its effectiveness in defusing the problem
- ▲ Evaluating long-term effects of interventions in addressing problems
- ▲ Communicating with necessary administrative officials

Linking the Schoolwide and Student Support Teams

Designing, developing, and helping implement early interventions should be the designated responsibilities of specific members of the school community. Hence, to ensure your schoolwide goals for safety and achievement, your school should establish a student support team (SST), a highly trained team skilled in developing effective interventions for children found to be at risk. Just as staff rely on experts in curriculum, instruction, language, health, and special education, they must also have easy access to consultation from experts on emotional health, mental health, and behavior skill development. Teachers cannot be expected to

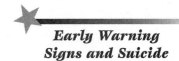

Early Warning Signs and Suicide

Suicide, which is the third leading cause of death among young people 15 to 24 years of age, often has a powerful impact on school communities. The strongest risk factors for attempted suicide in youth are depression, alcohol or other drug use disorder, and aggressive or disruptive behaviors. Resources that specifically focus on suicide are provided by the U.S. Department of Health and Human Services National Strategy for Suicide Prevention Web site, http://mentalhealth.samhsa.gov/suicideprevention/fivews.asp. This site provides links to other useful sites, such as fact sheets from the American Academy of Child and Adolescent Psychiatry and the American Psychiatric Association. Another useful site is the National Center for Suicide Prevention Training at http://www.ncspt.org.

be experts on mental health, but they can become proficient in knowing whom to consult. The school's capacity to intervene early begins with the knowledge that mental health and behavior problems in children are common, are preventable, and can be successfully treated. Teachers and other staff provided with adequate training and support can prevent risk factors from becoming disabilities.

The student support team should be incorporated into the School Improvement Program, with staffing overlap as described on page 5 of the *Action Guide*. See Figure 8, Linkage Between Schoolwide and Student Support Teams.

✓

A Useful Tool for Threat Assessment

The United States Secret Service and the Department of Education have developed a guide on threat assessment for school personnel, law enforcement officials, and others with protective responsibilities in schools. The guide includes suggestions for developing a threat assessment team; steps to take in response to threats; and a discussion of information sharing, when to involve law enforcement personnel, and how to develop a safe school climate. The guide, *Threat Assessment in Schools: A Guide to Managing Threatening Situations and to Creating Safe School Climates* (Fein, Vossekuil, Pollack, Borum, Modzeleski, & Reddy, 2002), is available at http://www.ed.gov/offices/OSDFS/threatassessmentguide.pdf and www.secretservice.gov/ntac.

Threat Assessment

All threats are NOT created equal. However, all threats should be assessed in a timely manner, and decisions regarding how they should be handled must be made quickly.

In today's climate, some schools tend to adopt a one-size-fits-all approach to any mention of violence. The response to every threat is the same, regardless of its credibility of the likelihood that it will be carried out. In the shock wave of recent school shootings, this reaction may be understandable, but it is exaggerated—and perhaps dangerous, leading to potential underestimation of serious threats, overreaction to less serious ones, and unfairly punishing or stigmatizing students who are in fact not dangerous. A school that treats all threats as equal falls into the fallacy formulated by Abraham Maslow: "If the only tool you have is a hammer, you tend to see every problem as a nail." Every problem is not a nail, of course, and schools must recognize that every threat does not represent the same danger or require the same level of response.

Some threats can herald a clear and present danger of a tragedy on the scale of Columbine High School. Others represent little or no real threat to anyone's safety. Neither should be ignored, but reacting to both in the same manner is ineffective and self-defeating. In every school, an established threat assessment procedure managed by properly trained staff can help school administrators and other school staff distinguish between different levels of threats and choose different appropriate responses.

Threat assessment seeks to make an informed judgment on two questions: How credible and serious is the threat itself? And to what extent does the threatener appear to have the resources, intent, and motivation to carry out the threat?

The School Shooter: A Threat Assessment Perspective. (2000). Federal Bureau of Investigation.

School improvement goals, visions, and universal interventions developed by the schoolwide team must be aligned with the individualized student supports and teacher and family consultation that the student support team provides. The principal, a master teacher, and a school mental health professional should serve on both teams so that schoolwide decisions are made with sensitivity to their impact on children who are at greater levels of need and early and intensive interventions take into account how schoolwide factors contribute to individual problems. Figure 8, Linkage Between Schoolwide and Student Support Teams, illustrates the relationship between the two teams.

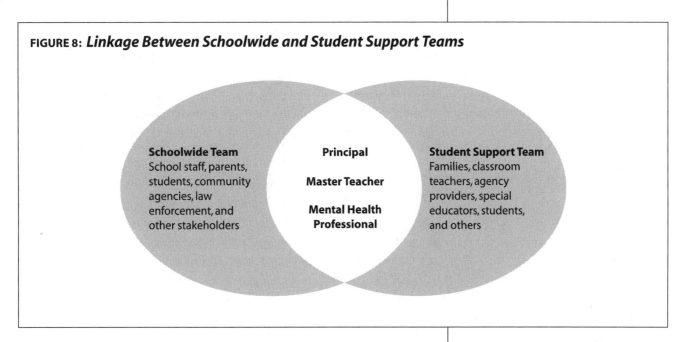

FIGURE 8: *Linkage Between Schoolwide and Student Support Teams*

Schoolwide Team
School staff, parents, students, community agencies, law enforcement, and other stakeholders

Principal

Master Teacher

Mental Health Professional

Student Support Team
Families, classroom teachers, agency providers, special educators, students, and others

Student support team members need the following problem-solving and consultation skills. If the team lacks these skills, they can be developed by training, consultation, and new membership.

Student Support Team Problem-Solving Skills

▲ Redefine concerns in clear behavioral terms.

    – What are the measurable behaviors?

    – When do they occur or not occur, and what is happening before or when they occur?

    – Where do they occur, where do they not occur, and at what frequency?

▲ Identify desired replacement behaviors.

    – What behaviors do we want?

▲ Develop testable hypotheses.

    – What can we observe that is behind the negative behaviors?

▲ Collect data and assessing hypotheses.

  – What information is needed to test the hypotheses?

▲ Design an intervention plan that is based on verified hypotheses.

  – Select validated interventions that best fit hypotheses.

  – Clearly determine where to begin.

  – Who may need training, modeling, coaching (teacher, parent, bus driver)?

  – What in the environment needs to be addressed?

▲ Implement the plan.

  – Who does what, when?

  – Are replacement skill levels appropriate? Is instruction needed?

  – Is there consistency of reinforcements from individuals who can reinforce behaviors in the settings in which they occur (e.g., teachers, aides, or parents)?

  – Are intervention steps effectively carried out?

Note: In many situations, an intervention may require new or replacement behaviors from the child, family members, and caregivers as well as from teachers and other staff. Therefore, your intervention plan may specify several specific objectives. (See the sidebar Student Support Team in Action.)

▲ Monitor and evaluate the results.

  – Who monitors the fidelity to the intervention plan?

  – What needs to be modified?

  – Are objectives reached at the desired rate?

Many models use these problem-solving steps. The Refer-Question-Consult functional problem-solving model (ACHIEVE) and Positive Behavioral Interventions and Supports (PBIS) are two popular examples. (See Appendix A for descriptions of both.)

Consultation Skills

▲ Understand and articulate the schoolwide plan and model and apply the school's universal prevention strategies.

▲ Know the school's climate, instructional program, curricula, discipline procedures, resources (including interagency), and school-community demographics.

▲ Consult with teachers, parents, and team members providing training and support for academic learning and behavior.

▲ Manage behavior.

▲ Measure developmental learning and behavior.

- Collaborate with parents and the community.

- Assess functional behavior and behavioral planning.

- Select and use proven interventions for learning and behavior problems.

- Monitor and evaluate interventions.

- Use culturally competent approaches and be culturally self-aware.

Examining Your Referral Process

A responsive referral process is key to the success of the student support team (see "Principles for Developing a Referral Process," *Action Guide*, p. 21). Teachers, families, and others will not make necessary referrals if the process is cumbersome or if the responses are not timely or effective.

Does your school have an effective referral system in place? Do parents know how to seek consultation from the student support team? How do your staff and families rate your present student support team's referral-response process? Can your plan reduce referral-response time?

The referral process should be simple and known to all staff, families, and agency partners. There should be no barriers to the student support teams or to informal consultation services. For example, the process should provide teacher peer support to develop and expand skills, as well as access to informal consultations from student support teams, staff, and others. Examine your existing referral process and eliminate the barriers you find. For an example of a well-functioning team, see the sidebar Student Support Team in Action.

A Student Support Team in Action

The following example is about a child from a Florida school district. The student support team initially consisted of the principal, counselor, classroom teacher, reading teacher, school psychologist, and parent. It is important to note that all members were provided with the information before the student support team met to help them prepare. The school also has grade-level support meetings so that teachers can share techniques prior to making a referral. In this example, look for connections between the student support team process and the schoolwide prevention program. Note that time is saved by the preparation and that no one individual is responsible for data gathering or analysis. Also note how important the mother's input was in forming hypotheses and in identifying strengths. Compare this early intervention plan with your plan.

Referral

Problem: Marty, age nine and in third grade, is sleeping in class in the morning during reading and math, six to ten days a month. He is passively noncompliant when the teacher gives directions. He does not complete eight to ten math assignments each week. Sleeping and defiance behavior are not as frequent in the afternoon. **Interventions tried**: Seating change, points and rewards for alertness, teacher aide, family contact, reduced workload, referral to school nurse. **Results**: No change in pattern.

Other Information. Marty can read on grade level. He was retained in first grade. He received speech-language therapy in first grade. He has been in five schools this year. His mother, a low-income single parent, told teacher about stress and wants to help.

Desired Replacement Behaviors. Stay awake and alert. Complete eight to ten math assignments. Make good choices by following teacher-given directions.

Principal Convenes a Student Support Team
(including classroom teacher and parent by conference phone)

- Information is provided to all team members prior to meeting.
- Hypotheses generation:
  - Not getting enough sleep at home
  - "Escaping" the work in reading and math—work too hard
  - Math curriculum above his level—he lacks fundamentals
  - Does not have independent work skills
  - Does not have good listening and attending skills
  - Does not feel "connected" to the school
  - ADHD/health disorder
  - Not using his social skills
  - Not receiving enough positive reinforcement
- Behavior is not noticed at home. He is compliant and sleeps eight-plus hours daily.
- He tells his mother that he likes his new school and has made friends.

Note: Information gathered in hypotheses setting enables team to reject and redefine hypotheses selected for assessment.

Data Collection and Assessment to Validate and Eliminate Hypotheses

Obtain baseline data for desired and undesired behaviors. Carry out a functional behavioral assessment. Compare Marty's behavior with that of his peers and with his behavior in other environments (e.g., reading, science, lunch, and bus). Observe Marty in several settings over the school day (counselor/school psychologist). Carry out curriculum-based assessment of math skills (teacher and reading teacher). Administer a child behavior checklist (to parent and teacher by school psychologist).

Assessment of Hypotheses

- Marty is deficient in specific curriculum math skills.
- Marty is unfamiliar with the social skills "choices" model used by the school.
- Staff is not frequently reinforcing Marty positively for appropriate compliance following directions.
- Marty has adequate emotional strengths and no serious problems.
- Marty appears to use sleep to avoid defiance when frustrated.

Interventions

- Set concrete measurable objectives for each validated hypothesis.
- To improve math assignment completions from two to eight-to-ten with 80% accuracy within nine weeks, provide remedial tutoring in math (to help Marty to master missing skills). Begin Marty on self-monitoring while completing math assignments (remedial instructor and aide).
- Provide frequent positive behavior reinforcements for compliance with academic expectations (teacher and aide).
- Begin counseling to learn and practice social skills (counselor/teacher/aide/staff).
- Frequently remind Marty about social skills choices model (in class and other settings).
- Increase social skill reinforcement opportunities (in-class counselor/teacher).
- Provide frequent feedback about successful progress to parent (teacher).

- Seek adult mentor to support progress (principal).
- Begin after-school extended school day program (counselor).
- Set times for weekly monitoring (school psychologist) and necessary support from team.

Evaluation

- Chart progress on all intervention outcomes.

- Identify progress (or its absence) in reaching objectives.
- Identify continued service needs and maintenance levels.
- Record and report effective interventions, academic progress (e.g., level of mastery), and demonstrated mastery of social skills.
- Prepare for unforeseen transitions by documenting "what works."

When Referral Behaviors Require More Complex Solutions

The same referral behaviors could occur if Marty had been seriously depressed. If this hypothesis had been generated and confirmed by assessment data, a more intensive behavior and treatment plan would be needed. In such a case, many of the interventions included in the example may be insufficient because there are also more serious mental health problems.

It is critical that the student support team avoid remedial instructional interventions alone when information suggests that serious mental health, discipline, or other problems are also present. Depression is treatable when consistent mental health services are provided. A child with a diagnosis of depression may benefit from medical interventions and cognitive treatments. In such a case, the student support team functions as an interagency team, designing, monitoring, and evaluating an intervention plan. An integrated model for a more intensive multiagency behavioral intervention plan will be discussed in Chapter 5. In cases of more serious mental health problems, remedial training and reinforcements should be integrated with other treatments to eliminate competing supports or service gaps. Planning for effective student support team operations requires the school to have in place an array of interventions and strategies to address both academic and psychosocial-behavioral support. Chapter 5 addresses service array.

Selecting Early Interventions

Appendix A includes descriptions of early interventions selected by our expert panel. These are denoted by ▲. In addition, a number of resources are available to help identify early interventions (as well as, in some cases, universal and intensive interventions). The following five resources are particularly relevant:

> ▲ *Addressing Student Problem Behavior.* Produced by the Center for Effective Collaboration and Practice, this

Special Education as Both an Early and an Intensive Intervention

Special education and Section 504 plans can be used as early interventions for problems that, if unaddressed, may result in severe and complex problems that would require more intensive interventions. For example, a child may need a 504 plan or special education support to address an attention or reading disability. Without special attention, the child may become progressively frustrated, which could lead to depression or a serious conduct disorder or both. However, for the purposes of this document, we generally consider special education as an intensive intervention because it most frequently requires multiple services to be effective.

Note

See "Conclusion: Selecting Interventions."

---

guide to functional assessment was developed by a team of teachers, family members, youth, teacher trainers, and researchers (Quinn, Gable, Rutherford, Nelson, & Howell, 1998a). It can be found at http://cecp.air.org/fba/default.htm.

▲ *Best Practices in School Prevention and Intervention* (Brock, Lazarus, & Jimerson, 2002). This book reviews a range of early intervention strategies, including bullying, peer mediation and conflict resolution, suicide prevention, and child maltreatment.

▲ *Safe and Sound: An Education Leader's Guide to Evidence-Based Social and Emotional Learning Programs*. Produced by The Collaborative for Academic, Social, and Emotional Learning, this guide identifies the critical elements of effective social and emotional learning (SEL) programs and assesses the effectiveness of 81 SEL curricula. Safe and Sound is available at http://www.casel.org/progrevfr.htm.

▲ *Youth Violence: A Report of the Surgeon General*. This science-based report reviews evidence of the relative effectiveness of different interventions. It includes data on what does not work and what can be harmful. It is available at http://www.surgeongeneral.gov/library/youthviolence/report.html.

▲ *SAMHSA Model Programs* (U.S. Department of Health and Human Services Administration, Center for Substance Abuse Prevention). Described at the end of Chapter 3, this tool helps you identify and compare science-based prevention programs, which are categorized as model, effective, or promising. This resource can be found at http://www.modelprograms.samhsa.gov.

▲ *Safe, Disciplined and Drug-Free Schools Expert Panel*. Described at the end of Chapter 3, the book and Web site identify and provide links to nine exemplary and 33 promising programs. This resource can be found at http://www.ed.gov/offices/OSDFS/expert_panel/drug-free.html.

Building a Capacity for Intensive Interventions

FEW

SOME

ALL

According to the Surgeon General's report on mental health (Office of the Surgeon General, 1999), a small percentage of children and youth, perhaps three to five percent, have emotional and behavioral problems that can severely impede learning and other functioning. For these students, schoolwide and early interventions may not be enough. Schools need access to clinical mental health services to help ensure that each child who needs effective intensive services gets them. In Chapter 4, you read about the student support team's response to Marty. What would that student support team do if it discovered through its assessment and family contact that Marty was sleeping in class because he was severely depressed? Would the team be able to connect Marty with needed clinical mental health services?

One of the critical reasons for including mental health agencies and providers on the schoolwide team is to ensure that intensive services are available to children who require them. The authorization from your school system's top administration, described in Chapter 1, should support the interagency agreements that may be necessary to implement intensive interventions. The tool Community Linkages Assessment Form (see Appendix B) can be adapted to track agencies and providers.

Your planning team should ask, What procedures does our school have in place to support the functioning of children with serious mental health problems? The Providing Intensive Interventions Checklist (see Appendix B) can frame an assessment of a school's capacity to provide the array of intensive interventions needed to address serious mental health problems.

Your comprehensive plan should include an interagency plan to provide intensive interventions across the school and community. The comprehensive plan should comprise an array of proven intensive interventions for students who have persistent emotional and behavioral problems. Multiagency service integration policies, procedures, and practices, including partnerships with families to enhance trust and ensure effective service outcomes, should support this array of interventions.

Your assessment of strengths and needs should determine not only the number of children needing such services but also the kind of services—or components of service—you already have available.

Overcoming Barriers to Providing Intensive Interventions

During the planning process, you may identify barriers to providing intensive services in the school. System policies, funding, time demands, competing priorities, and professional issues may challenge your team's ingenuity in developing solutions.

System policy may simply not grant "permission" to provide services in the school, or it may actually prevent non-system-employed professionals from providing services. Suggest to system administrators or the school board (when appropriate) that policies be adjusted to ensure that children can receive at the school the type of services they require.

Resources on Community Schools

Resources on Community Schools can be found on the Web sites of the Coalition for Community Schools (www.communityschools.org) and the Charles Stewart Mott Foundation (http://www.mott.org), which has supported community schools since 1935.

Full-Service Schools

One approach to providing services to students is through full-service schools. Full-service schools have been described as one-stop centers in which the educational, physical, psychological, and social needs of students and their families are addressed in a coordinated, school-based effort that integrates school and community services and supports (Dryfoos, 1994). Full-service schools can enhance the schoolwide foundation and early interventions. They also can be integrated into intensive interventions.

Full-service schools house a variety of health care, mental health, and related services for children and their families. By offering services on school grounds, these schools avoid many of the barriers to families' obtaining services for their children, such as transportation and lack of health insurance. These services are delivered through collaboration among the school, agencies, and families. Full-service schools often provide services before school and extend services until late at night, six or seven days a week, and also during vacations and summers (Warger, 2001).

For a description of the role of full-service schools in violence prevention, see *Preventing Youth Violence* (http://www.pcvp.org/pcvp/violence/policybrf/skoolfu3.shtml), which was developed by the Pacific Center for Violence Prevention.

For tools that you can use to develop a full-service school, see Calfee, Wittwer, & Meredith (1998), *Building a Full-Service School: A Step-by-Step Guide*, which includes needs assessment forms, interagency agreements, program evaluation tools, facilities criteria, funding sources, and family service coordination plans. Also see Dryfoos & Maguire (2002), *Inside Full-Service Community Schools*, which delineates the steps necessary to develop a full-service school.

Web Access to Comprehensive School-Based Health Clinics

The Bureau of Primary Health Care (BPHC)/Health Resources and Services Administration (HRSA), Department of Health and Human Services provides information (name of the clinic, address including zip code, and telephone number) on all its community-based services throughout the United States and territories. The information is provided on its Web site and includes the Comprehensive School-Based Health Clinics, the Federally Qualified Health Centers/Community Health Centers, and Migrant Health Centers, among others.

To access this information:

1. Enter www.bphc.hrsa.gov.

2. Go to the section titled "Data Sources" and click "Find a Health Center."

3. To locate contact information for service delivery sites, enter your search by using one or a combination of the following:

   a. Name of the service delivery site (it is not necessary to know this information)

   b. Geographic area (city, state, or zip code)

   c. Type of BPHC program (e.g., Healthy Schools, Healthy Communities)

   d. Type of service(s) (e.g., mental health/substance abuse, primary medical care)

4. Click "Submit Search."

The Web site will then provide information on all sites in that geographic area.

Funding for intensive services is difficult both to secure and sustain. Schools may be reluctant to fund intensive services from general school funds. Review your funding sources. (See Chapter 2 for ways to leverage Medicaid, EPSDT, and other resources to fund intensive services.) Many school systems have secured a Medicaid service provider number. Although Medicaid can pay for special education mental health services, some school systems use Medicaid only for non-mental health–related special education services.

Schools are more and more feeling the pressure of high-stakes achievement testing. Taking time away from academic instruction is often viewed as a negative. Aligning the need for intensive services with the opportunity for students to improve their academic performance requires planning. Some schools use the time before and after school for treatment services. Others integrate treatment into the child's regular school day—without removing the child from instruction—through consultation and in-class support for therapeutic behavioral interventions. Still others offer flextime to school mental health staff partnering with their clinical counterparts so that they can work evenings.

Guild issues, union contracts, and mental health service laws and policies sometimes create barriers (e.g., not providing reimbursement for meetings with parents or service providers). Case management and administrative costs are fundable under Medicaid and should not be a barrier to team services.

Fear that existing school staff will be replaced can generate resistance among individuals or groups of professionals. You can address this concern through clearly written agreements, trust building, and role delineation. School counselors, for example, may be marginalized when the plans do not consider them to be "providers." They may envision their services being replaced by agency mental health therapists whose training may actually be less structured and less child-focused than that of the counselors. The use of competency standards to determine who can provide specific services may resolve these issues.

Agency training for existing school staff may also reduce fear of job loss. Some agencies have allocated funds to supplement the school's budget so that they can hire dually licensed and certified mental health professionals. In Tennessee, for example, school psychologists are employed by the mental health agency to work in the schools. In Baltimore, Maryland, schools employ licensed clinical social workers. Just as in the case of teachers (see Chapter 1), trust is enhanced when the professionals affected by new arrangements participate in the planning process and receive assurance that services are supplementing what exists, rather than supplanting it.

Planning Centers for All Students in Westerly, Rhode Island

The elementary and middle schools in Westerly Public School District maintain planning centers within each building where all students can choose to get emotional support or "cool off," resolve conflicts, get assistance with school work, have a quiet space to work on homework, or work on problem-solving skills with an adult or on the computer. Although any student can choose to come to the planning center at any time throughout the school day, some students have written in their Individual Education Plan (IEP) a class period or more in the planning center. The planning centers have staff trained in behavior management. Planning center staff also help students and families access mental health or other community services.

Planning center staff can identify problems that students are having and intervene early; they can work with students to teach them coping and problem-solving skills to manage their difficulties. By addressing academic, emotional, or behavioral problems before they become crises, center staff can prevent the escalation of inappropriate behaviors. "The planning center," observed Joe, a seventh-grade student, "gives space to resolve conflicts." Combined with other programs, the planning centers have resulted in improved grades, achievement, and attendance and fewer disciplinary referrals, creating a positive, trusting, learning environment that promotes high academic and behavioral expectations.

Westerly Integrated Social Services Program, 1997.

School Collaboration

Intensive interventions also require collaboration within the school—between general and special educators and pupil service staff, between all school staff and the staff of alternative programs, and between school staff and the school's administration. Examining these relationships, as well as related policies, procedures, and practices, is essential to providing intensive services. For example, procedures or practices that segregate all students with complex, disabling emotional and behavioral problems are counterproductive. Segregation makes it difficult for these students to apply new skills in regular school settings and also prevents general education staff from learning how to reinforce and sustain the appropriate behaviors these students have learned. Collaboration is often necessary to provide students and teachers with sufficient support so that students can succeed in inclusive environments.

Resources that you can go to for examples of effective collaboration include *Safe, Drug-Free, and Effective Schools for ALL Students: What Works* (Quinn, Osher, Hoffman, & Hanley, 1998); *Handbook of School Mental Health* (Weist, Evans, & Lever, 2003); *The Role of Education in a System of Care: Effectively Serving Children With Emotional or Behavioral Disorders* (Woodruff et al., 1999); and *Mental Health, Schools, and Families Working Together* (Policymakers Partnership at the National Association of State Directors of Special Education, 2002).

Intensive Interventions

Chapter 4 of the *Action Guide* describes in detail the components of high-quality intensive interventions that have been shown to work for even the most challenging behavior problems. Here we elaborate on the information on pages 31–39 of the *Action Guide* and provide links to information that will enable you to employ these interventions.

Culturally Competent Intensive Interventions in the Navajo Nation

The Piñon Unified School District #4 serves Navajo students in schools in Piñon, which is in the center of the Navajo Nation. Although the district employs some interventions that may be found in other schools (e.g., after-school programs), staff have also developed culturally competent interventions that address the particular needs, and build on the particular strengths, of its students, their families, and their community. One universal intervention is Dual Language Classes. One early and intensive intervention, used by the Safe School/Healthy Student initiative, is the Sweat Lodge Program, which builds on Navajo spiritual tradition.

The Sweat Lodge Program is designed to reconnect youth to a spiritual perspective and to reinforce and rebuild their self-esteem, which, in turn, helps them improve their academic achievement. The Sweat Lodge Program is recognized for excellence throughout the Navajo Nation and is supported by the Navajo Nation Indian Health Service, Department of Human and Social Services, Navajo Nation Department of Law Enforcement, Department of Youth and Community Services, Behavioral Health, Diné Division of Education, and the judicial system. Its use is also consistent with a study of promising practices in another tribal community—the Three Affiliated Tribes: the Mandan, Hidatsa, and Arikara (Kendziora, Bruns, Osher, Pacchiano, & Mejia, 2001).

The Sweat Lodge Program provides services to students with emotional, personal, and/or behavioral problems who are at risk for placement out of the school or the community. A Child Study Team or staff member referral determines eligibility. Participation in the program is voluntary, although parental consent is required for juvenile participants. Students may also participate in the program for personal health reasons and to work off disciplinary points.

Navajo elders and/or trained Native American counselors offer group counseling and traditional prayers during the sweat. Participants are challenged to show concern and respect for their peers, family, elders, school, and community. A time for self-reflection is also included.

Participants are expected to maintain their efforts to address and acknowledge their problems and to understand that the sweat lodge is a meaningful step in reconnecting themselves to their traditional and cultural lives. Achieving well-being and academic success is the clearly defined goal.

Comprehensive, School-Based Mental Health Programs

In many schools, school mental health staff provide mental health services to both general and special education students. Some schools also maintain school health clinics; others use agencies or contractors to provide school-based mental health services. You should determine the most effective ways to integrate agency and school system mental health services in your district to ensure that children have access to a full array of effective services to improve their learning and other functioning—including counseling, screening, functional behavioral assessments, anger replacement training, behavioral consultation, and monitoring of behavior plans.

In what ways and at what level does your school's mental health service system function?

▲ What mental health services are in place within schools? How many trained and certified or licensed mental health providers serve your school (or each school in the district)?

▲ What methods are used to determine the competence of mental health services providers?

▲ How many children are served and at what levels of intensity?

▲ Who is not receiving effective research-based interventions, and how will your plan remedy this lack?

▲ How many children identified as needing comprehensive services are receiving less than comprehensive services?

▲ How many children are receiving no significant mental health services?

If your school district does not have a full cadre of trained, qualified staff who can provide the complete array of intensive services that your plan will require, you can complement existing school services with school- and home-based interventions delivered by other agencies. School-based mental health programs that include agency personnel can facilitate the student support teams' coordination and progress monitoring. Your plan for using school and agency staffs in a school-based mental health program requires clear lines of responsibility to maximize the use of skills and resources.

One approach to using agency staff is called Expanded School Mental Health (ESMH). ESMH programs build on collaboration between school and community agencies (e.g., community mental health centers or health departments). ESMH centers provide mental health evaluations and treatment services, including crisis intervention and individual, group, and family therapy. These services are available to children and youth, independent of their special education status.

School Health Opportunities for Overcoming Barriers to Intensive Interventions

Four models for school-based and school-linked services have been developed to provide all students with access to health (including mental health) and other community services. One of these models may already exist in your school or community and may have created some or all of the linkages, precedents, relationships, or memoranda of agreements necessary to support intensive interventions.

Support for Extended School Mental Health Programs

The Robert Wood Johnson Foundation has supported some extended school mental health models through its Caring for Kids: Expanding Dental and Mental Health Services Through School-Based Health Centers program, which is administered by the Center for Health and Health Care in Schools (CHHCS) at George Washington University in Washington, DC, (www.healthinschools.org). Two national centers, both funded by the Health Resources and Services Administration's Maternal and Child Health Bureau of the U.S. Department of Health and Human Services, provide useful information and technical assistance for these centers. They are the Center for School Mental Health Assistance (CSMHA) (http://csmha.umaryland.edu/csmha2001/main.php3) and the Center for Mental Health in Schools (http://smhp.psych.ucla.edu/). CSMHA and the National Assembly on School-Based Health Care (NASBHC) have compiled a directory of expanded school mental health programs, which can help you locate programs (http://csmha.umaryland.edu/csmha2001/dirprog.php3). Examples of existing funding for outcome-based programs can be found in *Exemplary Mental Health Programs: School Psychologists as Mental Health Service Providers* (3rd ed., 2002) found at www.nasponline.org.

Each model can be employed at the schoolwide foundation level and early intervention level. However, each can be particularly helpful in addressing the barriers to intensive interventions because they are not categorical (e.g., as is special education), they provide human and financial resources, and they address multiple risk factors across the home, school, and community.

Although these four models can be linked, they are distinct. In addition, they are frequently supported by different public and private funders and through different technical assistance centers. These four models are the Coordinated School Health Model, School Health Centers, Full-Service Schools, and Community Schools.

The Coordinated School Health Model

Working with more than 40 national organizations, the Centers for Disease Control (CDC) identified eight inter-active core components of school health (excerpted from http://www.cdc.gov/nccdphp/dash/about/school_health.htm):

- ▲ **Health Education.** A planned, sequential, K–12 curriculum that addresses the physical, mental, emotional, and social dimensions of health. The curriculum is designed to motivate and assist students to maintain and improve their health, prevent disease, and reduce health-related risk behaviors.

- ▲ **Physical Education.** A planned, sequential K–12 curriculum that provides cognitive content and learning experiences in a variety of activity areas. Quality physical education should promote each student's optimum physical, mental, emotional, and social development.

- ▲ **Health Services.** Services provided for students to appraise, protect, and promote health. These services are designed to ensure access or referral to primary health care services or both, foster appropriate use of primary health care services, prevent and control communicable disease and other health problems, provide emergency care for illness or injury, promote and provide optimum sanitary conditions for a safe school facility and school environment, and provide educational and counseling opportunities for promoting and maintaining individual, family, and community health.

- ▲ **Nutrition Services.** Access to a variety of nutritious and appealing meals that accommodate the health and nutrition needs of all students.

- ▲ **Health Promotion for Staff.** Opportunities for school staff to improve their health status through such activities as health assessments, health education, and health-related fitness activities.

▲ **Counseling and Psychological Services.** Services provided to improve students' mental, emotional, and social health, including individual and group assessments, interventions, and referrals.

▲ **Healthy School Environment.** The physical and aesthetic surroundings and the psychosocial climate and culture of the school. Factors that influence the physical environment include the school building and the area surrounding it, any biological or chemical agents that are detrimental to health, and physical conditions such as temperature, noise, and lighting. The psychological environment includes the physical, emotional, and social conditions that affect the well-being of students and staff.

▲ **Parent/Community Involvement.** An integrated school, parent, and community approach for enhancing the health and well-being of students, including school health advisory councils, coalitions, and broadly based constituencies for school health.

School Health Centers

School health centers provide school-based access to on-site immunizations, full health histories and physical examinations, or on-site therapy for children with special mental health needs in addition to core screening, management of medical emergencies, medication delivery, services for children with special health care needs, referral for common health problems (such as injury, asthma, or behavioral and emotional difficulties), and health screens (such as vision and hearing screens), which many schools have traditionally done (Duncan, 1998).

According to the American Academy of Pediatrics' Committee on School Health (2001), School health centers offer a variety of advantages:

▲ Students of all ages have reasonable access to medical services.

▲ Less classroom time is lost to travel time.

▲ Follow-up compliance may be better.

▲ Adolescents often will not seek out or take advantage of services in traditional settings.

▲ Families that are not accustomed to using primary or preventive services available to them in traditional settings can be taught to use them through schools.

▲ Behavioral risk assessments and ongoing preventive strategies that address major causes of youth mortality (suicide, homicide, accidental injury) often require a degree of access to health and mental health services that schools can provide. Mental health services on a school site can reduce time away from school needed to travel to regular mental health appointments. When a mental health clinic's presence on a school site is accompanied by close collaboration with school staff, enhanced behavioral observation and clinical management also occur.

The Bureau of Primary Health Care (BPHC)/Health Resources and Services Administration (HRSA), Department of Health and Human Services supports school-based health centers through a number of initiatives including Healthy Schools, Healthy Communities (HSHC), which was established in 1994 to encourage the development of comprehensive, full-time, school-based primary care programs that serve children at high risk.

Full-Service Schools

One approach to providing services to students is through full-service schools. Full-service schools have been described as one-stop centers in which the educational, physical, psychological, and social needs of students and their families are addressed in a coordinated, school-based effort that integrates school and community services and supports (Dryfoos, 1994). Full-service schools can enhance schoolwide foundation and early intervention. They also can be integrated into intensive interventions.

Full-service schools house a variety of health care, mental health, and related services for children and their families. By offering services on school grounds, these schools avoid many of the barriers to families' obtaining services for their children, such as transportation and lack of health insurance. These services are delivered through collaboration among the school, agencies, and families. Full-service schools often provide services before school and extend services until late at night, six or seven days a week, and also during vacations and summers (Warger, 2001).

Community Schools

Community schools extend both the range and scope of school-based or school-linked services. Community schools function as hubs for these services and are supported by collaborations of community- and school-based stakeholders. They can link the services and supports of multiple organizations and facilitate access to them by children, youth, and families. Most community schools link activities that focus on quality education; positive youth development; family support; family and community engagement in decision making; and community development.

The Coalition of Community Schools has visualized community schools as follows (2000):

A community school, operating in a public school building, is open to students, families and the community before, during, and after school, seven days a week, all year long. It is operated jointly through a partnership between the school system and one or more community agencies. Families, youth, principals, teachers, and neighborhood residents help design and implement activities that promote high educational achievement and use the community as a resource for learning.

The school is oriented toward the community, encouraging student learning through community service and service learning. A before- and after-school learning component allows students to build on their classroom experiences, expand their horizons, contribute to their communities and have fun. A family support center helps families with child-rearing, employment, housing, and other services. Medical, dental, and mental health services are readily accessible (*Community School: Partnerships for Excellence* at http://www.communityschools.org/partnerships.html).

Special Education and Related Services

Special education and related services are "an array of services and supports rather than a place" (*Action Guide*, p. 32). Special education is a very important resource for schools. In thinking about how to employ special education, you should consider the following facts described in the *Twentieth Annual Report to Congress on the Implementation of the Individuals with Disabilities Education Act* (U.S. Department of Education, 1998):

▲ Students with emotional disturbance tend to be under-identified. Epidemiological research suggests that between three and five percent of the student body have serious mental health problems. However, fewer than one percent of students are identified as having emotional disturbance under special education legislation. *How many students are identified in your school or district as having emotional disturbance? At what age? Are students with emotional and behavioral disorders served under any other special education category (e.g., learning disabilities)?*

▲ Although, in general, students with emotional disturbance may be underidentified, emotional disturbance among African American students may be overidentified, and emotional disturbance among girls and young women may be underidentified. *How do your statistics look when you factor in race and gender?*

▲ Students with emotional disturbance are identified as having such a disability later than students with other disabilities. Once identified as students with emotional disturbance, they are often placed in restrictive settings that remove them from mainstream environments. *At what age are students identified as having emotional disturbance in your school or district? How restrictive are their placements? Do race and gender affect these statistics?*

You can review school data to see whether under- or over-identification exists; whether once identified, students are placed in overly restrictive settings; and whether co-occurring issues such as learning problems or disabilities are addressed in students' IEPs as well as in the settings in which the students receive services. The schoolwide team should also consider the seven targets of the *National Agenda for Achieving Better Results for Children and Youth With Serious Emotional Disturbance* (see the sidebar—National Agenda for Achieving Better Results for Children and Youth With Serious Emotional Disturbance).

Students with emotional disturbance often have co-occurring disorders, such as learning disabilities. Other students with different disabilities also may need intensive mental health interventions. For example, youth with learning disabilities show increased depression, substance abuse, and behavior problems in high school compared with their nondisabled peers. Although they are not categorized as having emotional disturbance, they may have intensive mental health needs. Other youth with serious emotional problems may not be identified by the school as having emotional disturbance because they do not have any apparent academic achievement problems. Nonetheless, these students may have serious social and behavioral problems that block their adjustment.

National Agenda for Achieving Better Results for Children and Youth With Emotional Disturbance

TARGET #1: EXPAND POSITIVE LEARNING OPPORTUNITIES AND RESULTS

To foster the provision of engaging, useful, and positive learning opportunities. These opportunities should be result-driven and should acknowledge as well as respond to the experiences and needs of children and youth with emotional disturbance (ED).

TARGET #2: STRENGTHEN SCHOOL AND COMMUNITY CAPACITY

To foster initiatives that strengthen the capacity of schools and communities to serve students with emotional disturbance in the least restrictive environments appropriate.

TARGET #3: VALUE AND ADDRESS DIVERSITY

To encourage culturally competent and linguistically appropriate exchanges and collaborations among families, professionals, students, and communities. These collaborations should foster equitable outcomes for all students and result in the identification and provision of services that are responsive to issues of race, culture, gender, and social and economic status.

TARGET #4: COLLABORATE WITH FAMILIES

To foster collaborations that fully include family members on the team of service providers that implements family-focused services to improve educational outcomes. Services should be

→

open, helpful, culturally competent, accessible to families, and school- as well as community-based.

TARGET #5: PROMOTE APPROPRIATE ASSESSMENT

To promote practices ensuring that assessment is integral to the identification, design, and delivery of services for children and youth with emotional disturbance. These practices should be culturally appropriate, ethical, and functional.

TARGET #6: PROVIDE ONGOING SKILL DEVELOPMENT AND SUPPORT

To foster the enhancement of knowledge, understanding, and sensitivity among all who work with children and youth with and at risk of developing emotional disturbance. Support and development should be ongoing and aim at strengthening the capacity of families, teachers, service providers, and other stakeholders to collaborate, persevere, and improve outcomes for children and youth with ED.

TARGET #7: CREATE COMPREHENSIVE AND COLLABORATIVE SYSTEMS

To promote systems change resulting in the development of coherent services built around the individual needs of children and youth with and at risk of developing emotional disturbance. These services should be family-centered, community-based, and appropriately funded.

U.S. Department of Education. (1994).
http://cecp.air.org/resources/ntlagend.html

Special Education Technical Assistance

The U.S. Department of Education's Office of Special Education Programs supports an extensive technical assistance network. School teams can obtain information and support from this network. Descriptions of some important technical assistance centers follow.

Technical Assistance Centers

The Access Center: Improving Outcomes for All Students K–8

Address: The American Institutes for Research
1000 Thomas Jefferson St.
Washington, DC 20007-3835

Phone: (202) 999-5300

Fax: (202) 944-5454

TTY: (877) 334-3499

E-mail: accesscenter@air.org

Web site: www.k8accesscenter.org

The mission of the Access Center is to create a national infrastructure that states and local school districts can rely on for scientifically based practices that can be used with elementary and middle school students with disabilities. The Access Center seeks to enhance a student's engagement and learning in the general education curriculum through information and services. It facilitates strategic partnerships to help identify and implement scientifically based practices in schools and classrooms. It offers training for regional, state, and local educators to be better consumers of research. The Access Center also provides a broad menu of technical assistance (TA) methods, most of which can be found on its Web site, www.k8accesscenter.org. The Access Center's information, resources, and strategies address the cultural, contextual, and instructional aspects of student participation that lead to success in general education settings and mastery of general education content.

→

Center for Effective Collaboration and Practice (CECP)

Address: Center for Effective Collaboration and Practice
American Institutes for Research
1000 Thomas Jefferson Street NW, Suite 400

Washington, DC 20007

Phone: (888) 457-1551 or (202) 944-5400

Fax: (202) 944-5454

E-mail: center@air.org

Web site: http://cecp.air.org

The Center for Effective Collaboration and Practice, which developed the Early Warning, Action, and Step by Step guides, facilitates local, state, and national collaboration and has developed an extensive array of information to help build safe and supportive schools.

CECP's site connects you to several other essential resources. For example, go to "Strengthening the Safety Net" and then to Project SERVE. You can get a detailed staffing and task schedule for implementing Project SERVE, which you can also use as a template for designing "who does what" and costing out your hours of service for each child or intervention in your program. The Web site has "miniwebs" on cultural competency, functional and behavioral assessment, promising practices in children's mental health, violence prevention, and wraparound. You can download many federal documents and *PowerPoint*® presentations and do topic searches. CECP lists proven programs for prevention and early and intensive interventions and the contact information for each. Referenced, hot-linked, and Spanish versions of the Early Warning Guide and Action Guide are available on this site.

Center for Special Education Finance (CSEF)

Address: Center for Special Education Finance
American Institutes for Research
1791 Arastradero Road

Palo Alto, CA 94304-1337

Phone: (650) 843-8136

TTY: (650) 493-2209

Fax: (650) 858-0958

E-mail: csef@air.org

Web site: http://www.csef-air.org

The Center for Special Education Finance (CSEF) was established in October 1992 to work on fiscal policy questions related to the delivery and support of special education services throughout the United States. CSEF was recently refunded to continue to meet these information needs and to conduct the first comprehensive, nationally representative study of special education spending in more than a decade, the Special Education Expenditure Study (SEEP).

This Web site is useful for finding financial resources. The cost information that CSEF provides can help you compare your costs with national averages and show administrators that restructuring your pupil services staff priorities may result in significant savings.

Using the Web Site

We used the CSEF Web site data to show our school board how we could provide teacher training and staff consultation services by reducing the number of unnecessary assessments for special education eligibility.

Phil Bowser, school psychologist, Roseberg, Oregon

Center on Positive Behavioral Interventions and Supports (CPBIS)

Address: Center on Positive Behavioral Interventions and Supports
Behavioral Research and Training
5262 University of Oregon

Eugene, OR 97403-5262

Phone: (541) 346-2505

Fax: (541) 346-5689

E-mail: pbis@oregon.uoregon.edu

Web site: http://www.pbis.org

The goal of the Center on Positive Behavioral Interventions and Supports (CPBIS) is to increase "the capacity of schools, families, and communities to support and educate children and youth with significant problem behaviors" by (1) increasing both awareness and knowledge of positive behavioral interventions and supports and (2) emphasizing the features of a comprehensive systems approach to sustaining positive behavioral interventions and supports.

You can read research that supports PBIS, find schools using PBIS, get details on costs, find coaches, learn what you have to do to train staff or become a coach yourself, and see examples of forms used to maintain fidelity to the program. You can download information, as well as many useful *PowerPoint*® presentations, on implementing PBIS. This site is particularly useful for prevention and early intervention.

→

Consortium for Appropriate Dispute Resolution in Special Education (CADRE)

Address: Consortium for Appropriate Dispute
Resolution in Special Education
Direction Service, Inc.
P.O. Box 51360
Eugene, OR 97405-0906

Phone: (541) 686-5060

TTY
(NICHCY): (800) 695-0285

Fax: (541) 686-5063

E-mail: cadre@directionservice.org

Web site: http://www.directionservice.org/cadre/

CADRE aims to systematically survey the technical assistance (TA) and information needs of a broad range of stakeholders (e.g., state and parallel entities, families, underrepresented and underserved populations, general educators, and information and TA providers) and to provide dynamic technical assistance on dispute resolution procedures to all state and parallel entities. Information about the mediation process used to address disputes about special education and related services for children with disabilities can help you defuse the tension around disagreements and enable all to see the value of mediation over more adversarial procedures. The site also connects you to other sites that can help schools become more culturally competent when dealing with families with children with disabilities. Many of the materials are translated into Spanish.

National Information Center for Children and Youth with Disabilities (NICHCY)

Address: National Information Center
for Children and Youth
with Disabilities
Academy for Educational Development
P.O. Box 1492
Washington, DC 20013-1492

Phone/
TTY: (800) 695-0285 or (202) 884-8200

Fax: (202) 884-8441

E-mail: nichcy@aed.org

Web site: http://www.nichcy.org/

NICHCY provides information and referral services on children and youth with disabilities to families, caregivers, professionals, and others to improve the educational outcomes of all children and youth. Its goal is to help families and professionals to ensure that all children participate as fully as possible in all aspects of life, including school, home, and community. Spanish translations are provided.

This technical assistance site gives you information about how to ensure that you have considered the family's rights and protections under IDEA and Section 504. It also contains information about partnering, ways to include students and families in your planning and implementation, and training information for teachers and staff, along with other valuable information about disability issues.

National Center on Education, Disability, and Juvenile Justice (EDJJ)

Address: National Center on Education,
Disability, and Juvenile Justice
Department of Special Education
University of Maryland
1224 Benjamin Building
College Park, MD 20742-1161

Phone: (301) 405-6462

Fax: (301) 314-5757

E-mail: edjj@umail.umd.edu

Web site: http://www.edjj.org/

EDJJ is a collaborative research, training, technical assistance, and dissemination program designed to develop more effective responses to the needs of youth with disabilities in the juvenile justice system or at risk for involvement with the juvenile justice system. Through regional meetings, technical assistance, research and evaluation activities, and publication and dissemination, the Center helps change the perceptions and understandings about youth with disabilities in communities and in the juvenile justice system.

The Web site offers extensive information and resources on juvenile delinquency for parents, practitioners, educators, and policymakers. It features professional development training materials for improving educational experiences for youth at risk of juvenile delinquency and incarceration. Links to several publications of interest to both parents and school practitioners are available.

Alternative Programs and Schools

Developing effective alternative programs as part of your school-wide plan will require significant effort and careful monitoring because little positive research exists about the effectiveness of such programs.

Alternative schools and programs can be hurtful as well as helpful. A strong body of research suggests that interventions that bring antisocial youth together risk reinforcing negative behaviors among those students (Dishion, McCord, & Poulin, 1999). Examine the material in the *Action Guide* (p. 33) that discusses this issue and make sure that your program contains the nine elements found helpful in developing an alternative program. Be sure to include a well-designed transition system for reintegrating students into the regular program.

Alternative programs may increase their positive effects when they combine proven manualized therapies and wraparound systems of care with instructional supports. Your plan should include family involvement and service system supports and should employ resources that enable both academic and mental health and behavioral supports. Some systems have developed alternative schools that do not permit special education services to continue. Planning that coordinates services to students with both special education and alternative education needs should be an imperative in your design.

Alternative schools require the sending and receiving schools to cooperate closely. Students whose serious mental health problems require their temporary or long-term removal from a general education setting require access to the school system's curriculum and appropriate instruction. If alternative programs are to produce generalized effects, the school improvement plan must address the role of alternative schools and the ways transitions to and from these programs will be accomplished. (For *Special Education in Alternative Education Programs*, see ERIC EC Digest #E585 at http://ericec.org/digests/e585.html.)

In-school coordination and collaboration for effectively addressing the needs of children with intensive needs is an imperative first step. Ensuring a full array of services for these students is the second step. This can be accomplished by integrating services and interventions with community agency services to supplement what schools can provide. This service integration requires policies, procedures, and practices that ensure partnerships between school and community providers; among the school, community providers, and families; and among the school, community providers, families, and their children.

Westside Alternative School, Hays, Kansas

Westside Alternative School is an intensive interagency program for children and youth. Recipient of the 1996 Award of Excellence from the National Community Mental Healthcare Council, Westside is supported by the Hays Unified School District, the Hays West Central Kansas Special Education Cooperative, High Plains Mental Health Center, Hays Area Social and Rehabilitation Services, the Ellis County Attorney, local substance abuse treatment agencies, juvenile intake, community corrections, and foster care and family preservation services.

Westside provides services to students with emotional or behavioral disabilities who are risk for placement out of school, home, or community. Eligibility is determined by an Interagency Referral Committee when outpatient services are not sufficient, but the child does not require 24-hour supervision or hospitalization. Westside students frequently need other services, such as courts, substance abuse treatment, or mental health or other family services. Westside is funded by Medicaid, Hays Social and Rehabilitative Services, and the school district.

Teachers and mental health center staff provide close supervision for the K–12 students who attend the school full- or part-time. Time is allowed for frequent discussion about how well students are doing in terms of being responsible, honest, respectful, and courageous. Group counseling focuses on building skills in self-evaluation and taking responsibility for solving personal problems. Students are challenged to show concern for peers and to help them resolve problems, helping themselves in return.

Mental health staff provide in-home family therapy, daily group counseling, family night meetings, case management, attendant (respite) care, and 24-hour crisis intervention. School district special education teachers provide individualized education through small groups and individual attention. Treatment planning involves the student's home school, and reintegration planning begins immediately upon placement at Westside.

Resources for Community Treatment and Support

Many resources can help you develop intensive community-based interventions. One that gives an overview of the evidence-based interventions is Barbara Burns and Kimberly Hoagwood's *Community Treatment for Youth: Evidence-Based Interventions for Severe Emotional and Behavioral Disorders* (2002). Three others that can serve as tools for developing a system of care are Sheila Pires's *Building Systems of Care: A Primer* (2002) and Beth Stroul's *Systems of Care: A Framework for System Reform in Children's Mental Health* (2002), which are available from The National Technical Assistance Center for Children's Mental Health at the Georgetown University Child Development Center, and Andres Pumariega and Nancy Winters' *The Handbook of Child and Adolescent Systems of Care: The New Community Psychiatry* (2003). A fifth resource, which reflects a youth development orientation, is Nicole Yohalem and Karen Pittman's *Powerful Pathways: Framing Options and Opportunities for Vulnerable Youth* (2001). It was produced for the Youth Transition Funders Group. A sixth, which addresses the relationships between cognitive and behavioral problems on the one hand, and juvenile justice outcomes on the other hand, is a set of seven monographs on improving outcomes for youth with disabilities who may or do come in contact with the juvenile justice system:

- *Addressing Invisible Barriers: Improving Outcomes for Youth With Disabilities in the Juvenile Justice System* addresses the need for disability-specific approaches in adjudication and placement.

- *Advocating for Children With Behavioral and Cognitive Disabilities in the Juvenile Justice System*, addresses the critical role of advocacy.

- *Best Practices for Serving Court Involved Youth With Learning, Attention and Behavioral Disabilities* describes best practices and model programs for reducing delinquency and preventing recidivism.

- *Collaboration in the Juvenile Justice System and Youth Serving Agencies: Improving Prevention, Providing More Efficient Services, and Reducing Recidivism for Youth With Disabilities* explains the role of collaboration in improving services for court-involved youth.

- *Corrections and Juvenile Justice: Current Education Practice for Youth With Learning and Other Disabilities* describes and evaluates the educational services that youth in the juvenile justice system receive.

- *The Role of Recreation in Preventing Youth With Disabilities From Coming Into Contact With the Juvenile Justice System and Preventing Recidivism* describes recreation and therapeutic recreation programs specifically designed to address the intensive needs of youth.

- *Youth With Disabilities in the Correctional System: Prevalence Rates and Identification Issues* examines prevalence rates and identification issues as a starting point for planning.

Produced by CECP in collaboration with The National Center for Education, Disability, and Juvenile Justice, these monographs are available at http://cecp.air.org/juvenilejustice/juvenile_justice.htm.

A seventh resource addresses systemic and financial issues: Anne Lezak and Gary MacBeth's *Overcoming Barriers to Serving Our Children in the Community* (http://www.olmsteadcommunity.org/Barriers2.pdf).

Systems of Care

School and community human services are generally organized around individual risk factors or "symptoms." Youth with co-occurring mental health and substance abuse disorders rarely receive the kind of help they need at the time they need it. Although effective substance abuse and mental health treatments are available (Drug Strategies, 2003; Christophersen & Mortweet, 2001; Burns & Hoagwood, 2002), services and supports are fragmented, isolated, and rigid. Yet, co-occurring substance abuse and mental health disorders are frequently inseparable problems that cannot be effectively addressed in isolation from one another (Federation of Families for Children's Mental Health, 2001). Similarly, schools and community services frequently separate mental health services from remedial and special education support. Yet students who need the most intensive services need a "system of care" that can address multiple risk factors simultaneously.

Developing a system of care requires multiagency service agreements that keep students and their families as the central focus. What must you do to ensure that this multiagency coordination is in place? What areas of tension, such as confidentiality versus sharing vital information, does your plan need to address? Design your plan so that procedures are in place to enable the student support team to include all agency service providers or case service coordinators as members of the team. While agency representatives may not be able to participate in the case of every student, they should participate in the development of student support team policies. Integrating the work of multiple agencies may require innovative funding models.

The language of service integration can be complex and may require staff to have cross-system training. Agencies frequently use different consent forms, rules for confidentiality, diagnostic categories, formulas for funding, and qualifications for providers, among other things. Some providers cannot be reimbursed for team meetings or for multiple services to a student's family on the same day.

Systems have resolved these difficulties in a variety of ways. Service funding laws and federal flexibility statutes that can support your interagency and schoolwide service plans do exist. For example, IDEA '97 permits local schools to access Medicaid reimbursement as the payer-of-first-resort for many related services. Related services can include an array of psychological, social work, and counseling services as well as case management and family supports to address the emotional disability or behavioral plan. Medicaid may also fund medication monitoring by schools.

Some memoranda or interagency contracts have provided waivers from state or local requirements. Waivers from licensing or Medicaid regulations, for example, generally require state authorization.

Resources About Promising Practices in Children's Mental Health

The Center for Mental Health Services has produced 13 monographs describing systems of care. They are available at http://www.air.org/cecp.

Promising Practices in Children's Mental Health 2001 Series

- *Wraparound: Stories From the Field, Volume I*

- *Learning From Families: Identifying Service Strategies for Success, Volume II*

- *Promising Practices in Early Childhood Mental Health, Volume III*

Promising Practices in Children's Mental Health 2000 Series

- *Cultural Strengths and Challenges in Implementing a System of Care Model in American Indian Communities, Volume I*

- *Using Evaluation Data to Manage, Improve, Market, and Sustain Children's Services, Volume II*

- *For the Long Haul: Maintaining Systems of Care Beyond the Federal Investment, Volume III*

Promising Practices in Children's Mental Health 1998 Series

- *New Roles for Families in Systems of Care, Volume I*

- *Promising Practices in Family-Provider Collaboration, Volume II*

- *The Role of Education in a System of Care: Effectively Serving Children With Emotional or Behavioral Disorders, Volume III*

- *Promising Practices in Wraparound for Children With Serious Emotional Disturbance and Their Families, Volume IV*

- *Training Strategies for Serving Children With Serious Emotional Disturbance and Their Families in a System of Care, Volume V*

- *Building Collaboration in Systems of Care, Volume VI*

- *A Compilation of Lessons Learned From the 22 Grantees of the 1997 Comprehensive Community Mental Health Services for Children and Their Families Program, Volume VII*

Conclusion: Selecting Interventions

FEW
SOME
ALL

Selecting effective interventions involves two tasks: identifying interventions and ensuring a good fit between interventions and your school or community.

A variety of sources provide information on effective interventions. Many sources can be accessed through Web sites, including these:

▲ Center for Effective Collaboration and Practice (www.air.org/cecp)

▲ Center for the Study and Prevention of Violence's Blueprints (http://www.colorado.edu/cspv/blueprints/)

▲ Center for Mental Health in Schools (http://smhp.psych.ucla.edu/)

▲ Center for Mental Health Services (http://www.mentalhealth.org/)

▲ Center for Substance Abuse Prevention (http://www.samhsa.gov/centers/csap/csap.html)

▲ Centers for Disease Control National Youth Violence Prevention Resource Center (http://www.safeyouth.org/home.htm)

▲ Centers for Disease Control and Prevention, National Center for Injury Prevention and Control (http://www.cdc.gov/ncipc/dvp/bestpractices.htm)

▲ The Collaborative for Academic, Social, and Emotional Learning's (CASEL) Safe and Sound: An Educational Leaders Guide to Evidence-Based Social and Emotional Learning Programs (http://www.casel.org/progrevfr.htm)

▲ Hamilton Fish National Institute on School and Community Violence (http://www.hamfish.org/)

- ▲ Positive Youth Development in the United States: Research Findings on Evaluations of Positive Youth Development Programs (http://aspe.hhs.gov/hsp/positiveyouthdev99/)
- ▲ Prevention Research Center for the Promotion of Human Development, Pennsylvania State University (http://www.prevention.psu.edu/)
- ▲ Surgeon General of the United States (http://www.surgeongeneral.gov/library/youthviolence/report.html)
- ▲ U.S. Department of Education's Safe and Drug-Free Schools Program's Model Programs (http://www.ed.gov/offices/OESE/SDFS/programs.html)

The Center for Mental Health Services, Substance Abuse, and Mental Health Services Administration, U.S. Department of Health and Human Services has prepared an excellent guide to online resources for those interested in youth violence prevention. This guide, *Youth Violence Prevention Resources*, can be requested for free from the Knowledge Exchange Network at (800) 789-2647.

It is important to understand that an intervention or program that has been demonstrated to work somewhere else will not necessarily work in your school or community with the types of children you want to serve (Weisz, Donenberg, Han, & Weiss, 1995). Be a skeptical consumer and ask questions about outcomes, costs, staffing implications, adaptability, and external support.

Outcomes. Ask whether the program can work with the types of students and staff that you have. What evidence shows that this program has worked in school communities similar to yours?

Costs. Determine the costs of implementing the intervention. Costs may include the purchase of materials, consultation, space, additional staff, and staff time. Program developers, technical assistance providers, and staff from schools that have implemented the interventions can help you determine costs.

Adaptability. School staff often adapt interventions to meet local needs and preferences. Although some components may be altered, certain key components of many programs should not be changed. Determine whether the key components of the program you select can address your needs and be implemented successfully—without alteration. Program developers and technical assistance providers should be able to give you answers.

External Support. Implementing new programs requires support. Support may be available from the developers, technical assistance centers, state department staff, regional or intermediate educational unit staff, district staff, or school staff who have been trained to implement programs.

Identifying effective interventions can be hard work. In addition, evidence of efficacy in clinical trials (where researchers have considerable control over who is included in the study and how the intervention is delivered) does not ensure that an intervention will work in schools or community settings (Hoagwood, Hibbs, Brent, & Jensen, 1995; Weisz et al., 1995). To help you select interventions, we convened an expert panel to determine the criteria you should use and to identify programs that meet these criteria. The panel, which included nationally recognized researchers, practitioners, and technical assistance providers, identified these six criteria for selecting programs:

▲ The program must have documented effectiveness and be based on sound theory.

▲ The program can be easily integrated with existing school practices.

▲ The program must have data that demonstrate effectiveness or ineffectiveness with particular student groups.

▲ Data must indicate that the program has a positive impact on student achievement.

▲ Program developers/sponsors must demonstrate that subscribing schools receive sufficient technical assistance.

▲ Program components must focus on promoting positive solutions to behavioral and emotional problems.

The panel then identified the interventions that are described in Appendix A: Program Briefs. To help you determine whether the interventions might be a good fit with your school and community, the briefs provide information on such matters as costs, risk factors targeted, types of children for which there is evidence that the intervention worked, adaptability (what can and cannot be changed), and technical assistance available.

References

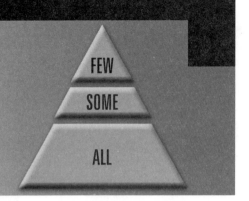

Aber, J. L., Jones, S. M., Brown, J. L., Chaudry, N., & Samples, F. (1998). Resolving conflict creatively: Evaluating the developmental effects of a school-based violence prevention program in neighborhood and classroom context. *Development and Psychopathology, 10*(2), 187–213.

Adelman, H. S. & Taylor, L. (2000). Promoting mental health in schools in the midst of school reform. *Journal of School Health,* 170–178.

American Academy of Pediatrics' Committee on School Health. (2001). School health centers and other integrated school health services (RE0030). *Pediatrics, 107*(1), 198–201.

Annie E. Casey Foundation. (1995). *The path of most resistance: Reflections on lessons learned from New Futures.* Baltimore: Author.

Bazelon Center for Mental Health Law. (1999). *Making sense of Medicaid for children with serious emotional disturbance.* Washington, DC: Author.

Bradley, D. F. & West, J. F. (1994). Staff training for the inclusion of students with disabilities: Visions from school-based educators. *Teacher Education and Special Education, 17,* 117–128.

Brock, S. E., Lazarus, P. J., & Jimerson, S. R. (2002). *Best practices in school prevention and intervention.* Bethesda, MD: National Association of School Psychologists.

Burns, B. J. & Hoagwood, K. (2002). *Community treatment for youth: Evidence-based interventions for severe emotional and behavioral disorders.* New York: Oxford University Press.

Calfee, C., Wittwer, F., & Meredith, M. (1998). *Building a full-service school: A step-by-step guide.* San Francisco: Jossey-Bass.

Cartledge, G. & Milburn, J. F. (1996). *Cultural diversity and social skill instruction: Understanding ethnic and gender differences.* Champaign, IL: Research Press.

Center for Health and Health Care in Schools. (1998). *Issues in financing school-based health centers: A guide for state officials.* Available: http://www.healthinschools.org.

Center for Mental Health in Schools. (2000). *Financial strategies to aid in addressing barriers to learning.* Available: http://smhp.psych.ucla.edu/pdfdocs/Finanacial/Fund2000.pdf.

Center for Mental Health Services, Substance Abuse and Mental Health Services Administration. (2001). *Youth violence prevention resources.* Rockville, MD: U.S. Department of Health and Human Services.

Center for Mental Health Services, Substance Abuse and Mental Health Services Administration. (2002). *Promising practices for safe and effective schools* [Videorecording]. Rockville, MD: U.S. Department of Health and Human Services.

Centers for Disease Control and Prevention, National Center for Injury Prevention & Control. (1993). *The prevention of youth violence: A framework for community action.* Atlanta, GA: Author.

Centers for Disease Control and Prevention, National Center for Injury Prevention and Control. (2000). *Best practices of youth violence prevention: A sourcebook for community action.* Atlanta, GA: Author.

Christophersen, E. R. & Mortweet, S. L. (2001). *Treatments that work with children: Empirically supported strategies for managing childhood problems.* Washington, DC: American Psychological Association.

Collaborative to Advance Social and Emotional Learning (CASEL). (2000). *Social and emotional learning (SEL) competencies.* Available: http://www.casel.org/competencies.htm.

Committee on Community-Level Programs for Youth; Board on Children, Youth, and Families, National Research Council and Institute of Medicine. (2002). *Community programs to promote youth development.* Washington, DC: National Academy Press.

Cross, T., Bazron, B., Dennis, K., & Isaacs, M. (1989). *Towards a culturally competent system of care, vol. I.* Washington, DC: Georgetown University Child Development Center, CASSP Technical Assistance Center.

Dishion, T. J., McCord, J., & Poulin, F. (1999). When interventions harm: Peer groups and problem behavior. *American Psychologist, 54,* 755–764.

Drug Strategies. (2003). *Treating teens: A guide to adolescent drug programs.* Washington, DC: Author.

Dryfoos, J.G. (1994). *Full-service schools: A revolution in health and social services for children, youth, and families.* San Francisco: Jossey-Bass.

Dryfoos, J. & Maguire, S. (2002). *Inside full-service community schools.* Thousand Oaks, CA: Corwin Press.

Duncan, P. I. (1998). School health services. In E. Marx & S.F. Wooley (Eds.), *Health is academic* (pp. 169–194). New York: Teachers College Press.

Dwyer, K. & Osher, D. (2000). *Safeguarding our children: An action guide.* Washington, DC: U.S. Departments of Education and Justice, American Institutes for Research.

Dwyer, K., Osher, D., & Warger, C. (1998). *Early warning, timely response: A guide to safe schools.* Washington, DC: U.S. Department of Education.

Elias, M. J., Zins, J. E., Weissberg, R. P., Frey, K. S., Greenberg, M. T., Haynes, N. M., Kessler, R., Schwab-Stone, M. E., & Shriver, T. P. (1997). *Promoting social and emotional learning: Guidelines for educators.* Alexandria, VA: Association for Supervision and Curriculum Development.

Federal Bureau of Investigation. (2000). *The school shooter: A threat assessment perspective.* Washington, DC: Author.

Federation of Families for Children's Mental Health. (2001). *Blamed and ashamed: The treatment experiences of youth with co-occurring substance abuse and mental health disorders and their families.* Alexandria, VA: Author.

Fein, R. A., Vossekuil, B., Pollack, W. S., Borum, R., Modzeleski, W., & Reddy, M (2002, May). *Threat assessment in schools: A guide to managing threatening situations and to creating safe school climates.* Washington, DC: U.S. Secret Service and U.S. Department of Education.

Flaxman, E. (Ed.). (2001). *Evaluating school violence programs*. New York: Teachers College, Institute for Urban and Minority Education, ERIC Clearinghouse on Urban Education.

Fleissner, D. & Heinzelmann, F. (1996). *Crime prevention through environmental design and community policing*. Washington, DC: National Institute of Justice, Office of Justice Programs.

Fullan, M. G. (1993). *Change forces: Probing the depth of educational reform*. Bristol, PA: Falmer Press.

Fullan, M. G. & Miles, M. B. (1992). Getting reform right: What works and what doesn't. *Phi Delta Kappan, 73*, 744–752.

Furlong, M. J. & Morrison, R. (2001). *California School Climate and Safety Survey—short form*. Santa Barbara, CA: University of California, Santa Barbara School Climate and Safety Partnership.

Hall, G. E. & Loucks, S. F. (1978). Teacher concerns as a basis for facilitating and personalizing staff development. *Teachers College Record, 80*, 36–53.

Haynes, N. M., Comer, J. P., & Hamilton-Lee, M. (1988). The school development program: A model for school improvement. *Journal of Negro Education, 57*, 11–21.

Hoagwood, K. I., Hibbs, E., Brent, D., & Jensen, P. (1995). Efficacy and effectiveness in studies in child and adolescent psychotherapy. *Journal of Consulting and Clinical Psychology, 63*, 683–687.

Hord, S. M., Sparks, D., Brown, W., Havens, S., & Calderon, M. (2000). *Voices from the field: Success in school reform*. Austin, TX: Southwest Educational Development Laboratory.

Illinois State Board of Education. (1997). *Illinois learning standards*. Springfield, IL: Author. Available: http://www.isbe.state.il.us/ils/.

Isaacs, M. & Benjamin, M. (1991). *Towards a culturally competent system of care, Vol. II: Programs which utilize culturally competent principles*. Washington, DC: Georgetown University Child Development Center, CASSP Technical Assistance Center.

Janas, M. (1998). Shhhhh, the dragon is asleep and its name is resistance. *Journal of Staff Development, 19*, 3.

Kendziora, K. T., Bruns, E., Osher, D., Pacchiano, D., & Mejia, B. (2001). *Wraparound: Stories from the field. Systems of care: Promising practices in children's mental health, 2001 Series*. Washington, DC: Center for Effective Collaboration and Practice, American Institutes for Research.

Krueger, R. A. (1988). *Focus groups: A practical guide for applied research*. Newbury Park, CA: Sage.

Learning First Alliance. (2001). *Every child learning: Safe and supportive schools*. Washington, DC: Author.

Learning First Alliance. (2003). *Beyond islands of excellence: What districts can do to improve instruction and achievement in all schools—a leadership brief*. Washington, DC: Author.

Loucks-Horsley, S. (2002). *The Concerns-Based Adoption Model (CBAM): A model for change in individuals*. Washington, DC: National Academy of Science, Current Project System. Available: http://www.nationalacademies.org/rise/backg4a.htm.

Marx, E. & Wooley, S. F. (Eds). (1998). *Health is academic: A guide to coordinated school health programs*. New York: Teachers College Press.

Miles, M. B. & Louis, K. S. (1996). Mastering the will and skill for change. *Educational Leadership, 47*(8), 57–61.

Nansel, T. R., Overpeck, M., Pilla, R. S., Ruan, J., Simons-Morton, B., & Scheidt, P. (2001). Bullying behaviors among U.S. youth: Prevalence and association with psychological adjustment. *Journal of New England Medical Association, 285,* 16.

Nastasi, B. K., Varjas, K., & Bernstein, R. (1998). *Exemplary mental health programs: School psychologists as mental health service providers.* Washington, DC: National Association of School Psychologists.

National Coalition for Community Schools. (2000). *Community schools: Partnerships for excellence.* Washington, DC: Author. Available: http://www.communityschools.org/partnerships.html.

National Education Association Health Information Network (NEA HIN) and Center for Mental Health Services, Substance Abuse, and Mental Health Services Administration. (2001). *Violence in communities and schools: A stress reduction guide for teachers and other school staff.* Washington, DC: Author.

National Youth Development Information Center. (2002). *Definitions of youth development (and related terms).* Washington, DC: Author. Available: http://nydic.org/nydic/devdef.html.

Office of the Surgeon General. (1999). *Mental health: A report of the Surgeon General.* Rockville, MD: U.S. Department of Health and Human Services.

Osher, D. & Osher, T. (1996). The national agenda for children and youth with serious emotional disturbances. In M. Nelson, R. Rutherford, & B. Wolford (Eds.), *Comprehensive collaborative systems that work for troubled youth: A national agenda* (pp. 149–164). Richmond, KY: National Coalition for Juvenile Justice Services.

Osterman, K. F. (2000). Students' need for belonging in the school community. *Review of Education Research, 70,* 323–367.

Pires, S. (2002). *Building systems of care: A primer.* Washington, DC: Georgetown University Center for Child and Human Development.

Policymakers Partnership at the National Association of State Directors of Special Education. (2002, April). *Mental health, schools and families working together for all children and youth: Steps toward a shared agenda.* Alexandria, VA: Author.

Pumariega, A. & Winters, N. (Eds.). (2003). *The handbook of child and adolescent systems of care: The new community psychiatry.* San Francisco: Jossey-Bass.

Quinn, M. M., Gable, R. A., Rutherford, Jr., R. B., Nelson, C. M., & Howell, K. W. (1998). *Addressing student problem behavior.* Washington, DC: Center for Effective Collaboration and Practice.

Quinn, M. M., Osher, D., Hoffman, C. C., & Hanley, T. V. (1998). *Safe, drug-free, and effective schools for ALL students: What works!* Washington, DC: U.S. Department of Education.

Quinn, M. M., Osher, D., Warger, C. L., Hanley, T.V., Bader, B. D., & Hoffman, C. C. (2000). *Teaching and working with children who have emotional and behavioral challenges.* Longmont, CO: Sopris West Educational Services.

Robinson, G. K., Barrett, M., Tunkelrott, T., & Kim, J. (2000). *School-based mental health services under Medicaid managed care* (DHHS Publication No. [SMA] 00-3456). Rockville, MD: Substance Abuse Mental Health Services Administration, Center for Mental Health Services.

Sims, A., King, M., & Osher, D. (1998). *What is cultural competency?* Washington, DC: Center for Effective Collaboration and Practice.

Sparks, D. (1993). Thirteen tips for managing change. *Pathways to school improvement.* Naperville, IL: North Central Regional Educational Laboratory. Available: http://www.ncrel.org/sdrs/areas/issues/educatrs/leadrshp/le5spark.htm.

Stroul, B. (2002). *Systems of care: A framework for system reform in children's mental health.* Washington, DC: Georgetown University Center for Child and Human Development.

U.S. Department of Education. (1994). *The national agenda for achieving better results for children and youth with serious emotional disturbance.* Washington, DC: Author.

U.S. Department of Education. (1998). *Implementing schoolwide programs: An idea book on planning, volume 1.* Washington, DC: Author.

U.S. Department of Education. (1998). *Twentieth annual report to Congress on the implementation of the Individuals with Disabilities Education Act.* Washington, DC: Author.

U.S. Department of Education, Office of Special Education Programs. (1997). School-wide behavioral management systems. *Research Connections in Special Education, 1*(1).

U.S. Department of Health and Human Services, Substance Abuse and Mental Health Services Administration, Center for Substance Abuse Prevention. (n.d.). *SAMHSA model programs.* Rockville, MD: Author. Available: http://modelprograms.samhsa.gov.

Wandersman, A., Imm, P., Chinman, M., & Kaftarian, S. (1999). *Getting to outcomes: Methods and tools for planning, evaluation and accountability.* Rockville, MD: Center for Substance Abuse Prevention.

Warger, C. (2001). *Research on full-service schools and students with disabilities.* Arlington, VA: ERIC Clearinghouse on Disabilities and Gifted Education.

Weist, M. D., Evans, M. D, and Lever, N. (Eds.). (2003), *Handbook of school mental health.* New York: Kluwer.

Weisz, J. R., Donenberg, G. R., Han, S. S., & Weiss, B. (1995). Bridging the gap between lab and clinic in child and adolescent psychotherapy. *Journal of Consulting and Clinical Psychology, 63,* 688–701.

Westerly Integrated Social Services Program. (1997). *Westerly integrated social services program.* [Brochure]. Westerly, RI: Author.

Woodruff, D. W., Osher, D., Hoffman, C. C., Gruner, A., King, M. A., Snow, S. T., & McIntire, J. C. (1999). The role of education in a system of care: Effectively serving children with emotional or behavioral disorders. In *Systems of care: Promising practices in children's mental health, 1998 series, volume III.* Washington, DC: Center for Effective Collaboration and Practice, American Institutes for Research.

Yankelovitch, D. (1991). *Coming to public judgment: Making democracy work in a complex world.* Syracuse, NY: Syracuse University Press.

Program Briefs

Matrix of Effective Programs

PROGRAM	Preschool	Lower Elementary	Upper Elementary	Middle/Junior High School	High School	Schoolwide/Universal	Early Intervention	Intensive Intervention	Classroom	School	Home/Family Involvement	Community Involvement	Academic Achievement	Social/Emotional Learning	Self-Control	Problem-solving	Antisocial/Aggressive Behavior, Violence	Delinquency	Alcohol, Tobacco, Other Drug Use (ATOD)	Page Number
ACHIEVE: A Collaborative School-Based Reform Process (Project ACHIEVE)		x	x	x		x	x		x	x	x	x	x	x	x	x	x			136
Aggression Replacement Training (ART)		x	x	x	x		x		x	x				x	x	x	x	x		141
Bullying Prevention Program		x	x	x		x			x	x	x	x		x			x			148
Child Development Project (CDP)		x	x			x			x	x	x	x	x	x			x	x	x	148
Class-Wide Peer Tutoring (CWPT)	x	x	x	x	x	x			x	x			x	x						◆ 15
First Step to Success		x					x		x		x						x			◆ 26
Functional Family Therapy (FFT)		x	x	x	x		x	x		x	x						x	x	x	152
The Good Behavior Game	x	x	x			x			x								x			155
High/Scope Preschool Curriculum Framework	x					x	x		x		x		x	x						158
I Can Problem Solve (ICPS)	x	x	x			x			x	x	x		x	x	x	x	x			162
Life Skills Training			x	x	x	x			x					x	x	x			x	165
Linking the Interests of Families and Teachers (LIFT)		x	x			x	x		x	x	x		x	x	x		x	x	x	169
Multidimensional Treatment Foster Care (MTFC)	x	x	x	x	x			x		x			x	x	x	x	x	x	x	173
Multisystemic Therapy (MST)				x	x			x			x	x	x	x	x	x	x	x	x	177
PeaceBuilders	x	x	x	x	x	x			x	x			x	x	x	x	x	x	x	183
Peacemakers		x	x	x		x		x	x	x				x	x	x	x			188
Positive Adolescent Choices Training (PACT)				x	x		x		x					x	x	x	x			◆ 26

◆ = Action Guide

Matrix of Effective Programs

PROGRAM	GRADE LEVEL					LEVEL OF INTERVENTION			ENVIRONMENT OF PROGRAM IMPLEMENTATION				TARGETED AREAS							Page Number
	Preschool	Lower Elementary	Upper Elementary	Middle/Junior High School	High School	Schoolwide/Universal	Early Intervention	Intensive Intervention	Classroom	School	Home/Family Involvement	Community Involvement	Academic Achievement	Social/Emotional Learning	Self-Control	Problem-solving	Antisocial/Aggressive Behavior, Violence	Delinquency	Alcohol, Tobacco, Other Drug Use (ATOD)	
Positive Behavioral Interventions and Supports (PBIS)	x	x	x	x	x	x	x	x	x	x				x	x		x			191
Primary Mental Health Project (Primary Project)	x	x					x			x				x	x		x			195
Project ALERT				x		x			x	x					x	x			x	198
Project Northland				x		x			x	x	x	x		x					x	203
Project STAR: Students Taught Awareness and Resistance (Midwestern Prevention Project)				x	x	x			x	x	x	x		x			x		x	206
Promoting Alternative Thinking Strategies (PATHS)		x	x			x	x		x	x	x		x	x	x	x	x			209
Resolving Conflict Creatively Program (RCCP)		x	x	x	x	x				x	x			x		x	x			◆ 9
Responding in Peaceful and Positive Ways (RIPP)				x		x			x					x	x	x	x			214
School Transitional Environment Program (STEP)				x	x		x		x	x			x	x						217
Second Step	x	x	x	x		x			x	x				x	x	x	x			220
SOAR, The Seattle Social Development Project		x	x			x			x	x	x		x	x		x	x	x	x	225
Social Decision Making/ Problem Solving Program (SDM/PS)		x	x	x	x	x	x	x	x	x	x			x	x	x				228
Strengthening Families Program: For Parents and Youth 10–14 (SFP 10–14)		x	x			x				x	x	x		x			x	x	x	231
Syracuse Family Development Research Program (FDRP)	x							x		x			x	x						234
The Think Time Strategy		x	x	x		x	x	x	x	x				x	x	x	x			238

◆ = Action Guide

Expert Panel Members

Howard Adelman
University of California, Los Angeles

George Batsche
University of South Florida

Barbara Bazron
Institute for Research, Education, and Training in Addictions

Lucy Davidson
Center for Child Well Being

Celene Domitrovich
Penn State University

Kellie Dressler-Detrick
Office of Juvenile Justice and Delinquency Prevention

Kevin Dwyer
American Institutes for Research

Theodore Feinberg
National Association of School Psychologists

Susan Gorin
National Association of School Psychologists

Pat Graczyk
University of Illinois, Chicago

Pat Guthrie
Council for Administrators of Special Education

Tom Hanley
Office of Special Education and Rehabilitative Services, U.S. Department of Education

Norris Haynes
Southern Connecticut State University

Stephanie Jackson
American Institutes for Research

Sheppard Kellam
American Institutes for Research

Anne Mathews-Younes
Substance Abuse and Mental Health Services Administration (SAMHSA), U.S. Department of Health and Human Services

Denise Middlebrook
Substance Abuse and Mental Health Services Administration (SAMHSA), U.S. Department of Health and Human Services

John Mitchell
American Federation of Teachers

Eve Moscicki
National Institutes for Mental Health

David Osher
American Institutes for Research

Ron Palomares
American Psychological Association

John Reid
Oregon Social Learning Center

Peter Sheras
University of Virginia

Russell Skiba
Indiana University

George Sugai
University of Oregon

Carlos Sundermann
National Resources Center for Safe Schools

Linda Taylor
University of California, Los Angeles

Richard Verdugo
National Education Association

Darren Woodruff
American Institutes for Research

Program Selection Criteria

This Appendix provides information on 28 programs that the Implementation Guide Expert Panel identified as meeting the criteria that they established. The criteria are as follows.

▲ The program must have documented effectiveness and must be based on sound theory.

▲ The program can be easily integrated with existing school practices.

▲ The program must have data that demonstrate effectiveness or ineffectiveness with particular student groups.

▲ The data must indicate that the program has a positive impact on student achievement.

▲ Sufficient technical assistance or other resources must be available to support the effective implementation of the program.

▲ Program components must focus on promoting positive solutions to behavioral and emotional problems.

With the exception of two comprehensive programs (ACHIEVE and PBIS), the programs selected were either included in *Youth Violence: A Report of the Surgeon General* or identified by the Safe, Disciplined and Drug-Free Schools Expert Panel as being an exemplary or promising program.[1]

References

Gottfredson, D. C. (2001). *Schools and delinquency*. New York: Cambridge University Press.

Office of the Surgeon General. (2001). *Youth violence: A report of the surgeon general*. Washington, DC: Author.

Quinn, M. M., Osher, D., Hoffman, C. C., & Hanley, T. V. (1998). *Safe, drug-free, & effective schools for ALL students: What works!* Washington, DC: American Institute for Research, Center for Effective Collaboration and Practice.

Program Information Format

The briefs offer program information in each of the following categories:

▲ Program Purpose

▲ Program Background

▲ Scope of Program

▲ Specific Problems/Targeted Risk Factors

▲ Program Operations

▲ Determining Your School's Readiness for the Program

▲ Getting Training to Begin the Program

▲ Program Costs

▲ Other Resources Required to Implement the Program

▲ Modifying for Your School/Classroom Context

▲ Program Components That Cannot Be Modified or Excluded

▲ Program Outcomes

▲ Possible Negative Outcomes Related to Implementation

---

[1] The comprehensive programs were included because they are likely to be more powerful in schools than single interventions alone. However, they are newer and harder to study in an experimental manner (Gottfredson, 2001). The panel selected two that show great promise and have been identified in science-based lists compiled by The Hamilton Fish Institute and the Federal Center for Substance Abuse Prevention. In addition, a panel of researchers, administrators, teachers, paraprofessionals, youth, and families found the two programs to be effective in improving academics and school safety (Quinn et al., 1998).

ACHIEVE: A Collaborative School-Based Reform Process

Contact:
Howard Knoff, Ph.D.

Position/Title:
Director, ACHIEVE

Phone Number:
(813) 978-1718

Fax:
(813) 978-1718

Address:
8505 Portage Ave.
Tampa, FL 33620–7750

E-mail:
knoffprojectachieve@earthlink.net

Web Address:
http://www.coedu.usf.edu/projectachieve

For more information regarding program materials, contact:

> Sopris West Educational Services
> 4093 Specialty Place
> Longmont, CO 80504
> Phone: (800) 547-6747
> www.sopriswest.com

Purpose

ACHIEVE is an innovative whole-school improvement and reform program that helps schools, communities, and families develop, strengthen, and solidify children and adolescents' resilience, and protective and self-management skills, better enabling them to resist unhealthy and maladaptive behavior patterns. ACHIEVE also meets many of the objectives and requirements of the No Child Left Behind legislation. Using its school effectiveness and professional development processes, ACHIEVE has been implemented in many low-performing schools; it places particular emphasis on increasing student performance in the areas of

▲ social skills and social-emotional development;

▲ conflict resolution and self-management;

▲ achievement and academic progress; and

▲ positive school climate and safe school practices.

ACHIEVE's target audience is predominantly elementary and middle school children, and the model has been replicated at more than 25 sites across the United States. Program components also have been used in high schools, alternative schools, psychiatric and juvenile justice facilities, Head Start and after-school programs and, recently, in a number of specialized charter schools.

Students from diverse ethnic and multicultural backgrounds have been represented in the student populations at schools included in the program. ACHIEVE has similarly been implemented in diverse geographic locations throughout the country and in districts ranging from extremely small to very large.

Program Background

Since 1990, more than 1,000 schools in more than 40 states have been trained in one or more of ACHIEVE's components—schools in urban, suburban, and rural settings involving students at all socio-economic levels and representing the lowest- to highest-performing schools in the nation. All of the participating schools and districts have used ACHIEVE training and involvement to build on the strengths of an existing program, to "solve" existing problems or challenges, and to prevent future problems, thereby extending their current successes. ACHIEVE has received federal (through the Office of Special Education Programs and the Office of Educational Research and Innovation), state, and private foundation support. Schools often fund ACHIEVE by using federal (e.g., Title I, Safe and Drug-Free Schools), state, local, and special grant money.

Scope of Program

ACHIEVE uses a schoolwide professional development, in-service, and technical assistance process that provides direct training to school personnel in individual schools. ACHIEVE places particular emphasis on the areas of social skills and conflict resolution, schoolwide positive behavioral support systems, student achievement and academic progress, positive school climates and safe school practices, effective school and schooling processes, and parental involvement and support.

Other program goals are enhancing teachers' problem-solving skills with at-risk students; improving building- and classroom-management skills of teachers and other school personnel; helping students with potential problems receive early intervention services that reduce the need for later special education placements; and assisting children already receiving special education services to ultimately return to the general education classroom. Relative to this latter point, ACHIEVE implements prevention programs that focus on the needs of all students; it develops and implements strategic intervention programs for students who are at risk and underachieving; and finally, it coordinates comprehensive and multifaceted wraparound programs for students with intensive needs. A final underlying program theme is the creation of a school climate in which everyone—teachers, administrators, parents—believes that he or she is responsible for every student in the building and the community. Formative and summative evaluations using real-time data help determine whether project interventions and procedures are improving student, staff, home, and community outcomes.

In total, the scope of ACHIEVE includes the following components and activities:

- ▲ The Stop & Think Social Skills Program
- ▲ Discipline, behavior management, and school safety system at the student, individual classroom, grade-level team, and total building levels
- ▲ "Special situations" analysis of setting-specific and peer group-specific problems in the school
- ▲ Crisis prevention, intervention, and response planning and implementation
- ▲ Functional behavioral assessment, strategic behavioral interventions, and school-wide positive behavioral support systems
- ▲ Parent and community school safety outreach and involvement activities
- ▲ Referral question consultation (problem-solving) process
- ▲ Development and implementation of early intervention, student support, and child study teams
- ▲ Curriculum-based assessment (CBA/CBM), other functional academic assessment, and strategic instructional consultation intervention strategies and approaches
- ▲ General and special education inclusion, integration, and effective instruction procedures, strategies, and approaches
- ▲ Strategic planning, organizational change, and school improvement policies, procedures, and strategies
- ▲ Integrated "building committee" approaches to organization and personnel management
- ▲ Professional development, peer consultation, and technical assistance procedures, strategies, and activities
- ▲ Clinical supervision and peer- or co-teaching strategies and procedures

- Parent and community involvement, training, and support assessments, procedures, strategies, and activities

- Formative and summative program evaluation and accountability procedures, strategies, and activities, along with the creation of functional, interactive, real-time databases

- Training-of-trainers program along with other systemic capacity-building and long-term institutionalization policies, strategies, and activities.

Specific Problems/Risk Factors Targeted by ACHIEVE

The ongoing collection of longitudinal data to evaluate the formative and summative efficacy of ACHIEVE and to facilitate functional problem solving and the development of strategic interventions is critical to the overall success of the project. Focusing on both the academic and the social-behavioral progress of all students, ACHIEVE has been shown to reduce discipline referrals to the principal's office, grade retention, and special education referrals and placements while increasing academic-engaged time in the classroom and academic achievement scores. More individualized interventions reduce student aggression while increasing impulsive and self-control strategies, resulting in more socially appropriate behavior, positive school climate, and safe school settings.

Program Operations and Readiness for ACHIEVE

ACHIEVE is implemented in a series of carefully sequenced steps over three years. Before implementation, a detailed overview is provided to the entire school staff, and an 80 percent acceptance vote is required to implement the program. Once accepted, an organizational analysis and needs assessment is completed, the school's committee structure is analyzed, different support teams are identified, and preproject baseline data are collected.

The components are generally implemented in the following manner:

Year 1 involves social skills training; referral question consultative (RQC) problem solving/functional analysis training; release time for planning, meetings, and technical assistance.

Year 2 includes social skills/RQC training and booster sessions; Behavioral Observation and Instructional Environment Assessment training; curriculum-based assessment and measurement (CBA/CBM) training; release time for planning, meetings, and technical assistance.

Year 3 requires booster sessions in all prior components; parent involvement in planning, training, and facilitation; grade-level intervention planning and implementation; release time for planning, meetings, and technical assistance.

Beyond Year 3, ACHIEVE schools provide approximately one day a month of release time for all grade-level teams to plan and implement the activities identified in their action plans. All training is facilitated by pupil services personnel and involves general and special education teachers, school staff (custodial, cafeteria, office, paraprofessionals, bus drivers), parents, and volunteers. A "training of trainers" model is also used.

Getting Training to Begin ACHIEVE

The project director and a cadre of trainers are available to provide district and school training and technical assistance at $1,500 per day plus expenses. Information about ACHIEVE is available from its Web site. Some support materials are available for individual purchase, especially the Stop & Think Social Skills Program, which is available at the prekindergarten through grade 1, grades 2 and 3, grades 4 and 5, and middle school levels. In addition, a training-of-trainers program is available with ongoing modeling and coaching relative to content, implementation, and technical assistance. Training sessions are conducted at national and state conferences for general and special education teachers, pupil personnel and related service professionals, and other professional and community groups. In addition, regional workshops are available that are open to individuals in local areas around the country.

Program Costs, Training Time, and Implementation

Training time for the initial Schoolwide Positive Discipline and School Safety component of ACHIEVE involves two workshop days plus one-to-three days of on-site technical consultation. The initial training goal is to help schools develop a comprehensive, buildingwide discipline, behavior management, and school-safety system with procedures and strategies that focus on prevention, strategic intervention (when needed), and wraparound approaches for students with intensive needs. On the first in-service day, staff learn the Stop & Think Social Skills curriculum. Staff then begin to implement the Stop & Think curriculum in their classrooms for four-to-six weeks. A return, two-day visit involves a full day of on-site consultation (where Stop & Think advanced demonstrations are provided with students in the school and meetings with grade-level teams and leaders occur) and a second full in-service day where the staff train on approaches toward student accountability, staff consistency, and "special situations" (e.g., cafeteria behavior, teasing, and bullying). The total cost for this, assuming a 750-student building with 50 teachers and staff members, is approximately $12,700 ($6,000 for the honorarium plus travel expenses, $6,500 in Stop & Think materials, and $200 in duplication costs), or about $17 per student.

Other ACHIEVE components involve additional workshop and technical consultation days.

At the school building level, ACHIEVE can be implemented with the staff and resources typically found in most schools, especially when a large number of special or Title I students are referred or already in a program. In addition to existing staff, school districts should identify one project coordinator for every three-to-five project buildings during the first three years of implementation and a project coordinator for every five-to-eight buildings thereafter.

As noted, the major costs for ACHIEVE are for staff materials and training. Cost savings, however, result from reducing referrals and placements into special education, student grade retentions, and additional costs for Title I services

when students are not academically achieving at appropriate state standards levels.

How ACHIEVE "Looks"

Although the evidence-based strategies, approaches, and techniques underlying the success of ACHIEVE are evident in every ACHIEVE school, each school "looks different" in the way it implements the program. However, the evidence-based elements are indeed universal: strategic planning, organizational assessment, and planned change; effective school and schooling practices; professional development, inservice training, and clinical supervision and staff consultation; community and family involvement, training, and outreach; data-based problem solving and decision making; functional assessment, and formative and summative evaluation; social skills, discipline/behavior management, and school safety approaches; behavioral and curriculum-based assessment leading to strategic intervention; and interagency partnerships and collaboration to facilitate intensive and wraparound service needs. When schools have been using effective and evidence-based processes prior to ACHIEVE implementation, these are integrated into Project activities. When gaps are identified, through ongoing needs assessments, ACHIEVE components are introduced as appropriate.

Program Outcomes

Overall, ACHIEVE has consistently demonstrated its ability to reduce student discipline referrals to the principal's office, reduce student suspensions and expulsions, reduce student grade retention, reduce special education referrals and placements, increase parent and teacher satisfaction, increase positive school climates and perceptions of school safety, and increase academic achievement.

Given these demonstrated and research-based successes, ACHIEVE has been designated an exemplary national model prevention program by the U.S. Department of Health and Human Services' Substance Abuse and Mental Health

Services Administration (SAMHSA) and Center for Substance Abuse Prevention (CSAP). It has been identified as a Select Evidence-Based Social and Emotional Learning Program by the Collaborative for Academic, Social, and Emotional Learning (CASEL). It was cited in the National Association of School Psychologists' 2002 publication, *Exemplary Mental Health Programs*.

Possible Negative Outcomes Related to the Implementation of ACHIEVE

None known.

References and Resources

Gottfredson, D. C. (2001). *Schools and delinquency*. New York: Cambridge University Press.

Knoff, H. M. & Batsche, G. M. (1995). Project ACHIEVE: Analyzing a school reform process for at-risk and underachieving students. *School Psychology Review, 24* (5), 579–603.

Quinn, M. M., Osher, D., Hoffman, C. C., & Hanley, T. V. (1998). *Safe, drug-free, and effective schools for ALL students: What works!* Washington, DC: U.S. Department of Education.

U.S. Department of Health and Human Services, Substance Abuse and Mental Health Services Administration, Center for Substance Abuse Prevention. (n.d.). *SAMHSA model programs*. Rockville, MD: Author. Available: http://modelprograms.samhsa.gov.

Aggression Replacement Training (ART)

Contact:
Mark Amendola

Position/Title:
Board Member, International Center for Aggression Replacement Training (ICART)

Phone Number:
(814) 881-2438

Address:
301 Julian Plaza
Syracuse, NY 13210

E-mail:
icart-usa@oasen.com

Web Address:
http://www.aggressionreplacementtraining.org

Purpose

ART is a response to antisocial behavioral excesses and prosocial behavioral deficits. ART consists of three interventions: Skillstreaming, Anger Control Training, and Moral Reasoning Training, which seek to enhance interpersonal skill competence, enhance self-mediated ability to control anger, and enhance the young person's moral reasoning ability and social problem-solving skills, respectively.

Program Background

Aggression Replacement Training was designed to serve a diverse group of males and females aged 11 to 19. Since its inception in 1986, the program has been implemented at 700 sites, including schools and various delinquency and mental health settings.

Scope of Program

Aggression Replacement Training subjects have been a diverse population, including students of various ethnic, cultural, and class backgrounds. The majority of ART interventions have been implemented in urban areas, but many also have occurred in suburban and rural settings.

Specific Problems/Risk Factors Targeted by ART

Chronic aggressive behavior; inability to control anger when provoked; a deficit in expressing one's feelings; poor response to failure; ineffective coping skills with group pressure; and refusal to follow reasonable requests all are targeted.

Program Operations

Aggression Replacement Training has three basic components: Skillstreaming, Anger Control Training, and Moral Reasoning Training. The training is integrated into the school day—from homeroom to classes to after-school detention. Teachers, counselors, psychologists, behavior specialists, correctional officers, and other school or center personnel (trainers) offer youth training in anger management over a ten-week period in three one-hour sessions per intervention per week. These trainers teach children what to do, what not to do, and why they need to practice certain types of behavior as opposed to others.

Skillstreaming builds student knowledge of positive, commendable social behavior. Small groups of chronically aggressive adolescents with shared psychological skill deficiencies are provided with modeling, role-playing, and performance training.

During Anger Control Training, students are taught to recognize negative behavior and taught what not to do in social situations. Moral Reasoning Training is designed to enhance the youth's sense of fairness, justice, and concern for the needs and rights of others.

Determining Your School's Readiness for ART

An effective ART program utilizes trainers who are willing and highly capable of working with adolescents individually and in groups. Effective trainers are comfortable with adolescents, recognize adolescents' challenges and concerns in this developmental period, support and reward positive behavior, and contribute to a positive self-image. The ability to motivate troubled youth is a prized and highly sought-after characteristic of an ART teacher.

Getting Training to Begin ART

The first of the steps recommended to trainers is to read *Aggression Replacement Training: A Comprehensive Intervention for Aggressive Youth* (Goldstein & Glick, 1987). A trainer can supplement his or her understanding of written program material either by attending workshops taught by the program developers or by observing a site that has implemented the ART program.

Once the trainer has completed these steps, he or she can conduct and/or participate in mock Skillstreaming, Anger Control Training, and Moral Reasoning Training. A more experienced teacher or trainer might lead the sessions while less experienced trainers role play as adolescent trainees.

Program Costs

Trainers may attend a two-day workshop on proficiency in implementation at a cost of $6,600 per program. This fee takes into account all related costs for supplies, materials, and salaries.

Resources Required to Implement ART

n/a

Modifying ART for Your School/ Classroom Context

The ART program can be used in a school or in a mental health or correctional facility, which illustrates the extent to which the program is easily adaptable to different environments and contexts. There is a high degree of flexibility in the ART curriculum.

In the Skillstreaming exercises, trainers are encouraged to choose ten skills they deem to be most needed by the children in their program. Although the ART program offers specific and detailed intervention strategies for aggressive youth, it is constructed within a framework that facilitates flexibility and adaptability.

Components That Cannot Be Modified or Excluded From ART

The Skillstreaming exercise, the Anger Control Training, and the Moral Reasoning training are all essential components of the ART program. For purposes of effectiveness, none of these elements should be excluded from the program, but they may be modified.

Program Outcomes

ART has been nationally recognized for the positive outcomes it has produced for children. It received the 1994 US OJJDP (Office of Juvenile Justice and Delinquency Prevention) Model Program Award.

ART promotes acquisition and performance of prosocial skills, improves anger control, decreases frequency of acting-out behaviors, reduces levels of impulsiveness, and increases frequency of prosocial behaviors. In one of two sample studies conducted by ART, the reduction in frequency and intensity of acting-out behaviors and the enhancement of participants' levels of moral reasoning were verified.

ART was compared to two control conditions, moral education and a no-treatment control, using a sample of aggressive male students in a Brisbane high school. The study concluded that the students completing the ART program showed a significant decrease in the incidence of aggressive behavior and a significant increase in the incidence of positive coping. The students also demonstrated improved social skills.

References and Resources

Curulla, V. L. (1990). *Aggression Replacement Training in the community for adult learning disabled offenders*. Unpublished manuscript. University of Washington, Seattle.

Goldstein, A. P. & Glick, B. (1987). *Aggression Replacement Training: A comprehensive intervention for aggressive youth*. Champaign, IL: Research Press.

Goldstein, A. P. & Glick, B. (1994). *The prosocial gang: Implementing Aggression Replacement Training*. Thousand Oaks, CA: Sage Publications.

Positive Alternative Learning Program. (1996). *Program manual*. (Available from Ferguson-Florissant School District, 6038 Caroline Ave., Berkeley, MO 63134).

Bullying Prevention Program

Contact:
Dan Olweus, Ph.D. or Susan P. Limber, Ph.D.

Position/Title:
Program Developers

Phone Number:
47–55–58–23–27 (Olweus)
(864) 656–6271 (Limber)

Address (Olweus):
Research Center for Health Promotion
Bergen, Norway

Address (Limber):
Institute on Family and Neighborhood Life
Clemson University
158 Poole Agricultural Center
Clemson, SC 29634–5205

E-mail:
olweus@psych.uib.no
slimber@clemson.edu

Web Address:
http://modelprograms.samhsa.gov/pdfs/
FactSheets/Olweus%20Bully.pdf

Purpose

The Bullying Prevention Program is a universal intervention for the reduction and prevention of bully/victim problems. The main arena for the program is the school, and school staff has the primary responsibility for the introduction and implementation of the program. The program aims to effect systematic changes of the "opportunity" and "reward structures" for bullying and similar behavior in the school and other relevant contexts. In addition, positive, friendly, and prosocial behaviors are encouraged and rewarded.

Program Background

The Bullying Prevention Program, developed in 1983 in Bergen, Norway, is a schoolwide violence prevention program that seeks to reduce the incidence of bully/victim problems among primary and secondary school children. It is based on a child-rearing model applied in a school setting to reduce low-level aggression and conflict. The program's developer, Dan Olweus, designed it to increase awareness and knowledge about bullying behavior in the school community; to promote the active involvement of parents, teachers, and other responsible adults; to help establish clear rules against bullying; and to provide support and protection for victims.

The Bullying Prevention Program is built around a limited set of key principles and findings derived chiefly from research on the development and modification of problem behaviors, particularly aggressive behavior. More specifically, the program strives to develop a school (and ideally, a home) environment that

- ▲ is characterized by warmth, positive interest, and involvement by adults;
- ▲ has firm limits on unacceptable behavior that are clearly stated;
- ▲ consistently applies nonhostile, nonphysical negative consequences in cases of violations of rules and other unacceptable behaviors; and
- ▲ provides positive adult role models and adult authority.

Scope of Program

The program serves students in elementary, middle, and junior high schools. All students within a school participate in most aspects of the program. Additional individual interventions are targeted at students who are identified as bullies or victims of bullying.

Specific Problems/Risk Factors Targeted by the Bullying Prevention Program

Bullying is characterized by the following three criteria:

▲ It is aggressive behavior or intentional harm-doing.

▲ It is carried out repeatedly over time.

▲ It occurs within an interpersonal relationship characterized by an imbalance of power.

One might add that bullying behavior often occurs without apparent provocation.

A student is being bullied or victimized when he or she is exposed, repeatedly and over time, to negative actions on the part of one or more other students. Such negative actions include intentionally inflicting, or attempting to inflict, injury or discomfort upon another. These behaviors can be carried out physically (e.g., hitting, kicking, pushing, choking), verbally (e.g., by calling names, threatening, taunting, malicious teasing, spreading nasty rumors), or in other ways, such as making faces or obscene gestures, or intentional exclusion from a group.

In order to be considered bullying, there should also be an imbalance in power or strength (an asymmetric power relationship). In other words, students who are exposed to the negative actions generally have difficulty in defending themselves and are somewhat helpless against the student or students who harass.

Bullying can be supported by peers who witness, egg on, or reward bullying behavior.

Program Operations

Core components of the program are implemented at the school level, the class level, and the individual level.

Schoolwide components include the administration of an anonymous questionnaire to assess the nature and prevalence of bullying at each school, a school conference day to discuss bullying at school and plan interventions, formation of a Bullying Prevention Coordinating Committee to coordinate all aspects of the school's program, and increased supervision of students at "hot spots" for bullying.

Classroom components include establishing and enforcing class rules against bullying and holding regular class meetings with students. Individual components include interventions with children identified as bullies and victims and discussions with parents of involved students. Teachers may be assisted in these efforts by counselors and school-based mental health professionals.

An important premise of the Bullying Prevention Program is that bullying behavior can be checked and rerouted into a more prosocial direction through a systematic restructuring of the social environment. Among other outcomes, this restructuring is expected to result in fewer opportunities for bullying behavior and fewer or smaller rewards (e.g., in the form of prestige or peer support) for displaying such behavior.

Determining Your School's Readiness for the Bullying Prevention Program

Before program implementation, schools administer the Olweus Bully/Victim Questionnaire to students. Results are used to assess the severity of the school's bullying problem by age and gender, to focus the attention of adults on the need to address the problem, and to pinpoint the physical locations where bullying incidents are most likely to occur. The data provide a baseline against which improvement can be measured. Once this information has been gathered, the program provides a framework for intervention at the school, class, and individual levels.

Getting Training to Begin the Bullying Prevention Program

A coordinating committee to oversee the program should be established at the school- or district-level and should include a school administrator, teacher representatives from each grade, a guidance counselor, a school-based mental health/social service professional, and parent and student representatives. Committee members and program coordinators receive at least one-to-two days of professional training from expert consultants before implementation. These individuals lead a half- to one-day inservice training for all school staff. During the first year of implementation, classroom teachers participate in regular teacher discussion groups (held at least monthly for one hour each). Yearly "booster" professional development sessions are also provided to all staff members.

Program Costs

Program costs include funding for an on-site coordinator (part-time or full-time recommended), approximately $28 per school for the questionnaire and computer scoring program to assess bullying at school, approximately $65 per teacher for classroom materials, and approximately $2,700 to $3,750 for training and ongoing consultation by a certified trainer.

Other Resources Required to Implement the Bullying Prevention Program

Community outreach (e.g., PTA meetings or informal telephone contacts) are also recommended as an important way to achieve home-school cooperation and to provide parents with information about bully/victim problems and proposed solutions.

Modifying the Bullying Prevention Program for Your School/Classroom Context

The information gathered in the questionnaire is used to create a school plan, to coordinate counseling and other social services, and to prevent problems by ensuring adequate adult supervision during lunchtime, break periods, and other non-classroom times. The plan is individually tailored to meet the needs of the school, based on the results of the questionnaire.

Components That Cannot Be Modified or Excluded From the Bullying Prevention Program

n/a

Program Outcomes

Data gathered from schools in Bergen, Norway, between 1983 and 1985 show substantial reductions (by 50 percent or more in most comparisons) in student reports of bullying and victimization. A marked reduction in general antisocial behaviors, such as vandalism, fighting, theft, alcohol use, and truancy, was also noted. Significant improvements were also observed with respect to school climate, as reflected in reports by students of improved order and discipline, more positive social relationships, and a more positive attitude toward schoolwork and school. The reported effects of the intervention were found across teacher, student self-report, and peer-report measures. These effects are expected to be generalizable, given the very large and diverse population of the study.

Possible Negative Outcomes Related to Implementation of the Bullying Prevention Program

Although the Bullying Prevention Program is currently operating at several U.S. sites, the program's ability to provide technical assistance to start-up sites is very limited.

Resources

Limber, S. P. (2001, Spring). Understanding and preventing bullying among children. *National Dropout Prevention Center/Network Newsletter, 13*(2) [Special issue].

Olweus, D. (1993). *Bullying at school: What we know and what we can do.* Oxford, UK: Blackwell.

Olweus, D., Limber, S., & Mihalic, S. F. (1999). *Blueprints for violence prevention, book nine: Bullying Prevention Program.* Boulder, CO: Center for the Study and Prevention of Violence.

U.S. Department of Health and Human Services, Substance Abuse and Mental Health Services Administration, Center for Substance Abuse Prevention. (n.d.). *SAMHSA model programs.* Rockville, MD: Author. Available: http://modelprograms.samhsa.gov

Child Development Project (CDP)

Contact:
Denise Wood

Position/Title:
Dissemination Coordinator

Phone Number:
(510) 533–0213, ext. 239 or (800) 666–7270

Address:
Developmental Studies Center
2000 Embarcadero, Suite 305
Oakland, CA 94606–5300

E-mail:
info@devstu.org

Web Address:
http://www.devstu.org

Purpose

The CDP's primary goal is helping elementary schools to foster their students' academic, social, and ethical development by enhancing student literacy skills and by strengthening the students' "sense of community" in school.

Program Background

The CDP is 20 years old. An earlier version of the CDP (or major components of it) has been implemented in approximately 200 schools in ten states. As revised, the program includes state-of-the-art reading decoding and comprehension components, and its community-building component has been streamlined to be less challenging and less costly to implement.

The program is designed to serve elementary schools in any grade level configuration.

Scope of Program

All three intervention components (see Program Operations, below) are designed to be used school-wide to build a foundation for learning and development. The Systematic Instruction in Phoneme Awareness, Phonics, and Sight Words (SIPPS) component also can be used as an early intervention program with students who have not yet developed strong decoding skills.

Specific Problems/Risk Factors Targeted by the CDP

The revised CDP is designed to build the basic and higher-order literacy skills of the full range of students served by a school. It is also designed to foster healthy social, emotional, and ethical development, and thereby to prevent such problem behaviors as substance abuse and delinquency.

Program Operations

The revised CDP program offers three distinct but complementary components. Depending on its needs and circumstances, a school may choose to implement the entire program or particular components. Descriptions of the components follow.

CSC (Caring School Community). Four approaches designed to build students' sense of community and foster parent involvement:

- ▲ Class meetings (decision making, problem solving, and norm-setting)

- ▲ A cross-age buddies program (cross-grade mentoring program)

- ▲ Fifteen innovative schoolwide community building and service activities

- ▲ Eighteen home-based activities per grade level (K–6) that help students connect their experience at home with their experiences at school.

Print and video materials and professional development workshops are available for these approaches.

SIPPS (Systematic Instruction in Phoneme Awareness, Phonics, and Sight Words). SIPPS is a stand-alone instructional program in decoding that develops word recognition strategies and skills that enable students to become independent, confident, and fluent readers. A "decodable text" program, SIPPS is designed to be flexible and wide-ranging both across and within grades. SIPPS has three levels:

- ▲ *Beginning Level:* Short-Vowel Single-Syllable Decoding

- ▲ *Extension Level:* Complex-Vowel Single-Syllable Decoding

- ▲ *Challenge Level:* Polysyllabic Decoding, which can be used both as the third level in a developmental program to teach young children to read and as an intervention program for older students (fourth grade and up) who can read at the first-grade level or higher.

Making Meaning. A reading comprehension program that uses a constructivist approach as well as direct teaching strategies to integrate academic, ethical, and social development throughout. This program provides a clearly defined scope and sequence of specific comprehension lessons.

Each of the three components generally requires a year of focused effort for a broad cross-section of teachers in a school to reach comfort and proficiency. Implementing all three components with maximum effectiveness will take most schools three years.

Determining Your School's Readiness for the CDP

n/a

Getting Training to Begin the CDP

CSC. Multiple options for implementing the CSC program are available: one- or two-day program orientation workshops; site visits for observation, feedback, and demonstration; a midyear visit to assist with the evaluation of the school's implementation progress.

SIPPS. Options to choose from include an initial one- or two-day workshop; a midyear visit to analyze implementation progress and provide guidance; and during-the-year visits for classroom observation, feedback, demonstration, and coaching (at one- and four-month milestones).

Making Meaning. Training consists of an initial three-day faculty workshop on the reading comprehension strategies, the integration of social values, assessment, and classroom management, and one day of additional training for a school literacy leadership team. Follow-up visits for classroom observation, demonstration, feedback, and coaching are optional.

Program Costs

CSC. Costs range from $4,000 to $12,000, depending on the number of staff development days, the quantity of materials needed (based on the number of classrooms), and travel expenses.

SIPPS. Costs range from $9,000 to $15,000, depending on the number of professional development days, the quantity of materials needed, and travel expenses.

Making Meaning. Costs range from $20,000 to $30,000, depending on the number of professional development days, the quantity of materials needed, and travel expenses.

Optional follow-up support for all three components is $2,000 per day plus expenses.

All materials are included in the package prices.

Student Consumables and Other Costs

CSC. Student material costs are quite modest and will vary with the particular activities selected for implementation; $5 per student per year is a generous estimate. Staff costs include any stipends to attend the initial two-day training and any compensation paid to a few selected staff for attending periodic activities-planning meetings during the year.

SIPPS. Student consumable materials costs may average $10 per student in grades K–2. No consumables are needed for grades 3 and above. Staff costs include any stipends to attend the initial training and any follow-up training and the costs of a part-time literacy coordinator, who usually is staffed at 25–50 percent of his or her time.

Making Meaning. No consumables are needed. Staff costs include any stipends to attend the initial training and any follow-up training and the costs of a part-time literacy coordinator, who usually is staffed at 25% to 50% of his or her time.

Other Resources Required to Implement the CDP

n/a

Modifying the CDP for Your School/ Classroom Context

How the CDP's community-building component is implemented is explicitly tied to local needs and resources. It has been implemented and shown

effective in a wide range of settings. Also, because it can be adopted in whole or part, the revised CDP program can suit a range of circumstances.

Implementation of each component can vary with needs and circumstances.

Components That Cannot Be Modified or Excluded From the CDP

The SIPPS component is the most structured of the three; it involves very specific routines, procedures, and sequences. The CDP does not yet have an organized network of users. The CDP plans to develop a Web site capacity to support direct communication among users and is considering various means of bringing users together on a face-to-face basis.

Each component is supported by extensive implementation resources, including video as well as print materials. The Caring School Community program also offers video and print resources to support new trainers. Initial workshops are offered for each component, and on-site follow-up workshops either are required (in the case of Making Meaning) or are available optionally.

Program Outcomes

In two major evaluation studies, the CDP program showed significantly

▲ improved academic motivation, liking for school, and trust in and respect for teachers;

▲ decreased social anxiety and loneliness in school;

▲ improved interpersonal competence (e.g., strengthened conflict resolution skills);

▲ improved character-related attitudes and behaviors (e.g., altruistic behavior, positive classroom behavior, concern for others);

▲ reduced incidence of alcohol and marijuana use; and

▲ improved longer-term achievement in the middle schools, including effects on grade point average and standardized test scores.

The original CDP program was implemented and evaluated in schools serving very different settings and student populations—different economically, racially and ethnically, and geographically. Its effectiveness was documented across this range of settings and populations. Moreover, the quality of program implementation was not correlated with any of these contextual conditions—that is, the CDP was as likely to be well implemented in low-income and racially diverse settings as it was in more affluent, less diverse settings.

SIPPS has been shown in a recent study, still unpublished, to benefit second language learners.

Evidence of effectiveness is for students K–6. That evidence is for a great range of student populations, including urban, suburban, and rural students; low-income as well as affluent students; and students of all major ethnic and racial groupings.

Possible Negative Outcomes Related to the Implementation of the CDP

No negative schoolwide outcomes were found in schools that consistently implemented the CDP program.

Resources

Solomon, D., Battistich, V., Watson, M., Schaps, E., & Lewis, C. (2000). A six-district study of educational change: Direct and mediated effects of the Child Development Project. *Social Psychology of Education, 4*, 3–51.

U.S. Department of Health and Human Services, Substance Abuse and Mental Health Services Administration, Center for Substance Abuse Prevention. (n.d.). *SAMHSA model programs.* Rockville, MD: Author. Available: http://modelprograms.samhsa.gov.

Functional Family Therapy (FFT)

Contact:
Doug Kopp, Tom Sexton

Position/Title:
Implementation Directors

Phone Number:
(702) 528-5459

Address:
FFT
2538 57th Ave. SW
Seattle, WA 98116

E-mail:
dkfft@msn.com
thsexton@indiana.edu

Web Address:
http://www.fftinc.com

Purpose

Functional Family Therapy (FFT) is an intensive intervention therapy designed to reduce delinquency, conduct disorder, drug and alcohol abuse, and family conflict that may support these individual problems.

Program Background

Initiated 30 years ago, FFT is currently used in more than 40 settings, three of which are school-based, all of which include collaboration with school personnel.

Scope of Program

FFT is both an early intervention and intensive treatment program.

Specific Problems/Risk Factors Targeted by FFT

A range of specific risk/protective factors related to youth and family functioning are targeted. In many outcome studies since its inception 30 years ago, FFT has demonstrated effectiveness with youth who are at risk of violence or delinquency; who are conduct disordered; who have drug/alcohol disorders; and who are at risk of out-of-home placement or juvenile justice involvement.

Program Operations

FFT is a family-based intervention that ranges, on average, from 8 to 12 one-hour sessions for mild cases and up to 30 sessions for more difficult situations. In most programs, sessions are spread over a three-month period. FFT has been conducted both in clinic settings as an outpatient therapy and as a home-based model.

The three specific intervention phases—Engagement and Motivation, Behavior Change, and Generalization—are interdependent and are linked in a sequential manner.

Phase 1: Engagement and Motivation.
Enhance the perception that positive change might

occur (intervention credibility) and minimize factors that would decrease this perception.

Phase 2: Behavior Change. Develop intermediate and then long-term behavior change patterns that are culturally appropriate, context sensitive, and individualized to the unique characteristics of each family member, including cognitive, interactive, and emotional components. Clinicians provide concrete resources that both guide and symbolize specific changes in behavior. Particular emphasis is placed on individualized and developmentally appropriate techniques.

Phase 3: Generalization. In this phase FFT is guided by the need to move (generalize) positive family change into other problem areas and different situations.

FFT also includes a comprehensive, multi-domained, and multiperspective adolescent and family assessment system that is based in clinical observation and objective measurement of client, process, and outcomes of the interventions. In addition, FFT utilizes the comprehensive Clinical Services System (CSS) as a computer-based tool to track and monitor FFT service delivery, outcomes, and model adherence.

Determining Your School's Readiness for FFT

n/a

Getting Training to Begin FFT

Functional Family Therapy can provide informational workshops for school personnel on the FFT intervention. As part of site certification, up-front and ongoing supervision is a critical part of FFT training.

Program Costs

To become an FFT-certified site, the cost of year-long training (which includes comprehensive clinical training, supervision, and technical support) is $26,100 plus expenses for three to eight therapists. Certification is a three-year

process, with training costs decreasing by half in each subsequent year. The Clinical Service System (a comprehensive system to help therapists track cases and adhere to the FFT model) is included in the cost for FFT site certification. Support and consultation during the first year of training is also included in the cost for FFT site certification. Including expenses, schools should budget approximately $34,500 to cover first-year training fees and expenses. Funding for a certified site would require multiagency or outside agency resources.

Other Resources Required to Implement FFT

FFT sites range from three to eight therapists (or FTEs). Program costs are dependent on the size of the site and the number of FFT therapists employed by the site. Training costs in year two are to maintain site certification and to train site therapists to provide clinical supervision at the site.

Modifying FFT for Your School/ Classroom Context

n/a

Components That Cannot Be Modified or Excluded From FFT

FFT effectiveness is based on strict adherence to the clinical model. Program fidelity is achieved by a specific training model and a sophisticated client assessment, tracking, and monitoring system that provides for specific clinical assessment and outcome accountability.

Program Outcomes

FFT has been demonstrated to be effective in both at-home and at-in-clinic settings in 12 states. Clinical trials have shown that FFT is effective in treating adolescents with conduct oppositional defiant or disruptive behavior disorders, alcohol and other drug abuse disorders, and delinquent and violent youth. Significant outcomes include lower recidivism rates (e.g., 11 percent compared with 67 percent for controls in one 1995 study), reduced foster care placement referrals, and improved family interactions. A cost-benefit analysis indicated that FFT had significantly lower direct costs than the usual probation services.

The program has been replicated with youth and families of varying ethnicities (African American, Hispanic/Latino, White, Native American, Asian American, and multiracial youth). The intervention has been replicated with populations in rural areas and major urban centers, and internationally (Sweden). Over the years, females have represented between 10 percent and 50 percent of participating youth.

Possible Negative Outcomes Related to the Implementation of FFT

None known.

Resources

Alexander, J., Barton, C., Gordon, D., Grotpeter, J., Hansson, K., Harrison, R., Mears, S., Mihalic, S., Parsons, B., Pugh, C., Schulman, S., Waldron, H., & Sexton, T. (1998). *Blueprints for violence prevention, book three: Functional Family Therapy*. Boulder, CO: Center for the Study and Prevention of Violence.

Barton, C., Alexander, J. F., Waldron, H., Turner, C. W., & Warburn, J. (1985). Generalizing treatment effects of Functional Family Therapy: Three replications. *American Journal of Family Therapy, 13*, 16–26.

The Good Behavior Game

Contact:
Shannon Cleary

Position/Title:
Dissemination Manager, Center for Integrating Education and Prevention Research in Schools, American Institutes for Research

Phone Number:
(202) 944-5300

Address:
1000 Thomas Jefferson St., NW, Suite 400
Washington, DC 20007

E-mail:
scleary@air.org

Web Address:
http://www.modelprograms.samhsa.gov/pdfs/
2001exemplary.pdf

Purpose

The purpose of the Good Behavior Game (GBG) is to reduce classroom disruption, aggression, and social withdrawal.

Program Background

In 1984, the Good Behavior Game was adapted by Dr. Sheppard Kellam and his colleagues at the Johns Hopkins University School of Public Health for use in several preventive intervention studies. It is this version, discussed below, that has the strongest evidence of positive effects out of the several versions of the game that have been tried. The Game uses a team-based approach to manage student behavior.

Scope of Program

GBG is implemented in early elementary grades to provide students with the skills they need to respond to later, possibly negative, school and other life experiences and societal influences. The program is universal. However, the most significant benefits have been found for children whose behavior suggests that they are at a high level of risk. The Good Behavior Game is an easy and effective universal classroom behavior management strategy. The Game could easily be adapted and expanded beyond the classroom to involve other personnel and other parts of the school day—for example, rewarding good behavior on the part of lunchroom teams. Fishbein and Wasik (1981) used the Good Behavior Game in the school library. Salend, Reynolds, and Coyle (1989) applied it in a residential school for adolescents, and Swiezy, Matson, and Box (1992) implemented it in a preschool. Data from the Baltimore (MD) trials indicate that the Game can be used as one component of a comprehensive classroom academic and behavioral intervention plan.

Specific Problems/Risk Factors Targeted by the Good Behavior Game

A high level of aggressive, disruptive behavior in first-grade classrooms is a major risk factor for later aggressive behavior, especially for aggressive boys (Kellam, Ling, Merisca, Brown, & Ialongo, 1998). For individual students, aggressive behavior in the early grades may be predictive of a large number of later problems, including poor academic achievement, behavior problems, and substance abuse. The Good Behavior Game directly addresses individual and classwide disruptive behavior.

Program Operations

GBG is a behavior modification program that involves students and teachers. It enhances the teachers' ability to define tasks, set rules, and discipline students, and it allows students to work in teams in which each individual is responsible to the rest of the group. Before the game begins, teachers clearly specify those disruptive behaviors (e.g., noncompliance, verbal and physical disruptions) that, if exhibited, will result in a team's receiving a checkmark on the board. When the game is over, teams that have not exceeded the maximum number of marks are rewarded, but teams that exceeded this standard receive no rewards. In due course, the timing of the game is altered so that the teacher begins the game with no warning and at different periods during the day.

The Game is appropriate for use with young children and is most often used in the primary grades. In the Baltimore evaluation, all students were assigned to one of three behaviorally heterogeneous teams in each classroom. Each team can earn rewards by following class rules and avoiding precisely defined misbehaviors. These rules are explained to students, including a clear definition of prohibited behaviors, such as getting out of seat without permission, verbal or physical disruption, or noncompliance. If a student breaks a classroom rule during the Game, then his or her team gets a check mark. All teams with fewer than four check marks at the end of the Game period are declared winners. Winning teams receive a variety of rewards, such as play time, fun activities, stickers, erasers, and so on. Social reinforcers always accompany tangible reinforcers and eventually replace them. The teacher chooses a team leader, often a shy/withdrawn child, to help distribute prizes. Previous research indicates that when a child becomes repeatedly associated with

reinforcement, her or his social standing with other children will be enhanced such that he or she will be approached by other children for play. The goal is for all teams to win by exhibiting good behavior.

The Game initially is played three times per week for periods of ten minutes, with teachers announcing each session and rewarding teams following the period. The duration of the game is increased by about ten minutes each session every three weeks up to three hours per session; the number of check marks remains at four. As the game progresses, teachers also begin to initiate the Game without notice and to save rewards until the end of the school week. Eventually, the Game is played at any time of day, during any activity, and in any location.

Getting Training to Begin the Good Behavior Game

Interested schools are advised to look at the manuals available on the Internet, and then consider what additional implementation support may be necessary. Contact the Center for Integrating Education and Prevention Research in Schools to explore the possibilities for consultations, implementation support, and advice.

Program Costs

The Good Behavior Game manual and technical assistance are currently being revised and will be available in Spring 2003.

Other Resources Required to Implement the Good Behavior Game

Although the teacher is the only staff member needed to play the game, classroom paraprofessionals and other school-related personnel can be used to help in implementation.

Modifying the Good Behavior Game for Your School/Classroom Context

Where you implement the Good Behavior Game can be changed (classrooms, libraries, etc.). The population served by the program is flexible (preschool through elementary grades, and even adolescents who are on a behavioral program, such as in residential). How you set the rules can also be modified, because what is appropriate behavior in one setting may be different in another.

Components That Cannot Be Modified or Excluded From the Good Behavior Game

The critical elements of the Good Behavior Game are (1) having behaviorally heterogeneous teams and (2) having team-based rewards/consequences for following the rules.

Program Outcomes

After one year of implementation, teachers reported a reduction in first-grade students' shy and aggressive behaviors, with the most significant effects observed in students initially considered most aggressive.

Long-term effects were also reported, based on a follow-up sample of 590 children who received the Good Behavior Game in first and second grades, compared to a control group who received no intervention. At the end of sixth grade, positive effects on aggression were sustained, but only for boys. At ages 19–21, aggressive boys who had been involved in the Good Behavior Game were significantly less likely than boys in standard classrooms to abuse drugs and to have serious antisocial behavior.

Although the immediate benefits of the Good Behavior Game in the classroom are obvious, it appears that the long-term effects are confined to the most aggressive boys in the classroom. Because highly aggressive males are likely to be the most problematic students in terms of behavior management—and the target of most school discipline and violence prevention interventions—this may not be a significant consideration. Similar results are also reported by many other successful interventions, with the greatest benefits found in those males considered most at risk. Schools with widespread behavior manage-

ment problems or a large number of highly aggressive girls should note this limitation in long-term effects.

Possible Negative Outcomes Related to the Implementation of the Good Behavior Game

None known.

References and Resources

Fishbein, J. E. & Wasik, B. H. (1981). Effect of the good behavior game on disruptive library behavior. *Journal of Applied Behavior Analysis, 14,* 89–93.

Kellam, S. G., Ling, X., Merisca, R., Brown, C. H., & Ialongo, N. (1998). The effect of the level of aggression in the first grade classroom on the course and malleability of aggressive behavior into middle school. *Development & Psychopathology, 10,* 165–185.

Salend, S. J., Reynolds, C. J., & Coyle, E. M. (1989). Individualizing the Good Behavior Game across type and frequency of behavior with emotionally disturbed adolescents. *Behavior Modification, 13,* 108–126.

Swiezy, N. B., Matson, J. L., & Box, P. (1992). The Good Behavior Game: A token reinforcement system for preschoolers. *Child & Family Behavior Therapy, 14,* 21–32.

U.S. Department of Health and Human Services, Substance Abuse and Mental Health Services Administration, Center for Substance Abuse Prevention (n.d.). *SAMHSA model programs.* Rockville, MD: Author. Available: http://modelprograms.samhsa.gov

High/Scope Preschool Curriculum Framework

Contact:
Gavin Haque

Position/Title:
Program Manager

Phone:
(734) 485–2000

Address:
High/Scope Educational Research Foundation
600 North River Street
Ypsilanti, MI 48198–2898

E-mail:
GavinH@highscope.org

Web Address:
http://www.highscope.org

Purpose

The purpose of the High/Scope preschool curriculum framework is to contribute to young children's intellectual, social, and physical development so as to prepare them for success and responsibility in school and in life.

Program Background

First developed in 1962, the curriculum framework is for children three to five years old. Approximately 35,000 preschool teachers and assistants have been trained by 1,400 certified High/Scope trainers.

Scope of Program

The High/Scope curriculum was initially developed for use in early intervention programs for at-risk three- to five-year-olds and has proven to be successful with such children.

Specific Problems/Risk Factors Targeted by High/Scope

The High/Scope curriculum framework seeks to contribute to children's intellectual, social, and physical development so they can achieve success and social responsibility in school and in life. The curriculum framework is especially appropriate for children who are at risk of not developing along these lines.

Program Operations

The High/Scope curriculum framework promotes children's active learning in the classroom and, through parent education, in the rest of children's lives. High/Scope creates a setting for children to engage in active learning. High/Scope's key experiences in child development define opportune times and ways for teachers to facilitate children's intellectual, social, and physical development.

Determining Your School's Readiness for High/Scope

The human and physical resources required to implement the High/Scope curriculum framework are about the same as are required for any good preschool program. The classroom should operate at least four mornings or afternoons a week for 32 weeks a year, with monthly home visits.

Getting Training to Begin High/Scope

High/Scope has a network of 1,400 teacher trainers who were certified upon successful completion of the High/Scope training-of-trainers program, or teacher training plus the trainer certification program. These trainers can identify teachers and programs that use the High/Scope curriculum framework. In addition, High/Scope has certified 161 teachers and ten programs.

The High/Scope preschool curriculum framework training manual is *Educating Young Children: Active Learning Practices for Preschool and Child Care Programs*, by Mary Hohmann and David P. Weikart (1995), available from the High/Scope Press, 600 North River Street, Ypsilanti, MI 48198–2898; phone (800) 442–4329.

High/Scope offers training throughout the United States and around the world: a seven-week training-of-trainers program, a four-week teacher-training program, a three-week trainer certification program for trained teachers, workshops lasting from one to five days, and conference presentations providing overviews of the curriculum framework and supporting research.

Training is strongly recommended and is required for certification. However, it is possible to purchase curriculum materials without official certification.

In the four-week teacher training program, teachers learn about active learning, room arrangement, daily routine, adult-child interaction, key experiences in child development, observational assessment of programs and children's development, how to work with parents, and related topics. Participants in the seven-week training-of-trainers program or the three-week trainer certification program also learn an active learning approach to adult education.

Program Costs

The four-week teacher-training program costs $2,225 per participant at High/Scope. Elsewhere, it costs $1,654 per participant for a group of 40, $2,850 per participant for a group of 20. The three-week trainer certification program costs $3,500 per participant. The seven-week training-of-trainers program costs $6,000 per participant. Training materials are included in these costs.

Other Resources Required to Implement High/Scope

n/a

Modifying High/Scope for Your School/Classroom Context

High/Scope offers a set of principles and practices that are applicable to varying content, including content generated by the needs and interests of individuals, communities, and ethnic groups around the world.

Components That Cannot Be Modified or Excluded From High/Scope

High/Scope stands firm in the priority the curriculum framework gives to children's active learning and the practices that support it.

Program Outcomes

The *High/Scope Perry Preschool Study* (Schweinhart, Barnes, & Weikart, 1993) examines the effects through adulthood of a preschool program using the High/Scope curriculum framework with children living in poverty:

▲ Sixty-seven percent of the program group but only 28 percent of the no-program group was intellectually prepared for school (IQ of 90 or greater at school entry).

▲ Forty-nine percent of the program group but only 15 percent of the no-program group attained a basic achievement level at age 14.

▲ Fifteen percent of the program group, compared with 34 percent of the no-program group, required treatment for mental impairment while in school.

▲ Sixty-six percent of the program group but only 45 percent of the no-program group graduated from high school; 7 percent of the program group, compared with 31 percent of the no-program group, had been arrested as adults five or more times by age 27.

▲ Every taxpayer dollar invested in the program returned $7.16 in economic benefits to the public.

The *High/Scope Training of Trainers Evaluation* (Epstein, 1993) included a study of two- to six-year-olds in Michigan preschool programs, 97 children in High/Scope classes and 103 in comparison classes. The High/Scope and comparison groups experienced preschool programs of similar high quality and had similar background characteristics—similar in gender, mean age, ethnicity, and parents' schooling. Trained outside observers rated High/Scope children significantly higher than comparison-group children in initiative, social relations, music and movement, and overall development.

High/Scope has been used with and by many ethnic groups throughout the United States and around the world. The *High/Scope Perry Preschool Study* children were all African American. High/Scope has been used with children of most disabilities, both moderate and severe. Evidence of the effectiveness of the High/Scope curriculum framework is unusually strong at the preschool level, and there is evidence of its effectiveness at the early elementary level in improving school achievement (Schweinhart & Wallgren, 1993) and at the adolescent level in increasing college enrollment (Oden, Kelly, Ma, & Weikart, 1992). The High/Scope curriculum framework has been found effective in urban public schools and Head Start preschool programs and in urban elementary schools, all of which would qualify for Title I funding.

Possible Negative Outcomes Related to the Implementation of High/Scope

None known.

References and Resources

Berrueta-Clement, J. R., Schweinhart, L. J., Barnett, W. S., Epstein, A. S., & Weikart, D. P. (1984). *Changed lives: The effects of the Perry Preschool Program on youths through age 19.* Ypsilanti, MI: High/Scope Press.

Epstein, A. S. (1993). *Training for quality: Improving early childhood programs through systematic inservice training.* Ypsilanti, MI: High/Scope Press.

Greenwood, P., Model, K. E., Rydell, C. P., & Chiesa, J. (1996). *Diverting children from a life of crime: Measuring costs and benefits* (MR-699.0-UCB/RC/IF). Santa Monica, CA: RAND.

Hohmann, M. & Weikart, D.P. (1995). *Educating young children: Active learning practices for preschool and childcare programs.* Ypsilanti, MI: High/Scope Press.

Oden, S., Kelly, M. A., Ma, Z., & Weikart, D. P. (1992). *Challenging the potential: Programs for talented disadvantaged youth.* Ypsilanti, MI: High/Scope Press.

Parks, G. (2000). *The High/Scope Perry Preschool project.* Washington, DC: U.S. Department of Education, Office of Juvenile Justice and Delinquency Prevention.

Schweinhart, L. J., Barnes, H. V., & Weikart, D. P. (1993). *The High/Scope Perry Preschool study through age 27* (Monograph no. 10 of the High/Scope Educational Research Foundation). Ypsilanti, MI: High/Scope Educational Research Foundation.

Schweinhart, L. J. & Wallgren, C. R. (1993). Effects of a follow through program on school achievement. *Journal of Research in Childhood Education, 8,* 43–56.

Schweinhart, L. J. & Weikart, D. P. (1980). *Young children grow up: The effects of the Perry Preschool Program on youths through age 15.* Ypsilanti, MI: High/Scope Press.

Schweinhart, L. J. & Weikart, D. P. (1997). The High/Scope preschool curriculum comparison study through age 23. *Early Childhood Research Quarterly, 12,* 117–143.

U.S. Department of Health and Human Services, Substance Abuse and Mental Health Services Administration, Center for Substance Abuse Prevention. (n.d.). *SAMHSA model programs.* Rockville, MD: Author. Available: http://modelprograms.samhsa.gov

Weikart, D. P., Bond, J. T., & McNeil, J. T. (1978). *The Ypsilanti Perry Preschool Project: Preschool years and longitudinal results through fourth grade.* Ypsilanti, MI: High/Scope Press.

I Can Problem Solve (ICPS)

Contact:
Myrna B. Shure

Position/Title:
Program Developer

Phone Number:
(215) 762–7205

Address:
MCP Hahnemann University
245 N. 15th St. MS 626
Philadelphia, PA 19102

E-mail:
mshure@drexel.edu

Web Address:
http://www.researchpress.com

Purpose

I Can Problem Solve (ICPS) is a school-based, primary prevention, universal program to teach children ages 4–12 how to think through and solve interpersonal problems with peers and adults.

Program Background

ICPS, designed for preschool through grade 6, was made available for mass dissemination for three age groups in 1992. The exact number of schools implementing ICPS is unknown. Each year since 1992, the publisher (Research Press) has documented 1,500 to 2,000 manuals sold each year, with many of those being multiple orders for single schools or districts.

Scope of Program

Although it is recommended that the program be phased-in a few grades at a time, the goal is exposure for the entire school. ICPS can also function as additional early intervention for students at particular risk with further training by the guidance counselor or other support staff.

Specific Problems/Risk Factors Targeted by ICPS

Most negative social behaviors are targeted:

- ▲ Physical aggression
- ▲ Verbal aggression
- ▲ Nagging, demanding behavior
- ▲ Overemotionality
- ▲ Impatience
- ▲ Rejection
- ▲ Lack of empathy
- ▲ Social withdrawal
- ▲ Poor academic readiness (preschool/ kindergarten) or academic achievement

Program Operations

Trained teachers provide the students with 30- to 45-minute sessions at least three times a week over four months. Students learn to use problem-solving skills to find solutions to interpersonal problems. Children are taught awareness of their own and others' feelings, alternative solutions to interpersonal problems, consequences to negative acts, and (beginning at age eight) sequenced step-by-step planning to reach a goal. Interpersonal concepts are integrated into the academic curriculum. Teachers and parents are taught a problem-solving style of discipline to use when actual problems arise.

Determining Your School's Readiness for ICPS

The best procedure for implementing the program within a school is to present the program to the entire faculty in an inservice meeting, and begin with only those teachers who desire the program for their classrooms. The school guidance counselor or other support staff should be trained to maintain the program in the school and to work individually with children at high risk.

Getting Training to Begin ICPS

Typically, a trainer will present a workshop to the entire faculty of a school during an inservice meeting. Then, either the entire school implements the program, or grades are gradually phased in, starting with the early grades. In addition, workshops for parent trainers are given.

Program Costs

Initial training costs $1,500 for a full-day workshop regardless of the number of trainees in the workshop and $2,000 to $2,500 for two full days. Travel expenses are additional.

The cost for ongoing support and consultation varies from $500 to $1,000 per day. Local school consultations average $250 per day. Follow-up phone consultation is available at no cost.

The *I Can Problem Solve Training Manual* (Shure, 1992) costs $39.95 and contains pictures and dialogues used to teach the program. One manual is needed per teacher, teacher aide, or other staff member who uses the program with the children. The *Raising a Thinking Child Workbook* (Shure, 2000) costs $19.95. One manual is needed for each family.

Other Resources Required to Implement ICPS

The only other materials needed are storybooks (already in the classroom) to be adapted to ICPS questions (e.g., how story characters feel and solve problems), and two-to-four animal hand puppets for each classroom of younger children as well as people hand puppets for the intermediate grade classrooms.

Modifying ICPS for Your School/Classroom Context

Because ICPS is a process of learning how to think (not what to think) in order to successfully solve interpersonal problems, teachers are free to modify the content of a given lesson-game to teach the required concept, sequenced strategically.

The actual number of lessons, or number of group teacher or parent meetings, can be reduced from the original ten meetings, as conducted during the formal research period, to as few as six. Implementation of ICPS should take place every day for 20 to 30 minutes in preschool and kindergarten, and three times a week for 40 minutes for the elementary grades. Parents can choose the time to conduct the lessons with their children at home, preferably at some consistent time such as before dinner, after dinner, or before bedtime.

Components That Cannot Be Modified or Excluded From ICPS

Although the number of actual formal lesson-games can be reduced, the practice of applying the problem-solving approach to real problems when they arise must not be excluded.

Program Outcomes

In preschool, and in kindergarten and the primary grades, the intended cognitive outcomes include gains in the interpersonal cognitive problem-solving (ICPS) skills trained: sensitivity to interpersonal problems, causal thinking (e.g., why one child might hit another), generating alternative solutions to interpersonal problems (e.g., one child wants a toy another has), and consequential thinking (e.g., what might happen if one child grabs a toy from another). In third through sixth grades, measured gains were made in generating alternative solutions and consequential thinking, as well as sequenced planning skills (steps to reach a stated interpersonal goal, potential obstacles that could interfere, and how long it might take to reach a goal).

At all ages studied, the following effects occurred:

- ▲ A decrease or prevention of negative behaviors:
  - Physical aggression (hitting, kicking) and verbal aggression (bossing, threatening)
  - Emotionality (easily upset by peers and/or adults, unable to cope with frustration)
  - Impatience (unable to wait, share, cooperate; persistent nagging and demanding)
  - Social withdrawal (inability to express feelings or stand up for rights; timid, fearful of peers and/or adults)
- ▲ An increase in positive outcomes and prosocial behaviors:
  - Liked by peers (others seek child out, enjoy being with him/her)
  - Shares/cares/cooperates

Possible Negative Outcomes Related to the Implementation of ICPS

None known.

References and Resources

Shure, M. B. (1992). *I can problem solve (ICPS): An interpersonal cognitive problem-solving program [3 volumes: Preschool; kindergarten/primary grades; intermediate elementary grades].* Champaign, IL: Research Press.

Shure, M. B. (2000). *Raising a thinking child workbook: Teaching young children how to resolve everyday conflicts and get along with others.* Champaign, IL, Research Press.

Shure, M. B. & Spivac, G. (1980). Interpersonal problem solving as a mediator of behavioral adjustment in preschool and kindergarten children. *Journal of Applied Developmental Psychology, 1,* 29–44.

Shure, M. B. & Spivac, G. (1982). Interpersonal problem-solving in young children: A cognitive approach to prevention. *American Journal of Community Psychology, 10* (3), 341–355.

Life Skills Training

Contact:
Gilbert Botvin, Ph.D.

Position/Title:
Professor and Director

Phone Number:
(212) 746–1270

Fax:
(212) 746–8390

Address:
Institute for Prevention Research
Weill Medical College of Cornell University
411 E 69th Street, KB–201
New York, NY 10021

E-mail:
gbotvin@mail.med.cornell.edu or
lstinfo@nhpanet.com

Web Addresses:
http://www.lifeskillstraining.com
http://www.med.cornell.edu/ipr

Purpose

Life Skills Training (LST) is a three-year intervention designed to prevent or reduce gateway drug use (i.e., tobacco, alcohol, and marijuana), primarily implemented in school classrooms by school teachers. The LST program is based on scientific evidence of what causes drug abuse and how to best prevent it. It is designed to do the following:

▲ Provide students with the necessary skills to resist social (peer) pressures to smoke, drink, and use drugs.

▲ Help them develop greater self-esteem, self-mastery, and self-confidence.

▲ Enable children to effectively cope with social anxiety.

▲ Increase their knowledge of the immediate consequences of substance abuse.

▲ Enhance cognitive and behavioral competency to reduce and prevent a variety of health risk behaviors.

Program Background

LST is a universal drug abuse prevention program that is based on an understanding of the causes of smoking, alcohol, and drug use/abuse. The LST intervention has been designed to target the psychosocial factors associated with the onset of drug involvement. The main goals of the LST program are to teach prevention-related information, to promote antidrug norms, to teach drug refusal skills, and to foster the development of personal self-management skills and general social skills.

Scope of Program

LST is a three-year intervention offered to all students in the grades targeted by the program. Originally LST focused on middle/junior high school students (initial intervention in sixth or seventh grade depending on the school structure, with booster sessions in the two subsequent years). Recently, Dr. Botvin and his associates developed an age-appropriate version of the LST program for upper elementary school students. It contains material for 24 classes (eight classes per year) to be taught during either grades 3–5 or grades 4–6.

LST has been tested with a broad range of adolescents. Evaluation studies show that it works for white, black, and Latino youth. It works for boys and girls alike and for adolescents living in suburban, urban, and rural environments.

Specific Problems/Risk Factors Targeted by LST

LST targets gateway substances (tobacco, alcohol, and marijuana) that are used at the beginning of the developmental progression. LST offers the potential for interrupting the developmental progression from use of these substances to other forms of drug use and abuse. A second reason for targeting this type of drug use is that the use of these substances accounts for the largest portion of drug-related annual mortality and morbidity.

Program Operations

The program is delivered in 15 sessions in Year 1, 10 sessions in Year 2, and 5 sessions in Year 3. Sessions, which last an average of 45 minutes, can be delivered once a week or as an intensive minicourse. LST consists of three major components that cover the critical domains found to promote drug use. Research has shown that students who develop skills in these three domains are far less likely to engage in a wide range of high-risk behaviors. Skills are taught using training techniques such as instruction, demonstration, feedback, reinforcement, and practice. The three components are:

- ▲ **Drug Resistance Skills** enable young people to recognize and challenge common misconceptions about tobacco, alcohol, and other drug use. Through coaching and practice, they learn information and practical ATOD (alcohol, tobacco, and other drugs) resistance skills for dealing with peers and media pressure to engage in ATOD use.

- ▲ **Personal Self-Management Skills** teach students how to examine their self-image and its effects on behavior; set goals and

keep track of personal progress; identify everyday decisions and how they may be influenced by others; analyze problem situations and consider the consequences of each alternative solution before making decisions; reduce stress and anxiety; and look at personal challenges in a positive light.

- ▲ **General Social Skills** teach students the necessary skills to overcome shyness, communicate effectively and avoid misunderstandings, initiate and carry out conversations, handle social requests, use both verbal and nonverbal assertiveness skills to make or refuse requests, and recognize that they have choices other than aggression or passivity when faced with tough situations.

Determining Your School's Readiness for LST

There are no specific requirements.

Getting Training to Begin LST

LST Provider Training is available for individuals interested in conducting the LST program with adolescent students in schools or other settings. All LST Provider Training is conducted by qualified trainers who are certified by National Health Promotion Associates, Inc. The LST Provider Training workshop is designed (1) to teach information concerning the background, theory, and rationale for the LST program; (2) to familiarize participants with the LST program; (3) to teach participants the skills needed to conduct the LST program; (4) to provide an opportunity to practice teaching selected portions of the LST program; and (5) to discuss practical implementation issues. LST has been shown to be effective regardless of whether it is taught by teachers, health professionals, or peer leaders.

Program Costs

LST can be implemented at a cost of approximately $7 per student per year (curriculum materials averaged over the three-year period). However, this does not include the cost of training, which is a minimum of $2,000 per day for one or two days. A single upper elementary teacher manual and student guide is $95. A single middle-school teacher's manual and student guide is $100. The student guides come in packs of 10 for both upper elementary and middle school.

The prices for a pack of 10 student guides are as follows:

▲ Upper Elementary Year 1, 2, 3 $50 (packs of 10)

▲ Middle School Year 1 $60 (packs of 10)

▲ Middle School Year 2 $50 (packs of 10)

▲ Middle School Year 3 $40 (packs of 10)

Other Resources Required to Implement LST

While teacher training is not required, it is highly recommended when a site desires to achieve the best program results. LST Teacher Training is designed to prepare providers to deliver the curriculum with content and process fidelity. Teacher training increases the effectiveness of the program and assists providers in developing implementation strategies for the program's comfort and fit in individual sites.

Modifying LST for Your School/ Classroom Context

LST has been successfully taught in a variety of settings, including school classrooms, after-school programs, summer camps, and community-based organizations. As long as the program is implemented according to the Fidelity Checklist, it can be taught in any setting. LST can be taught once a week or as often as every day. The effectiveness of both types of implementation is the same.

Components That Cannot Be Modified or Excluded From LST

To be optimally effective, LST must be implemented carefully and completely. If the material is only partially covered, studies have shown the program is likely to be less effective.

Implementation fidelity means teaching every unit of the program, in the sequence provided, for the specific number of sessions.

Program Outcomes

More than one-and-a-half decades of research with LST have consistently shown that participation in the program can cut drug use in half. These reductions (relative to controls) in both the prevalence (i.e., proportion of persons in a population who have reported some involvement in a particular offense) and incidence (i.e., the number of offenses that occur in a given population during a specified time interval) of drug use have primarily been with respect to tobacco, alcohol, and marijuana use. These studies have demonstrated that this prevention approach can produce reductions in drug use that are both long-lasting and clinically meaningful. For example, long-term follow-up data indicate that reductions in drug use produced with seventh graders can last up to the end of high school. Evaluation research has demonstrated that this prevention approach is effective with a broad range of students, including white middle-class youth and economically disadvantaged urban African American and Latino youth. It has not only demonstrated reductions in the use of tobacco, alcohol, or marijuana use of up to 87 percent, but studies show that it also can reduce more serious forms of drug involvement.

Based on outcomes averaged across more than a dozen studies, LST has been found to decrease tobacco, alcohol, and marijuana use by 50–75 percent.

Long-term follow-up results observed six years following the intervention show that LST

▲ decreases use of multiple illicit drugs up to 66 percent;

▲ reduces pack-a-day smoking by 25 percent; and

▲ decreases use of inhalants, narcotics, and hallucinogens.

Possible Negative Outcomes Related to the Implementation of LST

None known.

Resources

Botvin, G. J., Baker, E., Dusenbury, L., Botvin, E. M., & Diaz, T. (1995). Long-term follow-up results of a randomized drug abuse prevention trial in a white middle-class population. *Journal of the American Medical Association*, 273(14), 1106–1112.

Botvin, G. J., Griffith, K. W., Diaz, T., Scheier, L., Williams, C., & Espstein, J. A. (2000). Preventing illicit drug use in adolescents: Long-term follow-up data from a randomized control trial of a school population. *Addictive Behaviors*, 5, 769–774.

Botvin, G. J., Mihalic, S. F., & Grotpeter, J. K. (1998). *Blueprints for violence, book five: Life skills training*. Boulder: CO: Center for the Study and Prevention of Violence.

U.S. Department of Health and Human Services, Substance Abuse and Mental Health Services Administration, Center for Substance Abuse Prevention. (n.d.). *SAMHSA model programs*. Rockville, MD: Author. Available: http://modelprograms.samhsa.gov

Linking the Interests of Families and Teachers (LIFT)

Contact:
John Reid, Ph.D.

Position/Title:
Executive Director

Phone Number:
(541) 485-2711

Address:
Oregon Social Learning Center
160 East 4th Avenue
Eugene, OR 97401

E-mail:
johnr@oslc.org

Web Address:
http://www.prevention.psu.edu/LIFT.htm

Purpose

LIFT is a universal intervention designed for all first- and fifth-grade elementary school boys and girls and their families living in at-risk neighborhoods characterized by high rates of juvenile delinquency.

Linking the Interests of Families and Teachers (LIFT) is a school- and family-based intervention for the prevention of conduct problems such as antisocial behavior, involvement with delinquent peers, and drug/alcohol use. The main goal of LIFT is to decrease children's antisocial behavior and increase their prosocial behavior.

Program Background

LIFT is grounded on a developmental model of behavior that focuses on how the interactions of children with parents, peers, and school staff contribute to or exacerbate conduct problems (Patterson, Reid, & Dishion, 1992). LIFT attempts to lower the probability that parents, peers, and school staff will react coercively to a child's problem behaviors, and to increase the probability that children's prosocial behaviors will be supported.

Scope of Program

LIFT is a ten-week intervention consisting of parent training, a playground behavioral program, a classroom-based social skills program, systematic communication between teachers and parents, and a weekly newsletter. LIFT interventions involve peers, the school, and the family.

Specific Problems/Risk Factors Targeted by LIFT

LIFT specifically focuses on changing children's opposition, defiance, and social ineptitude and parents' discipline and monitoring.

The overarching focus of LIFT is to modify the reactions of parents, peers, and teachers to children's prosocial and antisocial behaviors. Specifically, in the family domain, LIFT promotes calm and consistent limit setting and parental involvement in the child's social life (especially school). In the peer domain, LIFT targets physical aggression in unstructured settings (i.e., the playground) by promoting positive peer interactions. In the classroom, LIFT promotes developmentally appropriate social relationships and peer group skills.

Program Operations

Parent Component. The parent component of LIFT consists of efforts both to improve family-school communication and to improve parental discipline and monitoring skills. The family-school communication component consists of a telephone and answering machine for each classroom on which teachers leave daily messages about class activities, homework assignments, and special events. Parents can call any time to learn about activities or assignments or leave messages regarding their child. A weekly newsletter keeps parents informed and provides suggestions for home activities that complement those at school.

LIFT parent instructors also meet with groups of 10 to 15 families once a week for six weeks. These sessions are held during the same three-month period of time that children are participating in the classroom and playground components at school. Each parent session follows a common format: (1) review of the results of the home practice from the previous week; (2) lecture, discussion, and role plays; and (3) presentation of the home practice activities for the following week. Videotaped scenarios are used in several sessions to present and illustrate certain skills. The basic skills presented in the first- and fifth-grade parent curricula are similar and link to the corresponding classroom curricula. To encourage attendance, sessions are offered each weekday evening and one weekday afternoon, free childcare is provided, and a prize drawing is held at the completion of each session. If parents are unable to attend, individual sessions are offered in their homes. If family commitments or circumstances make this option unworkable, parents are sent written materials. Additional parent sessions are arranged if necessary to discuss specific family problems and provide appropriate referrals.

Playground Component. The playground component of LIFT takes place during the middle of the free play portion of the classroom component. A modification of the Good Behavior Game (Barrish, Saunders, & Wolfe, 1969; Dolan et al., 1993) is used to actively encourage positive peer relations on the playground. At the beginning of the program, children within each classroom are divided into small groups. Individual and class rewards are based on the display of positive behaviors. Individual rewards are given by regular playground staff and by the LIFT instructor during the recess period. When a staff member observes a child acting in an overtly positive manner toward peers, the child is given an armband and verbally praised. At the end of recess, all armbands earned by class members are put into one class jar. When the jar is full, the entire class earns a special privilege.

Classroom Component. LIFT classroom instructors meet with all the students in a classroom for one hour twice a week for ten weeks. Each session follows the same general format:

▲ Brief lecture and role play on a specific set of social and problem-solving skills

▲ Opportunities for practicing these skills in structured small- and large-group sessions

▲ Free play employing a refinement of the Good Behavior Game

▲ Skills review and presentation of daily rewards

The second weekly session also includes a formal class problem-solving session. The regular classroom teachers assist the LIFT instructors in role plays and group practice.

Determining Your School's Readiness for LIFT

LIFT can be incorporated into school settings with relatively little difficulty. Many schools already provide some type of child problem-solving training within the regular curriculum, and many school districts provide parents at least some opportunity during the year to attend parent education classes. All schools monitor playground behavior and activities, and telephones are becoming increasingly common in classrooms. By integrating these activities and resources in a standardized program such as LIFT, schools could prevent at least some students on the path to delinquency from escalating to more extreme forms of antisocial behavior.

Getting Training to Begin LIFT

LIFT classroom instructors must be trained in the LIFT curriculum. Because regular classroom teachers assist the LIFT instructors in role plays and group practice, all LIFT instructors, school staff, and playground staff must be trained in the Good Behavior Game so that they can properly reinforce positive student behavior in both school and playground components of the program. LIFT parent trainers must be trained in the LIFT parent curriculum so they can lead sessions with groups of parents in the school or make home visits to parents who are unable to attend group sessions.

Program Costs

The LIFT program requires additional personnel in the school unless existing positions can be adapted to meet the needs of the program. LIFT classroom instructors and LIFT parent trainers may need to be hired. Childcare and prizes are offered as incentives for parents to attend parent training. A telephone with an answering machine or voicemail is placed in each LIFT classroom.

Other Resources Required to Implement LIFT

LIFT requires a high level of parent involvement, and strong parent commitment is extremely helpful to successful implementation of the program.

Modifying LIFT for Your School/Classroom Context

Each classroom must be outfitted with a telephone and answering machine (or voicemail). One hour twice a week for ten weeks is required for the LIFT curriculum in the classroom.

Components That Cannot Be Modified or Excluded From LIFT

The program needs to include each of the three domains: families, playground, and classroom, but components can be slightly modified to fit the needs of the school or community.

Program Outcomes

In short-term evaluations, LIFT decreased children's physical aggression on the playground (particularly children rated by their teachers as most aggressive at the start of the study), increased children's social skills, and decreased aversive behavior in mothers rated most aversive at baseline, relative to controls. Three years after participation in the program, first-grade participants had fewer increases in attention deficit disorder–related behaviors (inattentiveness, impulsivity, and hyperactivity) than controls. At follow-up, fifth-grade participants had fewer associations with delinquent peers, were less likely to initiate patterned alcohol use, and were significantly less likely than controls to have been arrested.

Possible Negative Outcomes Related to Implementation

None known.

References and Resources

Barrish, H. H., Saunders, M., & Wolf, M. M. (1969). Good Behavior Game: Effects of individual contingencies for group consequences on disruptive behavior in a classroom. *Journal of Applied Behavior Analysis, 2,* 119–124.

Dolan, L. J., Kellam, S. G., Brown, C. H., Werthamer-Larsson, L., Rebok, G. W., Mayer, L. S., Laudolff, J., Turkkan, J., Ford, C., & Wheeler, L. (1993). The short-term impact of two classroom-based preventive interventions on aggressive and shy behaviors and poor achievement. *Journal of Applied Developmental Psychology, 14,* 317–345.

Eddy, J. M., Reid, J. B., & Fetrow, R. A. (2000). An elementary school-based prevention program targeting modifiable antecedents of youth delinquency and violence: Linking the Interests of Families and Teachers (LIFT). *Journal of Emotional and Behavioral Disorders, 8*(3), 165–176.

Patterson, G. R. (1982). Coercive family process. Eugene, OR: Castalia Publishing.

Patterson, G. R., Reid, J. B., & Dishion, T. J. (1992). *Antisocial boys: A social interactional approach.* Eugene, OR: Castalia Publishing.

Reid, J. B., Eddy, J. M., Fetrow, R. A., & Stoolmiller, M. (1999). Description and immediate impacts of a preventative intervention for conduct problems. *American Journal of Community Psychology, 24,* 483–517.

Multidimensional Treatment Foster Care (MTFC)

Contact:
Gerard Bouwman

Position/Title:
Administrator

Phone Number:
(541) 485-2711

Address:
207 E. 5th Avenue
Eugene, OR 97401

E-mail:
gerryb@oslc.org

Web Address:
http://www.colorado.edu/cspv/blueprints/model/programs/MTFC.html

Purpose

Multidimensional Treatment Foster Care is an intensive intervention for youth with delinquency and behavioral problems, their families, and their communities. The goals of the program follow:

▲ Increase youth's normative/positive behaviors.

▲ Closely supervise youth at all times.

▲ Closely monitor peer associations.

▲ Specify clear, consistent rules and limits.

▲ Consistently follow through with consequences for both positive and problem behavior.

▲ Encourage youth to develop academic skills and positive work habits.

▲ Support family members to increase their parenting skills.

▲ Decrease conflict among family members.

▲ Teach youth new skills for forming relationships with positive peers and for bonding with adult mentors and role models.

Program Background

The MTFC program model is rooted in the research conducted in the early 1970s at the Oregon Social Learning Center in Eugene. Social learning theory and principles formed the earliest basis for the approach, and the subsequent isolation of predictors of problem behaviors through numerous research studies funded by NIMH, NIDA, and NICHD ultimately led to the development and adaptation of MTFC for a variety of populations. The first MTFC program was established in 1983 by Patricia Chamberlain, Ph.D., targeting serious and chronic juvenile offenders, and is funded by the Oregon Youth Authority. In 1992, a program was initiated for severely emotionally disturbed youngsters, funded collaboratively by the local Services to Families and Children office in Eugene and Title XIX Medicaid funds. In 1996, the Oregon State Office for Services to Families and Children funded a program for low-intelligence, emotionally disturbed youth of both genders between the ages of 6 and 18 who have problems with aggression, fire setting, self-harm, drug or alcohol abuse, or sexual acting out. In 1998, a program for developmentally delayed adolescents with sexual acting out or offending problems began under contract with Oregon's Office of Developmental Disability Services. And in 2000, under funding from the Lane Council of Governments, MTFC services were instituted for a regional population of serious and chronic juvenile offenders.

In 1999, all MTFC service activities were transferred from the Oregon Social Learning Center to OSLC Community Programs, an organization dedicated exclusively to the delivery of MTFC and other intensive home-based services. No changes in program staff accompanied this organizational change. No interruptions, terminations, or reductions of any MTFC programs have been experienced by either the Oregon Social Learning Center or OSLC Community Programs.

Scope of Program

MTFC provides services and supports to children and youth, foster parents, and youths' birth families.

Specific Problems/Risk Factors Targeted by MTFC

MTFC provides intensive and comprehensive individualized treatment, support, and supervision in a family setting to youth with delinquency, behavioral, or emotional problems.

Program Operations

Peer association is a key factor in the socialization process of children and youth, as is inclusion in a functional, well-adjusted family. The MTFC model is built around these realities. In this approach, community families are recruited, trained, and supported to serve as foster families for participating youth. No more than two children or youth are placed with any one family, so that counterproductive association with problem peers is restricted or eliminated. Intensive services are provided to the youth, the foster family, and, in

many cases, the biological family. The length of placement in MTFC is six to ten months, depending on population and other variables. Services vary by population:

For the Youth

▲ Participation in a structured, supportive, teaching-oriented placement in an MTFC home

▲ Close supervision of whereabouts, activities, and peer associations

▲ Daily monitoring of school participation and progress

▲ Skill building in academic and social activities

▲ Individual therapy

For the MTFC Parents

▲ 20 hours of preservice training

▲ Weekly training and technical assistance meetings

▲ On-call program staff backup and support, 24 hours/day, 7 days/week

For the Youth's Family

▲ Intensive training and support

▲ Access to program staff, 24 hours/day, 7 days/week

▲ Family therapy

▲ Aftercare services

Determining Your School's Readiness for MTFC

For more information on how to add MTFC to the treatment options available in your school's community, contact Gerard Bouwman.

Getting Training to Begin MTFC

In the MTFC model, the foster parents are the primary treatment agents. Case managers work with foster families to develop individualized treatment plans and strategies for each participant, aimed at addressing the specific needs of the youth. A system of clearly communicated and consistently applied rewards and consequences is a standard feature of the individual treatment plans. An important tool in MTFC treatment is the Parent Daily Report (PDR). Foster parents are contacted daily, by telephone, to provide information on the youth's behavior during the past 24 hours in the format of the PDR checklist. PDR information is used by the case managers to track progress and is reviewed during the weekly foster parent group meetings. Potential problems can be readily identified through the use of PDR data, and needed adjustments in treatment strategies can be made quickly on the basis of this information.

Program Costs

Depending on client population and duration of placement, MTFC services cost from $3,500 per month per child (child welfare population) to $4,030 per month per child (developmentally delayed adolescents who have had problems with sexual acting out or sex offending). This includes all services, supervision, and foster care placement.

Other Resources Required to Implement MTFC

None known.

Modifying MTFC for Your School/ Classroom Context

Although the treatment model is not open to modification without evidence of effectiveness supported through the clinical trials, programs may be modified somewhat to meet the needs of the community and the targeted treatment population. Program evaluation also may be modified.

Components That Cannot Be Modified or Excluded From MTFC

The MTFC model is not open to modification without co-occurring evaluation to determine effectiveness.

Program Outcomes

The Multidimensional Treatment Foster Care model has been tested in two early studies where researchers explored the feasibility of using this model for adolescents referred for delinquency and for youngsters leaving the state mental hospital. Results showed that MTFC was not only feasible but, compared to alternative residential treatment models, it was cost-effective and the outcomes for children and families were better. For example, during a two-year follow-up period, the number of days delinquent youngsters were incarcerated in the state training school was lower for participants in MTFC than for a comparison group of youngsters placed in group care programs. The savings in incarceration costs alone were $122,000.

Subsequent investigations of MTFC have shown that program youth compared to control group youth

- ▲ spent 60 percent fewer days incarcerated in follow-up;
- ▲ had fewer than half the number of subsequent arrests;
- ▲ ran away from programs three times less often;
- ▲ returned to live with parents/relatives more often; and
- ▲ had significantly less hard drug use in follow-up.

In the largest study so far conducted, boys in MTFC were compared with a control group of boys in group care (GC). The MTFC boys had less than half the number of arrests as the boys in GC one year after placement (i.e., an average of 2.6 offenses for MTFC boys and 5.4 offenses for GC boys). Boys in MTFC had an 83 percent higher rate of desistance from arrest than did boys in the control group. Nearly three times as many boys ran away or were expelled from their programs in the control group than in MTFC (5 out of 36 MTFC boys and 15 out of 38 GC boys). Boys in MTFC spent about twice as many days living with parents or relatives in follow-up than did boys in GC.

Possible Negative Outcomes Related to the Implementation of MTFC

None known.

Resource

Chamberlain, P. & Mihalic, S. F. (1998). *Blueprints for violence prevention, book eight: Multidimensional treatment foster care.* Boulder, CO: Center for the Study and Prevention of Violence.

Multisystemic Therapy (MST)

Contact:
Marshall E. Swenson, MSW, MBA

Position/Title:
Manager of Program Development, MST Services

Phone Number:
(843) 856-8226

Address:
P.O. Box 21269
Charleston, SC 29413–1269

E-mail:
ms@mstservices.com

Web Address:
http://www.mstservices.com

Purpose

Multisystemic Therapy (MST) is an intensive family- and community-based treatment that addresses the multiple determinants of serious antisocial behavior in juvenile offenders.

Program Background

MST was developed in the late 1970s to address several limitations of existing mental health services for serious juvenile offenders, including minimal effectiveness, low accountability of service providers for outcomes, and high cost.

Scope of Program

MST is an intensive intervention that should be reserved for youth at the highest level of risk for school failure and placement outside the home and community.

Specific Problems/Risk Factors Targeted by MST

With regard to MST in particular, interventions are designed to address those risk factors and protective factors that are closest to identified treatment goals. Thus, in any one case, MST will address an individualized subset of risk and protective factors.

Risk and Protective Factors

Individual Context

▲ Risk Factors
 – Low verbal skills
 – Favorable attitudes toward antisocial behavior
 – Psychiatric symptomatology
 – Cognitive bias to attribute hostile intentions to others

- ▲ Protective Factors
  - – Intelligence
  - – Being firstborn
  - – Easy temperament
  - – Conventional attitudes
  - – Problem-solving skills

Family Context

- ▲ Risk Factors
  - – Lack of monitoring
  - – Ineffective discipline
  - – Low warmth
  - – High conflict
  - – Parental difficulties (e.g., drug abuse, psychiatric conditions, criminality)
- ▲ Protective Factors
  - – Attachment to parents
  - – Supportive family environment
  - – Marital harmony

Peer Context

- ▲ Risk Factors
  - – Association with deviant peers
  - – Poor relationship skills
  - – Low association with prosocial peers
  - – Bonding with prosocial peers

School Context

- ▲ Risk Factors
  - – Low achievement
  - – Dropout
  - – Low commitment to education
  - – Aspects of the schools, such as weak structure and chaotic environment
- ▲ Protective Factors
  - – Commitment to schooling

Neighborhood and Community Context

- ▲ Risk Factors
  - – High mobility
  - – Low community support (neighbors, church, etc.)
  - – High disorganization
  - – Criminal subculture
- ▲ Protective Factors
  - – Ongoing involvement in church activities
  - – Strong indigenous support network

Program Operations

For each case, an assessment of family, peer, school, and social support systems is conducted rapidly (typically within one week to ten days). In conducting the assessment, the therapist interviews family members and others connected with the youth and family (e.g., friends, teachers, extended family, neighbors) to obtain multiple and independent views on the determinants of the identified problems and the strengths of the youth and family. Upon completion of the assessment, when problems have been specified satisfactorily, treatment goals are set by family members and the therapist. These goals are operationally defined in ways that enable the family and the therapist to monitor progress in concrete terms.

Treatment sessions focus on changing attitudes and behaviors that are needed to attain the goals. The therapist addresses treatment goals one at a time or in some logical combination. As progress is made toward meeting one goal, treatment sessions incorporate additional goals. At the conclusion of each session, family members are given explicit tasks designed to facilitate the attainment of identified goals. The first item on the agenda of the next session is the family members' performance of the tasks, and ameliorative plans are developed if tasks have not been completed.

The frequency and duration of sessions are determined by family need. Thus, sessions are held as often as every day early in treatment or when clinical progress is not being made. During the middle of treatment, the therapist may hold two to three sessions per week and call several times. As treatment termination nears, sessions may be held as infrequently as once a week. In addition, efficient use of therapist time is emphasized, with sessions ranging in length from 15 to 75 minutes. Thus, MST interventions have the flexibility to be relatively intense, in terms of both time in treatment (e.g., multiple sessions per week) and task orientation of treatment sessions (e.g., explicit goal setting and extensive homework assignments).

Weekly supervision is provided during scheduled times and as needed. Like MST interventions, supervision is pragmatic and goal-oriented. Therapists are expected to conceptualize cases in multisystemic terms. Supervision is directed toward articulating treatment priorities and obstacles to success and toward designing interventions to successfully navigate the obstacles. As members of therapist teams, therapists consult one another informally as well as during supervision. MST integrity is further supported and reinforced through weekly consultation with an MST expert. Thus, a high level of clinical support is provided to therapists from team members, supervisors, and MST consultants.

Following are some recommendations for effective implementation of the program:

- ▲ MST Therapists should be master's-level professionals.
- ▲ MST Clinical Supervisors should be Ph.D.-level professionals.
- ▲ MST Clinical Supervisors should have both clinical authority and administrative authority over the MST Therapists they supervise.
- ▲ Funding for MST cases should be in the form of case rates or annual program support funding in lieu of billing mechanisms that track contact hours, productivity, and so on.
- ▲ MST programs should have formal outcome tracking systems.
- ▲ MST programs should use outcome-focused personnel evaluation methods.
- ▲ Planning for cases after they are discharged from the MST program should be carefully managed and limited to aftercare referrals that target specific, well-defined problems. The assumption is that most MST cases should need minimal formal aftercare services.

Determining Your School's Readiness for MST

MST programs are typically housed within public mental health settings or private provider organizations that deliver mental health services. Such settings are more likely to have a culture (i.e., providing rehabilitative services for disadvantaged families versus being punishment oriented) and an infrastructure (e.g., case record-keeping system, staff knowledgeable about issues such as confidentiality, relations with formal community resources) that supports the provision of community-based mental health services. The ideal organizational context is one in which the provider administers a range of family- and community-based services that vary in restrictiveness from outpatient to home-based to therapeutic foster care, with perhaps a small short-term residential component.

Getting Training to Begin MST

Training is available only to persons implementing MST as a separate and distinct service with dedicated staff. Educators often participate in program design as stakeholders.

Therapists and supervisors receive training in MST in three ways. First, five days of intensive training are provided. Second, day-and-a-half "booster" sessions are offered quarterly. Third, treatment teams and their supervisors receive weekly telephone consultations from MST experts.

One aim of the training program is to help communities develop the necessary infrastructure to support ongoing MST implementation independently. This usually includes training a highly competent professional to provide training and consultation as an exclusive duty (as opposed to just another duty). The training protocol and quality assurance process are currently under development.

A training manual is provided to all participants in the formal training program. The text *Multisystemic Treatment of Antisocial Behavior in Children and Adolescents* (Henggeler, Schoenwald, Borduin, Rowland, & Cunningham, 1998) is available to the public.

Program Costs

Program costs vary greatly with the size of the program and the needs of the target population. The total cost of the operation of a single treatment team is estimated to range from $250,000 to $350,000 annually for treatment of 50 families. This translates into an average cost of $5,000 to $7,000 per family treated. Training and quality assurance costs usually account for 5–15 percent of total costs (smaller percentages for larger multiteam programs). All materials, support, and consultation fees are included in training costs.

Other Resources Required to Implement MST

MST services can be provided in existing community settings (e.g., homes, schools); little facility space is needed. Therapists require transportation and cellular phones.

Personnel resources and intense training are crucial to the success of MST programs. MST is conducted by master's-level therapists who receive on-site supervision from doctoral level mental health professionals. Therapists also can be highly competent bachelor's-level professionals. Therapists are selected on the basis of their motivation, flexibility, common sense, and "street smarts," the master's degree being viewed more as a sign of motivation than as evidence of a particular type or level of clinical expertise. Each MST treatment team consists of three or four therapists, each carrying a caseload of four to six families.

Modifying MST for Your School/Classroom Context

Although the treatment model is not open to modification without evidence of effectiveness supported through the clinical trials, programs may be modified in certain ways to meet the needs of the community and the targeted treatment population. Program evaluation also may be modified.

Components That Cannot Be Modified or Excluded From MST

▲ MST Therapists must be full-time employees assigned solely to the MST program.

▲ MST Therapists must be accessible at times that are convenient to their clients and, in times of crisis, very quickly. Issues to be addressed include the dedicated nature of the MST Therapist role, the use of flex-time/comp-time, policies regarding the use of personal vehicles, and the use of pagers and cellular phones.

▲ MST Therapists must operate in teams of no fewer than two and no more than four therapists (plus the Clinical Supervisor) and use the Family Preservation model of service delivery.

▲ MST Clinical Supervisors will be assigned to the MST program a minimum of 50 percent time (full-time carrying a partial caseload is also acceptable) per MST Team to conduct weekly team clinical supervision and facilitate the weekly MST telephone consultation. They must be available for individual clinical supervision for crisis cases. Supervisors carrying a partial caseload should be assigned to the program on a full-time basis.

▲ MST caseloads must not exceed six families per therapist; four to six families is typical. The accepted duration of treatment is three to five months.

▲ Consistent adherence to the MST model requires therapists to track progress and outcomes on each case weekly by completing case paperwork and participating in team clinical supervision and MST consultation.

- The MST program must have a 24 hrs/day, 7 days/week on-call system to provide coverage when therapists are taking personal time. The system must be staffed by professionals who understand MST and know the details of each MST case.

- With the cooperation of other organizations and agencies, MST Therapists must be able to take the lead for clinical decision making. The organization sponsoring the MST program is responsible for initiating collaborative relationships with other organizations. Each MST Therapist sustains these relationships through ongoing case-specific collaboration.

- MST program discharge criteria must be outcome-based and must ameliorate the referral problem or behavior.

Program Outcomes

Families who have received MST showed extensive improvements in family relations, and their youth evidenced decreased behavior problems. In a study contrasting MST versus behavioral parent training with abusive and neglectful families (Brunk, Henggeler, & Whelan, 1987), MST was significantly more effective at restructuring problematic parent-child relations. Borduin, Henggeler, Blaske, and Stein (1990), in the first controlled study of adolescent sexual offenders to appear in the literature, showed that MST reduced three-year recidivism for both sexual offenses and criminal offenses when compared with individual outpatient counseling. Preliminary findings from two studies (Borduin et al., 1995; Henggeler, Melton, & Smith, 1992; Henggeler, Melton, Smith, Schoenwald, & Hanley, 1993) showed that MST reduced drug use and abuse in samples of serious juvenile offenders (Henggeler et al., 1991). A long-term targeted outcome is that the youth's behavior can be managed in the least restrictive school setting and no longer presents problems that overwhelm the school's resources.

MST has been implemented in four randomized clinical trials with more than 300 serious, violent, or substance-abusing juvenile offenders and their families. Reflecting the demographics of youth in the juvenile justice system, the majority of youths receiving MST have been males and members of single-parent households that were characterized by economic disadvantage. MST has been equally effective with African American families and white families and with younger adolescents and older adolescents.

MST has been evaluated in both high-density and low-density population areas. MST programs typically cover a designated geographic area, and youth may come from anywhere within the defined territory. Most areas exhibit variation in population density that may meet any one of the definitions. In general, most of the young people treated in the clinical trials are at least old enough for middle school or junior high school, but many have not been academically successful enough to merit an age-appropriate grade placement.

Inappropriate referrals to the MST program include youth referred primarily for psychiatric behaviors (i.e., actively suicidal, actively homicidal, actively psychotic) and youth referred for sex offenses.

Possible Negative Outcomes Related to the Implementation of MST

None known.

References and Resources

Borduin, C. M., Henggeler, S. W., Blaske, D. M., & Stein, T. (1990). Multisystemic treatment of adolescent sexual offenders. *International Journal of Offender Therapy and Comparative Criminology, 35*, 105–114.

Borduin, C. M., Mann, B. J., Cone, L. T., Henggeler, S. W., Fucci, B. R., Blaske, D. M., & Wilson, R. A. (1995). Multisystemic treatment of serious juvenile offenders: Long-term prevention of criminology and violence. *Journal of Consulting and Clinical Psychology, 63*, 569–578.

Brunk, M., Henggeler, S. W., & Whelan, J. P. (1987). A comparison of multisystemic therapy and parent training in the brief treatment of child abuse and neglect. *Journal of Consulting and Clinical Psychology, 55,* 311–318.

Henggeler, S. W., Borduin, C. M., Melton, G. B., Mann, B. J., Smith, L., Hall, J. A., Cone, L., & Fucci, B. R. (1991). Effects of multisystemic therapy on drug use and abuse in serious juvenile offenders: A progress report from two outcome studies. *Family Dynamics of Addiction Quarterly, 1,* 40–51.

Henggeler, S. W., Melton, G. B., Brondino, M. J., Schere, D. G., & Hanley, J. H. (1997). Multisystemic therapy with violent and chronic juvenile offenders and their families: The role of treatment fidelity in successful dissemination. *Journal of Consulting & Clinical Psychology, 65,* 821–833.

Henggeler, S. W., Melton, G. B., & Smith, L. A. (1992). Family preservation using multisystemic therapy: An effective alternative to incarcerating serious juvenile offenders. *Journal of Consulting and Clinical Psychology, 60,* 953–961.

Henggeler, S. W., Melton, G. B., Smith, L. A., Schoenwald, S. K., & Hanley, J. H. (1993). Family preservation using multisystemic treatment: Long-term follow-up to a clinical trial with serious juvenile offenders. *Journal of Child and Family Studies, 2,* 283–293.

Henggeler, S. W., Mihalic, S. F., Rone, L., Thomas, C., & Timmons-Mitchell, J. (1998). *Blueprints for violence prevention, book six: Multisystemic therapy.* Boulder, CO: Center for the Study and Prevention of Violence.

Henggeler, S. W., Schoenwald, S. K., Borduin, C. M., Rowland, M. D., & Cunningham, P. B. (1998). *Multisystemic treatment of antisocial behavior in children and adolescents.* New York: The Guilford Press.

U.S. Department of Health and Human Services, Substance Abuse and Mental Health Services Administration, Center for Substance Abuse Prevention. (n.d.). *SAMHSA model programs.* Rockville, MD: Author. Available: http://modelprograms.samhsa.gov

PeaceBuilders®

Contact:
Michael I. Krupnick

Position/Title:
President

Phone Number:
(877) 4 PEACE NOW [(877) 473-2236]

Address:
P.O. Box 12158
Tucson, AZ 85732

E-mail:
info@peacebuilders.com

Web Address:
http://www.peacebuilders.com

Purpose

PeaceBuilders is intended to reduce violence and other negative behaviors (drug, alcohol, and tobacco use) and increase academic achievement for each child, while creating a safe learning environment. PeaceBuilders is a community-based model that is launched in the schools.

Program Background

PeaceBuilders has been in use for over nine years at the elementary school level. PeaceBuilders also offers a fully tested and proven middle school program and a K–8 model. Currently being tested are high school and Pre-K (early childhood) programs. PeaceBuilders has been implemented in more than 1,500 schools.

Scope of Program

PeaceBuilders is a comprehensive approach to environmental climate shift. The major component of the program is building a schoolwide foundation. However, PeaceBuilders also includes some early and intensive interventions. In the PeaceBuilders program, adult role models reinforce and model prosocial conflict prevention skills. The program includes solution-focused tools (such as recipes for reducing TV watching, sibling fighting, and angry outbursts) and strategies to increase homework completion. PeaceBuilders increases time on task throughout the learning environment, helping to improve academic achievement.

Specific Problems/Risk Factors Targeted by PeaceBuilders

- ▲ Lack of school attachment
- ▲ Lack of commitment to school
- ▲ Poor peer relations and peer rejection
- ▲ Problematic or distressing classroom atmosphere
- ▲ Academic failure in elementary school
- ▲ Deficits in social and emotional competency

- ▲ Community norms favorable toward drug use, firearms, and crime
- ▲ Media modeling of violence
- ▲ Transition and mobility
- ▲ Low neighborhood attachment
- ▲ Family management problems
- ▲ Family conflict
- ▲ Favorable parental attitudes and involvement in the risk behavior
- ▲ Early, persistent antisocial behavior
- ▲ Alienation and rebelliousness
- ▲ Friends who engage in problem behavior
- ▲ Hostile school climate
- ▲ Early initiation of the problem
- ▲ Constitutional factors

Program Operations

PeaceBuilders' instructional component is intended to be infused throughout academic classes, special events, and other strategies implemented at school. Through these activities, children learn six principles: Praise People; Give Up Put-downs; Seek Wise People as Advisors and Friends; Notice Hurts We Have Caused; Right Wrongs, and Help Others.

Teachers infuse PeaceBuilders principles and activities into all instructional courses, including language arts, social studies, science, math, arts and drama, and physical education, through simple lessons that help students learn a common language, common strategies, and common cueing systems. Adults reinforce, model, and use the behaviors at school, in the home, and throughout the community.

Activities of the PeaceBuilders program are designed to improve daily interactions among students, teachers, administration, support staff, parents, and community members and to make a difference on a schoolwide level. The PeaceBuilders program is woven into the school's everyday routine to make it a way of life, not just a time-limited or subject-limited curriculum. PeaceBuilders activities take place not only in the classroom but in the broader school environment. PeaceBuilder announcements

are made, and the Peace Pledge is recited over the school's PA system and at assemblies. Special lunchroom activities and other enjoyable PeaceBuilder activities are held for the entire school.

PeaceBuilders has been seen to work cross-culturally through repetitive studies in various countries—Australia, Tasmania, Scotland, and the United States—in both urban and rural areas with children of all socioeconomic backgrounds and has yielded similar results.

Determining Your School's Readiness for PeaceBuilders

Principal and administrator commitment bolster program success.

Getting Training to Begin PeaceBuilders

Training is required before implementing PeaceBuilders in your school. There are two training models, On-site and Train-the-Trainers, for elementary and middle school levels. For the elementary (K–5/6) school, the entire staff participates in a four-hour on-site training session.

For middle school, a two- to three-hour leadership training session is held for the leaders of the school and a core group of teachers, followed by a four-hour implementation training session for all staff members on how to implement the program and a full-day site visit by a certified trainer who will support the school as it implements PeaceBuilders.

Train-the-Trainers, for both elementary and middle school, requires that up to four participants from a school go to a central location and learn how to train the rest of the school staff. At this session they learn the nuts and bolts of PeaceBuilders, how to train their colleagues, and how to support the ongoing effectiveness of the program.

Standard handouts are provided for on-site trainings. Teachers receive an implementation schedule, lesson plans, instructional materials, and information regarding techniques for bringing PeaceBuilders to the classroom. Training manuals and related materials are given to all Train-the-Trainers attendees.

Program Costs

Elementary School Model. Elementary school program materials cost $8 per student plus $100 per site. On-site training costs $1,750 plus travel and lodging expenses for the certified trainer. The Train-the-Trainers Model costs $1,200 for up to four participants. The school is responsible for the travel and lodging expenses of the attendees.

Ongoing technical support by telephone is free and unlimited. On-site technical support costs $80/hour plus travel and lodging expenses.

Sites are encouraged to budget a minimum of $200/year for incentive materials. Every third year the site license must be renewed; the renewal fee is $250. Sites might also consider budgeting $300–$1,000/year for program expansion modules, such as parenting, intensive, after-school, and law enforcement.

Middle School Model. For a middle school, program materials cost $2,500 for sites with up to 800 students and $3,000 for sites with more than 800 students. The on-site model costs $3,500 plus travel and lodging expenses for the certified trainers.

The Train-the-Trainers Model costs $2,000 for up to four participants, and the school is responsible for the travel and lodging expenses of the attendees.

Ongoing phone technical support is free and unlimited. On-site support is $80/hour plus travel and lodging expenses.

Sites are encouraged to budget a minimum of $200/year for incentive materials. Every third year the site license must be renewed; the renewal fee is $250. Sites might also consider budgeting $300–$1,000/year for program expansion modules.

For larger school districts, PeaceBuilders recommends that a staff member be hired or assigned at 0.5–1.0 FTE for coordination and support.

Other Resources Required to Implement PeaceBuilders

The PeaceBuilders program is taught in all classrooms and areas of the school through common language and constant visual and oral cueing. Actual implementation time for the program involves teaching 10 lessons at 15 minutes/lesson (minimum) at the outset, plus four hours of staff training. Counselors and other school staff, in addition to classroom teachers, will spend some time supporting the program.

PeaceBuilders is constantly adding modular items to keep the program on the cutting edge and to serve the ever-growing base of schools, families, and communities that are part of the PeaceBuilders family. For licensed sites, some of these items are available through a password-protected section of the PeaceBuilders Web site, www.peacebuilders.com, for free download. Other items, which are more complete programs, are available for small fees and are added to the Web site or available from PeaceBuilders. One such module is the PeaceBuilders Banish Bullying Guide, which takes the PeaceBuilders principles and new activities and merges them with new research on bullying to produce a guide for banishing bullying through the PeaceBuilders lens. This guide, like many of our other new modules and programs, is being created through effective collaborations with international experts in the field, in this case the Anti-Bullying Network of Edinburgh University, Scotland.

The materials to implement the program are supplied at training sessions. Other school resources can be used to make items such as posters and booklets to support and reinforce program principles. In multischool locations such as school districts, monthly meetings of school representatives can raise the level of enthusiasm and improve the success of the program.

Modifying PeaceBuilders for Your School/Classroom Context

With a few unchangeable items such as the principles at its core, the program can be adapted to work in different environments. Aspects of the

PeaceBuilders program can be used as foundations on which to build integrated approaches or specific modules for school improvement and safety. Schools have created everything from special events (such as PeaceBuilders Olympics) to television programs and even housing projects that use and teach the program's principles. Some schools have worked closely with law enforcement and juvenile justice systems to include police officers and probation officers in PeaceBuilders events. Others have sponsored after-school programs, outdoor events in parks and recreation areas, and special cultural events related to PeaceBuilders. Catholic schools have held PeaceBuilders masses, and other organizations have applied the PeaceBuilders principles to businesses, commercial enterprises, and civic organizations.

Components That Cannot Be Modified or Excluded From PeaceBuilders

The basic PeaceBuilders language, principles, and icons cannot be modified, and the cueing systems must be maintained.

Program Outcomes

PeaceBuilders helps schools to become peaceful learning environments, where children achieve their highest potential academically. A common language is developed, and students acquire a sense of belonging and safety along with personal resources for making wise decisions.

Research on PeaceBuilders has shown that the program can reduce vandalism, weapons violations, suspensions, tardiness, and absences. In some schools, implementing the program has correlated with an increase in volunteer hours donated to the school, an increase in monetary sponsorship of the school by the community, and increased parent satisfaction. The program has shown positive correlations with academic achievement, specifically an increase in reading achievement scores.

Examples of improved test scores include an urban elementary school in the Bronx that increased its students' Language Arts scores on the state standardized test from 16.1 percent pre-implementation to 30.0 percent after two years of implementation. The principal attributes the score increase to the change in climate caused by PeaceBuilders. In a rural, native population school in Australia, reading scores across all grade levels K–9 increased from 6 percent above chronological age to an average of 34 percent above chronological age. The only programmatic change in this school during the 18-month test period was PeaceBuilders. In the same school, math and science test scores increased an average of 10 to 15 percentage points in the same period. In suburban Lake Washington School District, during its four-year Byrne Violence Prevention Grant studying the implementation of PeaceBuilders, schools in the study saw an increase in scores as well.

Possible Negative Outcomes Related to the Implementation of PeaceBuilders

None known.

Resources

Christie, G. (2001). *Prevention in context: What works under what conditions—PeaceBuilders.* Presentation at the National Technical Assistance Meeting, U.S. Department of Education, Washington, DC.

Embry, D. D., Flannery, D. J., Vazsonyi, A. T., Powell, K. E., & Atha, H. (1996). PeaceBuilders: A theoretically driven, school-based model for early violence prevention. *American Journal of Preventive Medicine, 12* (5), 91–100.

Krug, E. G., Brener, N. D., Dahlberg, L. L., Ryan, G. W., & Powell, K. E. (1997). The impact of an elementary school-based violence prevention program on visits to the school nurse. *American Journal of Preventive Medicine, 13* (6), 459–463.

Levy, H. O. (2001). *2000–2001 Annual school report district 9 CES 132 district 9*. New York: New York City Schools.

Thornton, T. N., Craft, C., Dahlberg, L. L., Lynch, B. S., & Baer, K. (Eds.). (2000). *Best practices of youth violence prevention: A sourcebook for community action*. Atlanta, GA: U.S. Department of Health and Human Services, Centers for Disease Control and Prevention, National Center for Injury Prevention and Control.

Vosskuhler, M. & Issman, S. (2002). *Raising standardized test scores and the role of Peacebuilders: A school climate shift program*. Manuscript submitted for publication.

Peacemakers

Contact:
Jeremy Shapiro, Ph.D.

Position/Title:
Independent Consultant

Phone Number:
(216) 292-2710

Address:
2669 Belvoir Blvd.
Shaker Heights, OH 44122

E-mail:
jeremyshapiro@yahoo.com

Web Address:
http://www.applewoodcenters.org/

Purpose

The purpose of the Peacemakers program is to reduce physical violence and verbal aggression and to increase positive interpersonal behavior among young people.

Program Background

Peacemakers evolved between 1994 and its publication in 2003. The program has been formally evaluated in fourth through eighth grades. It has been provided to youth in ninth grade with excellent participant feedback, but no outcome study has been completed to date. Peacemakers has been implemented in ten school districts and in approximately 50 schools.

Scope of Program

Peacemakers is a universal schoolwide intervention that works with all students in a school. There is also a counseling component that can be used for intensive intervention with students referred for problems with aggression. The coordination between the prevention and remediation components of the program is a unique feature of Peacemakers.

Specific Problems/Risk Factors Targeted by Peacemakers

Peacemakers targets the psychosocial risk factors that research has implicated in the development of violent behavior, namely, proviolence values, unstable self-esteem, hostile attributional bias, emotional dysregulation and impulsivity, weak consequential thinking, negative peer pressure, and weak skills in the areas of problem solving, assertiveness, communication, conflict resolution, and walking away from fights.

Program Operations

Peacemakers has four basic components:

▲ A teacher-delivered curriculum that teaches nonviolent attitudes and trains students in conflict-related psychosocial skills

- ▲ A set of procedures for infusing Peacemakers principles and techniques into the everyday culture of the school

- ▲ More flexible, less formal applications of Peacemakers interventions to individual students referred to school counselors for problems with aggression

- ▲ An interactive multimedia learning activity on CD-ROM that resembles a game and teaches the same attitudes and skills as the curriculum

The CD-ROM, produced by EDR Corporation, is an optional part of the program.

Peacemakers is delivered primarily by classroom teachers and also by counselors and other school staff. The curriculum takes 12–15 hours of classroom time to deliver. Program materials include Leader's Guides, Counselor's Manuals, Student Handbooks, and a CD-ROM.

Determining Your School's Readiness for Peacemakers

n/a

Getting Training to Begin Peacemakers

Peacemakers training is strongly recommended. The six- to eight-hour session provides an overview of the research on youth violence and prevention, consisting primarily of

- ▲ an introduction to delivering the program to young people with an emphasis on core psychosocial skills;

- ▲ common sources of resistance to internalizing the program; and

- ▲ strategies for overcoming obstacles.

Peacemakers trains directly; it does not have a train-the-trainer program. The *Leader's Guide* and the *Counselor's Manual* (Shapiro, 2002) are training manuals with instructions for program implementation that are much more detailed and specific than is typical for prevention program manuals.

Program Costs

Peacemakers figures costs in an a la carte manner, as the sum of the costs of materials and services. Different program components are provided by different vendors, although the core materials are published by National Educational Service. Program components, vendors, and costs are as follows:

The *Leader's Guide* ($169) and *Student Handbook* ($9) are published by National Education Service: www.NESonline.com, 800-733-6786.

The *Counselor's Manual* ($55.00) and the *Coolien Challenge* CD-ROM ($89 each; $440 for a set of 15) can be purchased from Applewood Centers, Inc.: www.applewoodcenters.org, 216-696-5800.

Training and consultation (fees vary) are provided by the program author, Jeremy Shapiro, Ph.D.: Jeremyshapiro@yahoo.com, 216-292-2710.

Other Resources Required to Implement Peacemakers

The program does not require hiring any additional staff. It is designed to be integrated into the everyday operations of schools by existing staff.

Modifying Peacemakers for Your School/Classroom Context

The Peacemakers curriculum includes ample provision for adapting the program to particular needs and characteristics of schools, locations, and cultural contexts while maintaining fidelity to the principles and methods of the program.

Components That Cannot Be Modified or Excluded From Peacemakers

The principles on which the program is based may not be modified or changed.

Program Outcomes

According to research conducted in the Cleveland Public Schools and published in 2002 in *Psychology in the Schools* (Shapiro, Burgoon, Welker, & Clough, 2002), the Peacemakers intervention increased student knowledge of psychosocial skills and reduced verbal and physical aggression as measured by both student self-report and teacher-report instruments. Peacemakers produced a 41 percent decrease in aggression-related disciplinary incidents and a 67 percent reduction in suspensions for violent behavior.

Research has indicated no difference in effects for African American and white students, slightly greater effects for boys than girls, and a slightly greater effect for middle school students than for elementary school students. The magnitude of intervention effects has been shown to be consistent between regular classrooms and special education classrooms.

Possible Negative Outcomes Related to the Implementation of Peacemakers

None known.

References and Resources

Shapiro, J. P. (2002). *The Peacemakers Program: Counselor's manual*. Cleveland, OH: Applewood Centers.

Shapiro, J. P. (2002). *The Peacemaker's Program: Leader's guide*. Bloomington, IN: National Education Service.

Shapiro, J. P. (1999). The Peacemaker Program: Effective violence prevention for early adolescent youth. *Communique: Newsletter of the National Association of School Psychologists, 27,* 6–8.

Shapiro, J. P., Burgoon, J. D., Welker, C. J., & Clough, J. B. (2002). Evaluation of the Peacemakers Program: School-based violence prevention for students in grades four through eight. *Psychology in the Schools, 39* (1), 87–100.

Positive Behavioral Interventions and Supports (PBIS)

Contact:
Dr. George Sugai or Dr. Robert Horner

Position/Title:
Center Co-Directors

Phone Number:
(541) 346-2505

Address:
Center on Positive Behavioral Interventions and Supports
1761 Alder Street
1235 College of Education
University of Oregon
Eugene, OR 97403–1235

E-mail:
pbis@oregon.uoregon.edu

Web Address:
http://www.pbis.org/

Purpose

The goal of Positive Behavioral Interventions and Supports (PBIS) is to improve the effectiveness, efficiency, and relevance of academic and social learning opportunities for all students. PBIS employs a broad range of systemic (universal) and individualized strategies (early and intensive interventions). The PBIS approach emphasizes the use of data collection and analysis to inform all decision making. PBIS is not a single intervention program, but rather is first and foremost a data-based problem-solving process that uses functional behavioral assessment to design interventions (to reduce problem behavior and/or teach new skills) and supports (maintaining positive changes). PBIS emphasizes the application of nonpunishing behavioral systems to achieve socially important behavior change.

Program Background

PBIS is a general approach to preventing problem behavior, not a specific practice or curriculum. It was developed initially as an alternative to aversive interventions that were used with students with severe disabilities who engaged in extreme forms of self-injury and aggression. More recently, the approach has been applied successfully with a wide range of students and has been extended from an intervention approach for individual students to an intervention approach for entire schools. At the schoolwide level, attention is focused on creating and sustaining school environments that improve lifestyle (personal, health, social, family, work, recreation, etc.) for all children and youth by making problem behavior less effective, efficient, and relevant, and desired behavior more functional. In addition, the most recent elaboration of PBIS emphasizes the use of culturally appropriate interventions.

Scope of Program

PBIS can be used for individual children with chronic behavior difficulties and with entire schools or districts for students of all ages. The approach is widely applicable to people with disabilities who exhibit severe behavior, as well as those with mild to moderate behavioral challenges. Typical intervention agents in everyday settings can apply the approach. Its use is not restricted to professionals such as psychologists or researchers.

The approach can be used for (1) schoolwide discipline; (2) general classroom and behavior management; (3) specialized or targeted group-based interventions; and (4) specialized behavior intervention planning. Prevention-based interventions and processes are emphasized at all levels.

Specific Problems/Risk Factors Targeted by PBIS

The goals of PBIS are to eliminate problem behavior, to replace problem behavior with more appropriate behavior, and to increase a person's skills and opportunities for an enhanced quality of life. Problem behaviors (such as aggression, self-injury, tantrums, or property destruction) have long been barriers to successful education, socialization, employment, and community adaptation. PBIS involves applying behavioral principles within community norms to reduce problem behaviors and build appropriate behaviors that result in durable behavioral changes and an improved lifestyle.

Program Operations

The focus of PBIS operations is to help schools

▲ respond effectively, efficiently, and relevantly to a range of problem behaviors occurring in school;

▲ engage in team-based problem solving;

▲ adopt, fit, and sustain research-based behavioral practices; and

▲ give priority to a unified agenda of prevention.

PBIS interventions have common features that include data-based planning and decision making, focusing on the behavior of adults in school, and providing a continuum of behavior supports. PBIS emphasizes environmental redesign (changing aspects of the setting), curriculum redesign (teaching new skills), modification of behavior

(teaching and changing student and adult behavior), and removing rewards that maintain problem behaviors.

Schools that implement PBIS on a schoolwide basis clarify expectations for student behavior and give students reminders when needed; simplify the rules students are expected to follow; teach students appropriate, prosocial behaviors; and reward students when they have been "caught doing something good." Consequences of inappropriate behaviors are understood and are quickly acted upon when warranted. In PBIS schools, classroom and special settings within the schools (e.g., lunchroom or playground) all have consistent behavioral expectations and procedures for monitoring and enforcing rules. For students whose behavior needs are beyond those addressed in these rules, a behavior support team establishes individual action plans.

Following is the process for implementing PBIS:

▲ Establish a school leadership team that includes an administrator; grade-level representation; a family member; and support staff such as counselors, special educators, and paraprofessionals. The team secures schoolwide agreements regarding positive behavioral supports that include a common purpose and approach to discipline, a clear set of positive expectations for behavior, procedures for encouraging expected behavior and discouraging inappropriate behavior, and procedures for ongoing monitoring and evaluation.

▲ Implement effective classroom management that includes behavior management, effective teaching, and appropriate curricula.

▲ Implement appropriate supports outside the classroom setting (e.g., lunchrooms, hallways, playgrounds) that include teaching expectations and routines, active supervision, proactive use of reminders, and use of positive reinforcement.

▲ Implement individual support systems that emphasize behavioral competence and self-management.

- ▲ Use a wraparound process that includes clear and measurable outcomes, data-based monitoring, targeted social skills instruction, and individualized instructional and curricular accommodations.
- ▲ Arrange for high fidelity implementation through team-based leadership and implementation. Provide direct support for staff that includes systematic staff development, instructional scripts/prompts, and positive reinforcement.
- ▲ Provide formative, data-based monitoring.

Determining Your School's Readiness for PBIS

Improving student behavior must be one of the top school priorities. Active administrator support and full participation from all staff are required. When problem behavior is chronic and intense, comprehensive linkages with other human service agencies (e.g., juvenile justice and corrections, mental health, public health, child and family services) are required.

Getting Training to Begin PBIS

Many individuals and centers provide training and technical assistance on PBIS. One center, the Center on Positive Behavioral Interventions and Supports, has been funded by the Office of Special Education Programs to provide technical assistance information and training on schoolwide implementation of a full continuum of PBIS. The Center does not have a standard or single training manual. Instead, individual trainers provide training materials developed for individual training events. These materials are represented on the Center's Web site (www.pbis.org). Trainers and consultants associated with the Center provide training and staff development opportunities before and during implementation of schoolwide PBIS. Training and staff development are strongly recommended.

The Center advocates an implementation of the systems approach to schoolwide positive behavior support that is based on a two-year staff development schedule involving four main staff levels:

- ▲ Building-based implementation teams composed of administrators, teachers, specialists, family members, and so on, who lead the implementation of schoolwide action plans
- ▲ Coaches or facilitators who assist teams in the sustained implementation of the action plans
- ▲ Local and regional trainers who prepare new teams and provide training on PBIS
- ▲ Regional, district, and state coordinators who lead PBIS implementation activities and receive five to eight days of training over a one-year period.

Program Costs

- ▲ Substitute teacher/release time for five-to-eight staff development days per team member per year
- ▲ Photocopying of approximately 200 pages of training and reference materials per team member per year
- ▲ Schoolwide implementation requires one to two staff development days, supporting materials at approximately $50 per staff member, and one to two hours per month for implementation monitoring.

Other Resources Required to Implement PBIS

PBIS emphasizes the use of data collection and analysis to inform decisions. A data collection system should be established to determine the students' current levels of functioning, the impact of the interventions on problem behavior, and improvements in other lifestyle results (e.g., family, work, recreation).

Modifying PBIS for Your School/Classroom Context

PBIS is a general approach, not a specific practice or curriculum. It goes beyond one approach—reducing challenging or impeding behavior—to multiple approaches that include changing systems, altering environments, teaching skills and focusing on positive behavior, and developing interventions based on an analysis of why challenging behavior occurs.

Components That Cannot Be Modified or Excluded From PBIS

Without strong leadership from school administrators, program efforts often are inefficient, incomplete, and ineffective. PBIS requires a schoolwide buy-in, team-based decision making, the systemic collection and use of data to determine and monitor strategies, and the systemic use of positive behavioral approaches (plus avoidance of negative reactive approaches) to discipline.

Program Outcomes

See the PBIS Web site (www.pbis.org) for articles describing program outcomes.

Possible Negative Outcomes Related to Implementation of PBIS

None known.

Resources

Lewis, T. J. & Sugai, G. (1999). Effective behavior support: A systems approach to proactive school-wide management. *Focus on Exceptional Children, 31*(6), 1–24.

Lewis, T. J. & Sugai, G. (Eds.). (1999). *Safe schools: School-wide discipline practices.* Miniseries Monograph, International Conference, Council for Children with Behavior Disorders.

Sprague, J. R., Sugai, G., Horner, R. H., & Walker, H. M. (1999). Using office discipline referral data to evaluate school-wide discipline and violence prevention interventions. *Oregon School Studies Council Bulletin, 42*(2), 1–17.

Sugai, G. & Horner, R. H. (1999). Discipline and behavioral support: Preferred processes and practices. *Effective School Practices, 17*(4), 10–22.

Todd, A. W., Horner, R. H., Sugai, G., & Sprague, J. R. (1999). Effective behavior support: Strengthening school-wide systems through a team-based approach. *Effective School Practices, 17*(4), 23–27.

Primary Mental Health Project (Primary Project)

Contact:
Deborah Johnson

Position/Title:
Director of Community Services
National Director, Primary Project

Phone Number:
(716) 295–1000, ext. 224 or
(877) 888-7647 (toll free)

Address:
Children's Institute
274 N. Goodman, D103
Rochester, NY 14607

E-mail:
djohnson@childrensinstitute.net

Web Address:
http://www.childrensinstitute.net

Purpose

Primary Project, a school-based early detection and prevention program, seeks to enhance learning and adjustment skills and other school-related competencies and to reduce social, emotional, and school difficulties in preschool through primary grade children by providing timely and effective one-on-one help to children who are just beginning to show adjustment difficulties.

Program Background

Primary Project began in a single school in Rochester, NY in 1957. The program has since been clarified, refined, and expanded. Today, Primary Project is in more than 1,500 schools internationally, serving children in preschool through third grade. The program has been adapted to meet the specific needs and interests of local communities and has adopted other names, such as Primary Intervention Program, Primary School Adjustment Program, and Healthy Learners Initiative.

Scope of Program

Primary Project, an early intervention program for students at risk, addresses risk factors and builds on protective factors related to school outcomes. It seeks to change behaviors related to school adjustment, including behavioral control, assertiveness, peer social skills, and task orientation.

Specific Problems/Risk Factors Targeted by Primary Project

▲ Poor classroom adjustment
▲ Mildly aggressive behavior
▲ Withdrawn behavior
▲ Shy disposition
▲ Anxious behavior

Program Operations

All aspects of Primary Project support the development and nurturing of positive therapeutic relationships between the paraprofessional child associates and the children. The project includes the systematic screening of all children in the target grades, which serves to identify children who stand to gain significantly from Primary Project, including those who exhibit social withdrawal, peer rejection, mildly aggressive behavior, shyness, and social anxiety. Once the screening and selection of children is complete, child associates begin to interact regularly with the children on a one-to-one basis. Children are typically scheduled for one 30- to 40-minute session per week for one to two school semesters, depending on the child's needs and the program's goals for the child. Child associates meet with children in specially equipped playrooms that provide age-appropriate, culturally suitable activities. Expressive play is a primary activity of the child, and the playroom offers a safe, welcoming, and facilitative environment in which the child and the adult can interact.

The child associate is central to the Project's effectiveness, and his or her performance is supported and strengthened through ongoing training and supervision by professionally trained mental health personnel. A year-long training program covers topics regarding school environment, confidentiality, communication skills, effective limit-setting strategies with aggressive children, and cultural and ethnic/racial differences.

Determining Your School's Readiness for Primary Project

Some schools hold a half-day training session for primary grade teachers and principals before implementing the project. Communities that incorporate this component find that teachers and other staff who attend this session are more receptive. Staff "buy-in" facilitates successful implementation.

Getting Training to Begin Primary Project

Several books and journal articles are available to help readers understand the Primary Project. Its program development and evaluation are summarized in *School-Based Prevention for Children at Risk: The Primary Mental Health Project* (Cowen et al., 1996). A comprehensive source of information

about implementing and maintaining the program is the *Primary Project Program Development Manual* (Johnson, 2000).

Training opportunities are geared to the local community. It is strongly recommended that project staff participate in a three-day intensive institute (offered nationally), which gives an in-depth orientation to the project, and visit nationally certified programs. A two-day initial training on-site for project teams is also strongly recommended for teams of professionals and paraprofessionals. A certified trainer from the Children's Institute typically conducts the first two-day training. During later sessions, the community takes more responsibility for training as its sense of ownership of the local program increases. In addition to attending trainings and reviewing program materials, school staff can learn about the Primary Project through internships and direct consultations.

National Certification of the Primary Project is offered on the basis of site-by-site visits. Applications for certification can be submitted after the program has been in place for three years. Following a self-study and independent review, a site review is conducted and the site is recommended for certification.

Program Costs

The average annual cost of seeing a single Primary Project child can be less than $250/year. The costs per site vary, as do the funding sources.

Playroom supplies cost about $1,000 in the start-up year. The program development manual is $40; the supervision manual is $30. The initial two-day training for more than 12 people is $1,200 a day. Travel costs are additional. The three-day intensive training is $400 per person. Ongoing personal support and consultation is available. Rates vary.

Other Resources Required to Implement Primary Project

n/a

Components That Cannot Be Modified or Excluded From Primary Project

The program is targeted to preschool and elementary school students, typically through third grade. All children are systematically screened, and selection criteria are based on the risk factors listed above. Highly qualified child associates are recruited and/or trained in child development. The roles of the school mental health professionals are clear. Program evaluation must be ongoing.

Program Outcomes

Tests of Primary Project's effectiveness as a prevention program have utilized varying evaluation designs. The project has been shown to be effective across racial/ethnic and SES subgroups.

The major group for which the project is not appropriate comprises children who have been diagnosed with a severe emotional disturbance or conduct/behavior disorder.

The project has not been proven to be effective for children served across multiple years or children in higher grades (fourth grade and up).

Possible Negative Outcomes Related to the Implementation of Primary Project

n/a

References

Cowen, E. L., Hightower, A. D., Pedro-Carroll, J. L., Work, W. C., Wyman, P. A., & Haffey, W. G. (1996). *School-based prevention for children at risk: The Primary Mental Health Project*. Washington, DC: American Psychological Association.

Johnson, D. B. (2002). *Primary Project program manual*. Rochester, NY: Children's Institute.

Project ALERT

Contact:
G. Bridget Ryan

Position/Title:
Executive Director,
BEST Foundation for a Drug-Free Tomorrow

Phone Number:
(800) 253–7810

Address:
725 S. Figueroa St., Suite 1615
Los Angeles, CA 90017

E-mail:
info@projectalert.best.org

Web Address:
http://www.projectalert.best.org

Purpose

Project ALERT focuses on alcohol, marijuana, cigarettes, and inhalants and is designed to prevent middle school youth from beginning to use drugs, to prevent those who have experimented from becoming regular users, and to prevent or curb risk factors demonstrated to predict drug use.

Program Background

Project ALERT was developed by RAND in the 1980s with funding from the Conrad N. Hilton Foundation. One of the few school-based prevention programs to be scientifically tested, it was implemented and evaluated in 30 highly diverse middle schools in California and Oregon between 1984 and 1990. Since 1991, it has been disseminated nationally. More than 15,000 trained teachers actively use Project ALERT in more than 3,500 school districts nationwide.

Scope of Program

The program is intended for all students in grades six through eight.

Specific Problems/Risk Factors Targeted by Project ALERT

Individual Domain
- ▲ Youth already using alcohol, tobacco, or other drugs
- ▲ Intention to use drugs in the future
- ▲ Belief that drug use is not harmful
- ▲ Inadequate resistance skills

Family Domain
- ▲ Parental drug use
- ▲ Lack of clear norms against use
- ▲ Poor communication

School Domain
- ▲ High levels of drug use
- ▲ Low norms against use

Peer Domain

▲ Peer drug use

▲ Peer approval of drug use

Program Operations

Project ALERT is delivered by the students' own classroom teachers, who guide and support them as they develop resistance skills and confidence. Project ALERT consists of 11 weekly lessons in sixth or seventh grade and three booster lessons 12 months later. The effect of the curriculum is cumulative. Lessons progress from motivating nonuse (Lessons 1–3), learning to identify and resist pressures to use drugs (Lessons 4–6), providing multiple opportunities to practice resistance skills (Lessons 7 and 9), and identifying the benefits of resistance (Lesson 11), to following up with reinforcement (Booster Lessons 1–3). Lessons 8 and 11, which focus on inhalants and smoking cessation, are introduced after the initial motivation and skill sequence.

Motivating Nonuse. The curriculum begins by setting the stage. The teacher produces Project ALERT and tells the students that during the course of the program, they will discuss why people do and do not use drugs, learn how to identify and resist prodrug arguments, and learn how to resist when they feel pressured to try alcohol, cigarettes, marijuana, or other substances.

Identifying Prodrug Pressures. Project ALERT focuses on reducing three key barriers to drug resistance: (1) the inability to identify internal and external pressures to use; (2) the belief that use is widespread; and (3) inadequate skills in countering prodrug arguments. This process consists of learning to identify where pressure comes from, getting an accurate picture of drug use, and learning to recognize techniques used by advertisers.

Learning Resistance Skills. The curriculum acknowledges that it can be difficult to say no to direct offers of alcohol and other drugs and to the more indirect pressures that come from within ourselves. Project ALERT stresses that there are several different ways to say no. If students find one way uncomfortable, they can choose another.

Reinforcing the Curriculum. At the end of the core program, students write down "Why I have chosen a healthy lifestyle free from drugs" on Project ALERT certificates. The teacher collects the certificates, reads volunteered responses, and returns them in a "graduation exercise." These statements of commitment help students express their feelings through writing and increase behavior change.

Booster Lessons. Project ALERT's Booster Curriculum is designed to extend the positive effects of the core curriculum. Cognitive research shows that booster lessons are critical for maintaining early prevention gains. The three Booster Lessons build on the core curriculum and on each other. Each lesson stresses motivating resistance to drugs, practicing resisting internal and external pressures to use drugs, and recognizing the benefits of resisting drugs.

Determining Your School's Readiness for Project ALERT

n/a

Getting Training to Begin Project ALERT

Teachers receive 14 detailed lesson plans and have access to a toll-free technical assistance phone line. A training manual has been developed for those trainers who conduct the teacher training workshops. All classroom teachers participate in a required one-day training workshop before implementing Project ALERT. The training workshop has four objectives:

▲ To help educators fully understand the content, process, and goals of Project ALERT

▲ To demonstrate key activities in the curriculum

▲ To motivate the implementation of Project ALERT with fidelity

▲ To increase confidence in the ability to teach the curriculum

The workshop is highly interactive, immersing teachers in a variety of classroom situations. Training is reinforced after the workshop by means of two "take home" demonstration videos that model how the curriculum, when taught with fidelity, plays out in the classroom, showing typical student responses.

Project ALERT has dozens of trainers located around the country. These trainers are periodically monitored and a high level of quality control is maintained. There is no train-the-trainer program.

Program Costs

For $125 per teacher, each teacher receives the complete training and materials package. This includes a one-day training workshop, a complete teacher's manual with 14 detailed lesson plans, two teacher demonstration videos, eight classroom videos and 12 classroom posters, an optional teen leader component, and periodic video and print curriculum updates at no charge. There are no ongoing costs for student materials except for a few reproducible handouts.

Ongoing support for trained Project ALERT teachers is provided through a free technical assistance newsletter, produced three times a year. A toll-free teacher assistance phone line is available to provide answers to questions from the field. Refresher workshops are available for trained teachers.

Other Resources Required to Implement Project ALERT

Eleven classroom periods of 45 minutes or more are required during the first year of the program. Three periods of 45 minutes or more are required during the booster year. The classroom should be equipped with a TV and VCR, chalkboard, newsprint, felt-tip markers, and masking tape. An overhead projector and screen are optional. The ability to photocopy student handouts is necessary. Teachers need to participate in a one-day training workshop where they receive the required lesson plans, videos, and

posters. Because Project ALERT spans two grade levels, it is important to train teachers who will deliver the booster lessons as well as teachers who will deliver the core lessons. Workshops are held at the district level when 20 or more teachers are interested in training. Regional workshops are available to accommodate districts training fewer teachers.

Modifying Project ALERT for Your School/Classroom Context

Project ALERT has been adapted and field tested over 13 years from a curriculum developed and longitudinally researched by RAND, the nation's leading think tank on drug policy. RAND initially tested Project ALERT with more than 7,000 seventh and eighth graders at 30 schools in California and Oregon. The scientifically rigorous study was designed to find out whether Project ALERT would work across a wide variety of schools and communities. In selecting a sample and a control group for the longitudinal study, RAND chose a diverse set of school districts. They specifically included districts that encompassed urban, suburban, and rural communities, as well as different population profiles, to give the curriculum the broadest possible test.

One of the things RAND learned in this variety of environments was the importance of continually adapting the curriculum to reflect the background and experiences of the children in each classroom and the changes in the broader social and cultural climate that surrounds them. Much of this adaptation is built right into the curriculum. Because the curriculum is so participatory, asking students questions and involving them in group activities and skits, it varies subtly from one classroom to another.

One group of students may believe myths about drugs that need correcting; another group may already have a pretty accurate picture. Teachers are constantly kept on their toes figuring out how to respond to what different students bring into the classroom. And because what students bring into the classroom changes over time, as well as from group to group, that adaptation goes on year in and year out in the hands of adept, culturally and ethnically diverse teachers across the communities of America. RAND and the BEST Foundation have revised and updated the curriculum, on the basis of input from the field, right from the beginning. During the experimental period, RAND met with teachers after every lesson, asking for suggestions about what worked and what didn't, how to improve the curriculum, and how to handle specific problems.

Components That Cannot Be Modified or Excluded From Project ALERT

The curriculum is designed to be taught as written. Successful replication of the Project ALERT model involves delivering all 14 lessons in sequence over a two-year period; setting proximal goals; teaching in ways that promote self-efficacy, active student involvement, and practice; use of modeling, reinforcement, validation, respect, and enthusiasm as teaching strategies; and providing home learning opportunities.

Program Outcomes

Outcome data involve two types of implementation: teen-led training and adult-led training. Project ALERT's most consistent results were for marijuana. The program not only curbed initiation, it also held down frequent (monthly) use among students who had already started smoking cigarettes. These effects appeared nine months after exposure to the seventh grade curriculum and were maintained by the booster lessons (15 months after baseline).

The program was most effective for students who had never smoked or used marijuana. Fifteen months after baseline, marijuana initiation rates among baseline nonusers were 30 percent lower for students who had gone through Project ALERT than for those who had not. Project ALERT also curbed frequent marijuana use in the high-risk groups, but the effects were smaller and less often statistically significant.

For cigarettes, Project ALERT's best results were for the high-risk baseline experimenters, who exhibited significant reductions in current, monthly, and even more frequent smoking levels. Current use rates declined by 25 percent in the adult teacher schools; similar reductions were found for monthly use in the teen leader schools. And, although Project ALERT had little effect on baseline nonsmokers, it stimulated some smokers to quit. These favorable results typically showed up 15 months after baseline.

Project ALERT also reduced levels of cigarette use that signal serious use, especially for baseline experimenters in the teen-leader schools. After delivery of the eighth-grade Booster Lessons, both weekly and daily smoking among baseline experimenters declined by 50 percent in these schools; weekly smoking declined by one-third in the adult-only schools. However, students who were confirmed smokers at baseline reacted negatively to the program.

Shortly after delivery of the seventh grade curriculum, Project ALERT produced modest reductions in drinking for nonusers, experimenters, and users. After the students entered the eighth grade, however, most of these early gains disappeared. Half of the control students with no prior drinking experience at baseline initiated alcohol use within 12 months. Participation in the seventh grade Project ALERT curriculum did not slow this acceleration for students in the treatment schools. Nor did the booster curriculum revive the programs' earlier success.

Project ALERT dampened prodrug beliefs—perceived consequences, normative beliefs, belief in ability to resist, and expectations of future use. Fifteen months after baseline, the reductions in the proportion of treatment students holding prodrug beliefs typically ranged between 15 and 40 percent. Program results for expectations of future use were much stronger for marijuana than for the other substances. In the normative category the program significantly reduced the treatment students' estimates of how many students used each target drug and helped those in the teen-leader schools believe that resisting cigarettes and marijuana can bring greater respect from one's friends.

By the ninth grade, program effects on behavior had eroded. But program effects on cognitive risk factors lasted considerably longer. As late as tenth grade, Project ALERT students in the teen-leader schools were more likely to believe that drug use would have negative personal consequences and that resistance would earn respect from friends. These effects also showed up in the adult-only schools but were marginally significant. Students in the teen-leader schools also were more likely to provide lower estimates of alcohol, cigarette, and marijuana use among their peers and to believe their friends disapproved of drug use. At 12th grade, students taught by adults plus teen leaders were more likely to provide lower estimates of peer drug use and to believe that drug use produces dependency.

Possible Negative Outcomes Related to the Implementation of Project ALERT

None known.

Resources

Bell, R. M., Ellickson, P. L., & Harrison, E. R. (1993). Do drug prevention effects persist into high school? How Project ALERT did with ninth graders. *Prevention Medicine, 22,* 463–483 [also RAND RP–237].

Ellickson, P. L. & Bell, R. M. (1990). Drug prevention in junior high: A multi-site longitudinal test. *Science, 247,* 1299–1305 [also RAND, R-3919–CHF, March 1990].

Ellickson, P. L., Bell, R. M., & Harrison, E. R. (1993). Changing adolescent propensities to use drugs: Results from Project ALERT. *Health Education Quarterly, 20*(2), 227–242.

Ellickson, P. L., Bell, R. M., Thomas, M. A., Robyn, A. E., & Zellman, G. L. (1988). *Designing and implementing Project ALERT: A smoking and drug prevention experiment.* (R-3754 CHF). Santa Monica, CA: RAND.

U.S. Department of Health and Human Services, Substance Abuse and Mental Health Services Administration, Center for Substance Abuse Prevention. (n.d.). *SAMHSA model programs.* Rockville, MD: Author. Available: http://modelprograms.samhsa.gov

Project Northland

Contact:
Ann Standing

Position/Title:
National Prevention and Education Sales Manager

Phone Number:
(651) 213-4030 or (800) 328-9000, ext. 4030

Address:
Box 176
15251 Pleasant Valley Road
Center City, MN 55012–0176

E-mail:
astanding@hazelden.org

Web Address:
http://www.hazelden.org/bookplace

Purpose

Northland is a research-based, multilevel, multi-year alcohol use prevention program for youth. Program goals are to delay the age when young people begin drinking, reduce alcohol use among young people who have already tried drinking, and limit the number of alcohol-related problems among young people.

Program Background

The program has been in use since 1991, when school districts were randomly assigned as intervention or control districts before any programs had begun. The first phase of Northland took place in the intervention schools and communities from 1991 to 1994. Northland programs provide state-of-the-art alcohol use prevention materials for sixth, seventh, and eighth grade students. This is the largest randomized community trial ever conducted, involving 24 school districts and 28 adjoining communities in northeastern Minnesota.

Scope of Program

The intervention consists of social-behavioral curricula in schools, peer leadership, parental involvement, parental education, and community-wide task force activities. Project Northland spans three years from sixth grade through eighth grade.

Specific Problems/Risk Factors Targeted by Project Northland

The program targets alcohol use among adolescents.

Program Operations

Northland invites participation and experiential learning at home and in peer-led classroom activities. It consists of classroom instruction, peer leaders, parent involvement, and parent education, as well as community-wide activities. The prevention curriculum is composed of ATOD instruction, violence prevention, conflict resolution, job skills training, social competency instruction, leadership skills training, and decision-making skills training. The educational enhancement activities consist of tutoring and study skills. The family-focused interventions consist of family/parenting skills training, services to improve family management practices, and family involvement in school activities.

Northland combines both individual behavior change (demand) and environmental change (supply) strategies in alcohol use prevention.

The components of the program include the *Slick Tracy Home Team Program*, a six-week classroom and home-based program for sixth-grade students and their parents, and *Amazing Alternatives!* for seventh graders, some of whom serve as peer facilitators who lead group discussions, class games, and role playing. *Powerlines* is an eight-session, 45-minutes-per-session, peer-led classroom-based curriculum that introduces students to "power" groups in the community that influence adolescent alcohol use and availability.

Project Northland is a multilevel program that involves teachers, students, parents, and the community. The role of the teacher is critical. The materials are designed to permit students and peer-leader directed activities where possible, but the teacher must ensure that the lesson plans are followed as presented. Teacher training is strongly recommended to maintain fidelity of implementation.

The efficacy of Project Northland is strongly linked to the peer leadership model. Same-age peers are among the most credible sources of social information concerning alcohol use. Peer-chosen students lead 70 percent of the small-group activities. Peer leaders are trained, and the role of the peer leader as team facilitator and reporter contributes to a positive self-image.

Getting Training to Begin Project Northland

All components of the curriculum and teacher training are available through Hazelden, a publisher of prevention resources that offers professional training in alcohol and drug prevention.

Program Costs

The components of the program include the *Slick Tracy, Amazing Alternatives!*, and *Powerlines* curricula for sixth-, seventh-, and eight-graders, respectively. Another component is Supercharged!, which features insights and practical techniques for implementing the program's parent and community component. The cost is $229.95 for each grade level or $755.00 for the entire collection including the *SuperCharged!* community component; $549.00 for the grades 6–8 collection only. The purchase of an entire collection includes one free seat at a registration training event.

The Project Northland toolbox also includes the *StudentView* survey (65¢ per copy) and a video for students called *Everyone's NOT Doing It: An Alcohol Prevention Video* ($225.00).

Other Resources Required to Implement Project Northland

n/a

Modifying Project Northland for Your School/Classroom Context

Project Northland is easily replicated in many settings, including classrooms, after-school programs, and community prevention programs.

Components That Cannot Be Modified or Excluded From Project Northland

Replication results may differ from the original research study if the program is not implemented in the same way as the original study.

Program Outcomes

Intended outcomes are to delay the age when young people begin drinking, to reduce alcohol use among young people who have already tried drinking, and to limit the number of alcohol-related problems of young people.

After three years (1991–1994) of Northland activities, students involved with the project from the sixth, seventh, and eighth grades showed a monthly drinking rate 20 percent lower than students from control communities; weekly drinking was 30 percent lower. Students in the intervention group who were never-drinkers at the beginning of the sixth grade not only drank significantly less than students in the control group, they also smoked fewer cigarettes and used less marijuana at the end of the eighth grade; cigarette smoking was 37 percent lower and marijuana use was 50 percent lower.

Project Northland was effective in changing peer influence to use alcohol, normative expectations about how many young people drink, parent-child communication about the consequences of alcohol use, and the importance of reasons for not using alcohol.

The program was less effective in changing perceptions of access to alcohol and actual access to alcohol, a central focus for the second phase of Northland.

Possible Negative Outcomes Related to the Implementation of Project Northland

None known.

Resources

Komro, K. A., Perry, C. L., Murray, D. M., Veblen-Mortenson, S., Williams, C. L., & Anstine, P. S. (1996). Peer-planned social activities for preventing alcohol use among young adolescents. *Journal of School Health*, *66*(9), 328–334.

Komro, K. A., Perry, C. L., Veblen-Mortenson, S., & Williams, C. L. (1994). Peer participation in Project Northland: A community-wide alcohol use prevention project. *Journal of School Health*, *64*(8), 318–322.

Perry, C. L., Williams, C. L., Komro, K. A., Veblen-Mortenson, S., Stigler, M. H., Munson, K. A., Farbakhsh, K., Jones, R. M., & Forster, J. L. (2002). Project Northland: Long-term outcomes of community action to reduce adolescent alcohol use. *Health Education Research*, *17*(1), 117–132.

Perry, C. L., Williams, C. L., Veblen-Mortenson, S., Toomey, T. L., Komro, K. A., Anstine, P. S., McGovern, P. G., Finnegan, J. R., Forster, J. L,. Wagenaar, A. C., & Wolfson, M. (1996). Project Northland: Outcomes of community-wide alcohol use prevention program during early adolescence. *American Journal of Public Health*, *86*(7), 956–965.

U.S. Department of Health and Human Services, Substance Abuse and Mental Health Services Administration, Center for Substance Abuse Prevention. (n.d.). *SAMHSA model programs*. Rockville, MD: Author. Available: http://modelprograms.samhsa.gov

Williams, C. L., Perry, C. L., Farbakhsh, K., & Veblen-Mortenson, S. (1999). Project Northland: Comprehensive alcohol use prevention for young adolescents, their parents, schools, peers, and communities. *Journal of Studies on Alcohol*, Supplement 13, 112–124.

Project STAR: Students Taught Awareness and Resistance (Midwestern Prevention Project)

Contact:
Karen Bernstein

Position/Title:
Project Manager

Phone Number:
(626) 457-6687

Address:
University of Southern California
Institution for Prevention Research
1000 S. Fremont Ave., Unit #8
Alhambra, CA 91803

E-mail:
karenber@usc.edu

Web Address:
http://www.projectstar.info

Purpose

Project STAR, also known as the Midwestern Prevention Project (MPP), is a comprehensive community-based, multifaceted program for adolescent drug abuse prevention. Project STAR involves an extended period of programming. Although initiated in a school setting, it goes beyond the school into the family and the community.

Program Background

STAR is a research-based project developed by USC's Institute for Disease Prevention and Health Promotion Research. Project STAR was developed specifically to focus on the prevention of drug abuse among youth.

Scope of Program

Project STAR is a universal, schoolwide program that bridges the transition from early and middle adolescence through late adolescence. Since early adolescence is the first risk period for gateway drug use (i.e., alcohol, cigarettes, and marijuana), programming is initiated with whole populations of middle school students in the sixth and seventh grades.

Specific Problems/Risk Factors Targeted by Project STAR

The issues targeted are peer use of drugs and peer approval of drugs and drug use.

Program Operations

Project STAR strives to help youth recognize the tremendous social pressures to use drugs and provides training skills in how to avoid drug use and drug use situations. These skills are initially learned in the school program and then reinforced through parents, media, and community organizations.

The school is the central program channel. STAR is initiated in the transition year to middle school or junior high (either sixth or seventh grade, depending on the local school district), delivered by trained teachers, and facilitated by peer leaders. The program contains 10–13 sessions focused on increasing skills to resist and counteract pressures to use drugs. The second year includes a five-session booster program to reinforce the previous year's message. Active social learning techniques (e.g., modeling, role playing, and discussion, with student peer leaders assisting teachers) are used in the school program, along with homework assignments designed to involve family members. The parental program involves a parent-principal committee that meets to review school drug policy, and parent-child communications training.

The classroom atmosphere must facilitate students' active involvement. Students are asked to share information about themselves and to practice ways of interacting with others. A classroom teacher encourages students to share feelings and experiences and to voice any questions they may have. It is important to create an emotionally safe environment and support high degrees of student involvement. Peer leaders can be helpful in creating such an environment.

Getting Training to Begin Project STAR

Training is required to implement Project STAR, but the project is not yet commercially available. Program developers are currently working with a small number of communities to pilot a plan for program dissemination. This information is expected to be available by 2004.

Program Costs

The total cost over a three-year period (including training and materials for teachers, parents, and community leaders) is approximately $200,000. Costs are based on up to 20 teachers trained as a group for the school program, 20 parent-group members trained as a group for the parent program, three or four principals, four student peer leaders, 12 parents, and 1,000 middle school students.

Other Resources Required to Implement Project STAR

n/a

Modifying Project STAR for Your School/Classroom Context

The Project STAR curriculum contains 15 sessions. Session A deals with identifying students as peer leaders. Session B details how the peer leaders are trained for their roles in the classroom. These sessions need to be completed before the actual program begins. Sessions 1–10 present the core drug prevention program, and Sessions 11–13 are the related sessions on violence prevention. If there are time constraints that prevent a group from completing all 15 sessions, the Project STAR staff is available for consultation and guidance on how to proceed.

Components That Cannot Be Modified or Excluded From Project STAR

Sessions 11–13 of the curriculum are intended to follow Sessions 1–10. They are not designed to be used as stand-alone violence prevention programs.

Program Outcomes

Evaluations of Project STAR have demonstrated for program youth, compared with control youth,

- ▲ reductions of up to 40 percent in marijuana use and smaller reductions in alcohol use maintained through grade 12;

- ▲ effects on daily smoking, heavy marijuana use, and some hard drug use shown through early adulthood (age 23);

- ▲ increased parent-child communications about drug use; and

- ▲ facilitated development of prevention programs, activities, and services among community leaders.

Possible Negative Outcomes Related to the Implementation of Project STAR

None known.

Resources

MacKinnon, D. P., Johnson, C. A., Pentz, M. A., Dwyer, J. H., Hansen, W. B., Flay, B. R., & Wang, E. Y. (1991). Mediating mechanisms in a school-based drug prevention program: First-year effects of the Midwestern Prevention Project. *Health Psychology, 10*(3), 164–172.

Pentz, M. A., Dwyer, J. H., & MacKinnon, D. P. (1989). A multicommunity trial for primary prevention of adolescent drug abuse. *Journal of the American Medical Association, 261*(22), 3259–3266.

Pentz, M. A., Mackinnon, D. P., Dwyer, J. H., Wang, E. Y. I., Hansen, W. B., Flay, B. R. et al. (1989). Longitudinal effects of the Midwestern prevention project on regular and experimental smoking in adolescents. *Preventive Medicine, 18,* 304–321.

Pentz, M. A., MacKinnon, D. P., Flay, B. R., Hansen, W. B., Johnson, C. A., & Dwyer, J. H. (1989). Primary prevention of chronic diseases in adolescence: Effects of the Midwestern Prevention Project on tobacco use. *American Journal of Epidemiology, 130*(4), 713–724.

Pentz, M. A., Mihalic, S. F., & Grotpeter, J. K. (1998). *Blueprints for violence prevention, book one: The Midwestern Prevention Project.* Boulder, CO: Center for the Study and Prevention of Violence.

Promoting Alternative Thinking Strategies (PATHS)

Contact:
Carol A. Kusché, Ph.D.
Mark T. Greenberg, Ph.D.

Position/Title:
Co-Directors, PATHS Training, LLC
Licensed Clinical Psychologist and
Psychoanalyst

Phone Number:
(206) 323-6688

Address:
927 10th Avenue East
Seattle, WA 98102

E-mail:
ckusche@attglobal.net

Web Addresses:

http://www.preventionscience.com/PATHS/
PATHS.html

http://www.prevention.psu.edu/PATHS/

http://www.colorado.edu/cspv/blueprints/
model/programs/PATHS.html

Purpose

PATHS is a comprehensive curriculum designed to be used by classroom teachers with elementary school–aged students for instruction in social and emotional literacy. PATHS promotes the internalization of prosocial values and reduces aggression, behavior problems, and emotional distress in children while enhancing the educational process by cultivating a caring, respectful classroom environment.

Program Background

PATHS has been in use for almost 20 years; the current version of the curriculum was published in 1994. PATHS is designed to be used throughout elementary school (grades K to 5 or 6, depending on the school). PATHS has been implemented in more than 1,000 schools in the United States, Canada, and New Zealand and in translated versions in Holland, France, and other countries. A Spanish version is available.

Scope of Program

PATHS has been shown to be beneficial in building a schoolwide foundation (to promote emotional literacy, mental and emotional wellness, a caring school environment, adaptive social problem-solving skills, positive discipline, etc.) and as an early intervention for students at risk.

Specific Problems/Risk Factors Targeted by PATHS

▲ Impulsiveness or poor self-control

▲ Deficits in social and emotional competency

▲ Early and/or persistent antisocial or aggressive behavior

▲ Disregard for societal rules and norms and rebelliousness

▲ Affective disorders (e.g., depression and anxiety)

▲ Deficits in social problem-solving, planning, and critical thinking skills

- ▲ Poor peer relations and peer rejection
- ▲ Lack of attachment or commitment to school
- ▲ Problematic or distressing classroom atmosphere.

Program Operations

PATHS is designed to be taught by the classroom teacher three times per week or more for at least 20 minutes per session. The curriculum contains more than 130 lessons with detailed scripts as well as other materials needed to teach the lessons. Descriptions for generalization strategies to use throughout the day and ways to integrate PATHS with academic curricula are also included, along with material to send home to parents. It is recommended that auxiliary staff be included as much as possible, and school counselors can be incorporated as appropriate.

The PATHS lessons focus on self-control, emotional awareness, understanding, regulation, empathy, respect for self and others, self-esteem, social problem-solving and critical thinking skills, improved peer relations, positive values, and the development of positive attitudes toward school, community, and life. One of the overarching goals of PATHS is to promote the optimum development of productive, creative, competent, well-balanced children through the dynamic integration of emotion, cognition, language, and behavior.

Different components are emphasized at various grade levels as appropriate to developmental growth. Thus, the components of grade K emphasize such things as motor control over behaviors, giving compliments, respect for self and others, and beginning emotional literacy. When the children move to first grade, they are ready for intermediate emotional literacy, self-control through use of cognition, manners, beginning group problem solving, beginning friendship skills, and so on. By the end of elementary school, they will be solving complex social problems (using an 11-step problem-solving model), discussing problem prevention (including alcohol and drug prevention), thinking about moral issues (e.g., discussing fairness vs. unfairness), and

learning advanced emotional literacy (e.g., cues we use to understand emotions in self and others).

Determining Your School's Readiness for PATHS

Years of experience have shown that strong principal and administrative support is crucial for effective implementation of PATHS. Effectiveness is also enhanced when teachers are positive participants. Parent support for the curriculum goals is beneficial. If there is little interest or support from school administrators, the school district is probably not ready to implement PATHS.

Getting Training to Begin PATHS

Training for PATHS is optional but is strongly recommended. The training is comprehensive and covers many different areas, such as the theories utilized in designing PATHS (including brain development), content areas, process issues, materials, research findings, and parent and family issues. On-site PATHS training workshops are available for up to 30 participants per workshop through PATHS Training LLC. Workshops generally run for two days, either consecutively or with time between days as desired. On-site or phone consultation and follow-up are also available. Continuing education units can be obtained for the workshops where state requirements permit and arrangements are made in advance.

PATHS also offers on-site workshops to train individuals (e.g., school counselors, liaisons, teachers) who then train others in their systems (e.g., teachers at schools in their areas). This train-the-trainer model is particularly effective when the original trainers are available to encourage and supervise implementation.

A training manual is included with the PATHS curriculum. The entire curriculum for grades K–6 consists of a *Teacher's Instructional Manual*, six volumes of detailed lessons, pictures, photographs, posters, *Feeling Faces*, and additional materials. Evaluation (research) materials, *Blueprints for Violence Prevention* (Greenberg, Kusché, & Mihalic,

1998), and a research book of the original PATHS Project (Greenberg & Kusché, 1994) are also available.

Program Costs

The cost of a training workshop for up to 30 people is $3,000 for two days, plus the cost of transportation for the trainer to and from the workshop city, hotel stay, and $30 per diem. Additional costs for the school might include costs for the workshop site, payment to teachers and auxiliary staff who attend (e.g., inservice pay), continuing education credits (if paid for by the school), and a snack or lunch for participants (if provided).

The complete PATHS curriculum (with Turtle) costs $640. The curriculum without Turtle is $550 and the Turtle Unit by itself is $145. Individual volumes can be purchased for $80 each, and extra posters, charts, puppets, and so on are also available on a unit price basis. All these materials can be ordered from the publisher. *Feeling Faces* can be purchased at $6 per set or can be made at cost (templates and permission are provided).

Ongoing support and consultation are available from PATHS Training at $50 per hour by phone, or on-site visits can be arranged for $1,500 per day plus transportation and accommodations if needed. These items are all optional.

The amount of per-pupil and/or per-staff cost varies greatly, depending on the year of implementation and on the way in which the school wants to implement PATHS. For example, the training workshop obviously adds a substantial cost for the first year, but it may not be required again if there is low to moderate staff turnover. Similarly, the purchase of the curriculum is a one-time investment because it can be used again each year. Costs for consumable products, such as *Feeling Faces*, are incurred annually. A school counselor or facilitator can be used or hired to supervise or support PATHS implementation, but this is optional.

Other Resources Required to Implement PATHS

Teachers must read and mentally prepare for each lesson as they would with any new curriculum. This is easier each time PATHS is taught, but in the beginning, preparation can require substantial time because teachers have had little or no training in emotional-social learning. Materials are included in the curriculum package (pictures, photographs, posters, stories, etc.), so costs are not incurred for teaching materials. An exception is *Feeling Faces*, which can be ordered from the publisher, but most teachers have them made and cut at a copy shop to reduce costs, using the templates included in the curriculum kit. Space requirements include classroom space for displaying a Feelings Chart, several PATHS posters, and each child's *Feeling Faces* (usually on desks or in individual cubby space).

Modifying PATHS for Your School/ Classroom Context

PATHS is designed to be flexible. Most lessons are designed with optional break points, so that one lesson can be done in one to six or more sessions, depending on the developmental needs of the students in a particular class. After the basic PATHS foundation has been taught, teachers are encouraged to select lessons and units that best fit the current needs of their students rather than teaching lessons in any set order (e.g., if teasing is a current problem, teachers can pull the teasing subunit out of the supplementary volume and teach it right away). PATHS can be easily integrated with existing school practices and can be adjusted to meet the varying needs of different schools, districts, and communities.

Scripts are provided for each PATHS lesson to furnish information and to assist teachers in presenting concepts. Teachers are encouraged to elaborate on and paraphrase ideas contained in these scripts, so that they are delivered in a manner that best suits their students and their own teaching style. As they adapt PATHS for their own classrooms, teachers can select examples and problems (solved during real-life problem-solving lessons) that are relevant to their students' lives and needs.

Components That Cannot Be Modified or Excluded From PATHS

A core set of lessons in PATHS serves as the foundation on which all other lessons build; the developers believe that these are necessary for the program to be effective. These core lessons include PATHS Kid for Today (ongoing self-esteem and respect for others), basic Feeling Lessons (anger management and self-control), and Informal Group Problem Solving.

It is important to note that children in grades 3, 4, and 5 who are receiving PATHS for the first time cannot be taught the level of material designed for children in those grades who have been through the core lessons of PATHS earlier. Children beginning the PATHS curriculum later must receive the basic foundation before proceeding to more advanced material.

Program Outcomes

Specific outcome objectives of PATHS include

- ▲ increasing self-control, including the ability to stop, think, and calm down before taking action, especially when feeling upset;

- ▲ developing emotional awareness, understanding, and regulation;

- ▲ promoting empathy, consideration, and respect for self and others;

- ▲ increasing social problem-solving, planning, and critical thinking skills;

- ▲ improving peer relations;

- ▲ developing positive attitudes toward school, community, and life; and

- ▲ enhancing classroom atmosphere to support academic development.

Research studies have demonstrated the effectiveness of PATHS with children in general education as well as with children in special-needs classes (learning disabled, emotionally challenged, mildly mentally delayed, deaf, hearing-impaired, and gifted). Studies have shown that, compared with matched controls, PATHS significantly increased children's ability to recognize and understand emotions, demonstrate self-control, tolerate frustration, understand social problems, develop effective alternative solutions, decrease the percentage of aggressive/violent solutions to problems, use effective conflict-resolution strategies, and plan ahead to solve complex tasks.

These studies further showed decreased behavioral difficulties in children who received PATHS, including decreased internalizing symptoms, externalizing symptoms, and conduct problems. In the domain of cognition and achievement, general education students showed significant improvements in nonverbal reasoning and quality of planning. Special education children showed a strong trend toward improvement in math achievement scores, and deaf children showed significant improvement in reading achievement.

Additional studies from the Fast Track Project reported lower peer aggression scores and lower peer hyperactivity scores based on peer ratings, lower reports by teachers of disruptive classroom behavior, and improved classroom atmosphere as assessed by independent observers. Research by independent researchers has also validated success with PATHS (e.g., higher nonverbal IQ subtest scores and scores of emotional understanding).

Possible Negative Outcomes Related to Implementation of PATHS

None known.

References and Resources

Denham, S. A. & Burton, R. (1996). A socio-emotional intervention program for at risk four-year-olds. *Journal of School Psychology, 34*, 225–245.

Greenberg, M. T. (1997). Promoting social and emotional competence: The PATHS curriculum and the CASEL network. *Reaching Today's Youth*, 49–52.

Greenberg, M. T. & Kusché, C. A. (1993). Preventive intervention for school-aged deaf children: The PATHS curriculum. *Journal of Deaf Studies and Deaf Education*, 3, 49–63.

Greenberg, M. T., Kusché, C. A., Cook, E. T., & Quamma, J. P. (1995). Promoting emotional competence in school-aged children: The effects of the PATHS Curriculum. *Development & Psychopathology*, 7, 117–136.

Greenberg, M. T., Kusché, C. A., & Mihalic, S. F. (1998). *Blueprints for violence prevention, book ten: Promoting Alternative Thinking Strategies (PATHS)*. Boulder, CO: Center for the Study and Prevention of Violence.

Kusché, C. A. & Greenberg, M. T. (1994). *The PATHS (Promoting Alternative Thinking Strategies) curriculum*. Seattle, WA: Developmental Research and Programs.

U.S. Department of Health and Human Services, Substance Abuse and Mental Health Services Administration, Center for Substance Abuse Prevention. (n.d.). *SAMHSA model programs*. Rockville, MD: Author. Available: http://modelprograms.samhsa.gov

Responding in Peaceful and Positive Ways (RIPP)

Contact:
Wendy Bauers Northup

Position/Title:
Co-Director

Phone Number:
(804) 798-1369

Address:
Prevention Opportunities, LLC
12458 Ashland Vineyard Lane
Ashland, VA 23005

E-mail:
ameyer@saturn.vcu.edu

Purpose

Responding in Peaceful and Positive Ways (RIPP) is a violence prevention curriculum for sixth graders that focuses on social/cognitive skill building to promote nonviolent conflict resolution and positive communication. The program combines classroom instruction and real-life opportunities for proactive peer mediation to resolve conflicts. Program goals include the creation of a caring community to support prosocial norms and expectations that acknowledge the interactive influences of behaviors, intrapersonal attributes, and environmental factors.

Program Background

The program is grounded in social/cognitive learning theory and targets the influence of intrapersonal attributes, behaviors, and environmental factors. It follows from Perry and Jessor's (1985) health promotion model to reduce risk factors associated with violence by promoting nonviolent alternatives.

Scope of Program

RIPP is a sixth-grade, universal violence-prevention program that has been tested in urban and rural middle schools.

Specific Problems/Risk Factors Targeted by RIPP

RIPP is a social and cognitive skill-building program that aims to prevent violence by promoting nonviolence among students in middle school. It alters students' attitudes toward violence, psychosocial variables, and conflict resolution skills.

Program Operations

The 25-session curriculum is taught during a 45-minute class period (usually social studies or health education) once a week. RIPP provides young people with new ways to respond to conflict. Using the acronym RAID, the students are taught four types of nonviolent options: Resolve, Avoid, Ignore, Diffuse.

Teaching that they have other choices in any conflict dispels the idea that fighting is a necessary response to an insult or a challenge. RIPP also teaches the need for everyone to accept differences, to affirm those with whom they come in contact, and not to engage in put-downs of others. The program uses adult role models to teach knowledge, attitudes, and skills that emphasize nonviolence and promote positive communication. The program uses team-building activities along with small-group work, role plays, relaxation techniques, and repetition and rehearsal.

Key elements include working in small groups; problem solving; identifying feelings; handling differences; peer mediation; clarifying values; dealing with prejudices; and avoiding, ignoring, defusing, and resolving conflicts. The problem-solving component includes several steps that students memorize and practice frequently. Students learn to stop, calm down, identify the problem and feelings about it, decide among nonviolent options (resolve, avoid, ignore, or defuse), do it, look back, and evaluate.

Determining Your School's Readiness for RIPP

The operations manual for RIPP, *Promoting Non-Violence in Early Adolescence: Responding in Peaceful and Positive Ways* (Meyer, Farrell, Northup, Kung, & Plybon, 2000), is designed to assist schools in adapting RIPP to their own purposes. The second chapter, "Getting RIPP Running," addresses specific issues related to getting a school ready to implement the program.

Getting Training to Begin RIPP

The curriculum is taught by trained prevention specialists rather than teachers. The detailed operations manual provides an overview for hiring as well as highlights for training. Training is available either on-site at your own school or at the Virginia Commonwealth University.

Program Costs

A new position in the school, known as prevention specialist, is required for the program. Costs are associated with training the specialist, materials to support the curriculum in the classroom, and a peer mediation program.

Training

- ▲ Five days, includes materials for each participant
- ▲ $650 per person plus expenses ($315 for additional people from same school)
- ▲ At your site, $6,100 for up to 20 participants (plus expenses for trainer)

Materials

- ▲ $27.50 for the operations manual, *Promoting Non-Violence in Early Adolescence: Responding in Peaceful and Positive Ways* (http://www.wkap.nl/prod/b/0-306-46386-5)
- ▲ $85 for sixth–eighth grade curriculum (training required)
- ▲ $20 for poster

Other Resources Required to Implement RIPP

A peer mediation program is recommended to accompany the program curriculum.

Modifying RIPP for Your School/Classroom Context

Chapter 8 of the operations manual, "Adaptation of RIPP for Cultural and Community Differences," articulates ways to modify RIPP to meet the needs of different communities and students. Following a summary of issues to consider, specific suggestions are offered for program implementers.

Components That Cannot Be Modified or Excluded From RIPP

One of the crucial components of the program is the person who facilitates it, the violence prevention facilitator, who is selected by the school administrator from a pool of qualified applicants. The peer mediation program to accompany RIPP is highly recommended.

Program Outcomes

An evaluation funded by the Centers for Disease Control and Prevention showed that at posttest, RIPP participants showed significantly lower rates of fighting, bringing weapons to school, and in-school suspensions than control subjects. RIPP students were also more likely to use the peer mediation program and scored higher than controls on the RIPP knowledge test. RIPP participants reported more frequent use of peer mediation and reductions in fight-related injuries at posttest. The program's impact on violent behavior was more evident among those with high pretest levels of problem behavior. RIPP is being refined for students with behavioral and learning disabilities.

Possible Negative Outcomes Related to Implementation of RIPP

The program requires giving up one day of health or social studies class per week for 25 weeks.

References and Resources

Farrell, A. & Meyer, A. (1997). Effectiveness of a school-based prevention program for reducing violence among urban adolescents: Differential impact on girls and boys. *American Journal of Preventive Medicine, 12*, 13-21.

Farrell, A. D. & Meyer, A. L. (1997). The effectiveness of a school-based curriculum for reducing violence among urban sixth-grade students. *American Journal of Public Health, 87*, 979–984.

Farrell, A. D., Meyer, A. L., & Dahlberg, L. L. (1996). Richmond youth against violence: A school-based program for urban adolescents. *American Journal of Preventive Medicine, 12*, 13–21.

Farrell, A., Meyer, A., & White, K. (2001). Evaluation of Responding in Peaceful and Positive Ways (RIPP): A school-based prevention program for reducing violence among urban adolescents. *Journal of Clinical Child Psychology, 30*(4), 451–463.

Meyer, A. (1999). The subjective impressions of sixth grade urban adolescents concerning their ability to achieve personal goals. *Journal of Primary Prevention, 19*(4), 315–349.

Meyer, A. & Farrell, A. (1998). Social skills training to promote resilience in urban sixth grade students: One product of an action research strategy. *Education and Treatment of Children, 21*(4), 461–488.

Meyer, A., Farrell, A, Northup, W., Kung, E, & Plybon, L. (2000). *Promoting non-violence in early adolescence.* New York: Kluwer Academic/ Plenum Press.

Meyer, A. & Lausell, L. (1996). The value of including a "Higher Power" in efforts to prevent violence and promote optimal outcomes during adolescence. In B. Hampton, P. Jenkins, & T. Gullotta (Eds.), *Preventing violence in America* (pp. 115–132). Thousand Oaks, CA: Sage.

Perry, C. L., & Jessor, R. (1985). The concept of health promotion and the prevention of adolescent drug abuse. *Health Education Quarterly, 12*, 169–184.

U.S. Department of Health and Human Services, Substance Abuse and Mental Health Services Administration, Center for Substance Abuse Prevention. (n.d.). *SAMHSA model programs.* Rockville, MD: Author. Available: http://modelprograms.samhsa.gov

School Transitional Environment Program (STEP)

Contact:
Peter Mulhall, Ph.D.

Position/Title:
Director of Center for Prevention, Research & Development

Address:
Institute of Government & Public Affairs
University of Illinois
Champaign, IL 61820

Phone Number:
(217) 333-3231

E-mail:
mulhall@uiuc.edu

Purpose

The School Transitional Environment Program (STEP) is a selective early intervention that focuses on providing supports to students who are at risk for potential problems at predictable school transition times (e.g., from elementary school to junior high or junior high to high school). It helps students through those transitions. STEP redesigns the high school environment to make school transitions less threatening.

Program Background

STEP is based on the Transactional-Ecological/Transitional Life-Events model in which children experience greater risks for negative outcomes during normative transitional events, such as moving from elementary to middle school or from junior to senior high school. The increased risk is due to the heightened complexity and developmental demands of the new setting, and the school's typical inability to provide the necessary support, resources, and information for students to transition successfully. STEP seeks to institute changes in the school environment to make the transition less threatening and disruptive, and to create a supportive environment in the receiving school.

Earlier research has shown that, for many students, changing schools leads to poor academic achievement, classroom behavior problems, heightened anxiety, and increases in school absenteeism, all of which may lead to dropping out of school and other behavioral and social problems. By reducing school disorganization and restructuring the role of the homeroom teacher, STEP aims to reduce the complexity of school environments, increase peer and teacher support, and decrease students' vulnerability to academic and emotional difficulties.

Scope of Program

The STEP program assists new students in their first year of high school. STEP does not require any full-school reform, only the restructuring of the physical school and class arrangements.

Specific Problems/Risk Factors Targeted by STEP

STEP best benefits those students at greatest risk for behavioral problems who attend large, urban junior or senior high schools that have multiple feeding schools and serve predominantly children of color and economically disadvantaged students. Large high schools with several feeder schools, high schools with economically disadvantaged or less academically successful students, and even schools with challenging academic programs may benefit most from STEP as each characteristic creates a difficult transition from one school to the next for students.

Program Operations

STEP's success is achieved through redefining the role of homeroom teachers and restructuring schools' physical settings. Together these changes increase students' beliefs that school is stable, well-organized, and cohesive. Students are assigned to homerooms in which all classmates are STEP participants. Teachers in these classrooms act as administrators and guidance counselors, helping students choose classes, counseling them regarding school and personal problems, explaining the program to parents, and notifying parents of student absences. This increased attention reduces student anonymity, increases student accountability, and enhances students' abilities to learn school rules and exceptions. All program students are enrolled in the same core classes, which are located close together in the school, to help participants develop stable peer groups and enhance their familiarity with school. STEP students take all primary classes (English, math, social studies, science, and homeroom) together, reducing the need to cope with constantly shifting peer groups. Each student receives a 15- to 20-minute homeroom counseling session about once a month. STEP teachers meet once or twice a week to identify students who may need additional help.

Determining Your School's Readiness for STEP

Since implementing the STEP program does not involve full-school reform or changes in instructional methods, extensive resources are not required. The intervention is designed to be easy to implement and not take time away from basic academic instruction—simply change the physical environment and give added support during homeroom.

Getting Training to Begin STEP

STEP teachers receive two days of training to build knowledge and skills on adolescent development and emotional issues, strategies to handle those issues, and team building before the school year begins. School guidance or mental health personnel deliver the training. If they are not available, outside experts can deliver the training and consult during the school year. STEP team members meet frequently to discuss issues and special student problems.

Program Costs

STEP aims to restructure the physical school and class arrangements, not instruction content or classroom time. STEP does not engage schools in full-school reform or changes in instructional methods. This makes STEP a less expensive, but still effective, form of intervention.

Other Resources Required to Implement STEP

STEP requires only restructuring the physical environment and training homeroom teachers.

Modifying STEP for Your School/Classroom Context

STEP's core components include creating "cohorts" of transitioning students who remain together as a group during core classes and homeroom, restructuring the arrangement of classes to create smaller "learning communities" within the school, and redefining the roles of the homeroom teacher and counselors to provide a greater support structure for transitioning students. The homeroom teachers become advisors to the students in the cohort and serve as liaisons between the students, their families, and the rest of the school. The homeroom teachers take on many of the administrative responsibilities of the traditional guidance counselor, such as helping students select classes and addressing truancy issues with families. The homeroom teachers also meet with the other teachers who provide core instruction to the cohort, to identify students who may need additional counseling or support. STEP classrooms are located near each other within the school building.

Components That Cannot Be Modified or Excluded From STEP

n/a

Program Outcomes

The STEP program focuses entirely on school environment as a risk factor and seeks to improve student outcomes through environmental change. Though it may be more effective as part of a more comprehensive prevention effort, studies of STEP have found it to be more effective than programs targeting transitional life events through individual skill building. Studies have demonstrated STEP's effectiveness with extremely high-risk schools when targeted at the transition points into both junior high/middle school and high school. Although its focus is somewhat narrow, studies have demonstrated significant outcomes with a relatively large sample across a wide range of behavioral and emotional indices, using both student and teacher reports.

Evaluations performed at the end of ninth grade demonstrate that STEP students, compared to control students, displayed (1) decreases in absenteeism and increases in GPA; (2) stability of self-concept (compared with decreases for control students); and (3) more positive feelings about the school environment, perceiving the school

as more stable, understandable, well-organized, involving, and supportive.

Long-term follow-up indicated that STEP students, compared with controls, had lower dropout rates (21 percent versus 43 percent), and higher grades and fewer absences in grades 9 and 10.

Replication showed that STEP students, compared to control students, had (1) fewer increases in substance abuse, delinquent acts, and depression; (2) fewer decreases in academic performance and self-concept; (4) lower dropout rates; (5) less self-reported delinquency, depression, and anxiety; and (6) higher self-esteem, academic performance, and school attendance.

Possible Negative Outcomes Related to Implementation of STEP

Although negative outcomes have not been identified, some research suggests that interventions that segregate children with problem behavior may exacerbate conduct problems (Dishion, McCord, & Poullin, 1999).

References and Resources

Dishion, T. J., McCord, J., & Poulin, F. (1999). When interventions harm: Peer groups and problem behavior. *American Psychologist, 54*(9), 755–764.

Felner, R. D. & Adan, A. M. (1988). The School Transitional Environment Project: An ecological intervention and evaluation. In R. H. Price, E. L. Cowen, R. P. Lorion, & J. Ramos-McKay (Eds.), *14 ounces of prevention: A casebook for practitioners*. Washington, DC: American Psychological Association.

Felner, R. D., Ginter, M., & Primavera, J. (1982). Primary prevention during school transition: Social support and environmental structure. *American Journal of Community Psychology, 10*, 277–290.

Reyes, O. & Jason, L. A. (1991). An evaluation of a high school dropout prevention program. *Journal of Community Psychology, 19*, 221–230.

Second Step

Contact:
Barbara Guzzo

Position/Title:
Director of Client Support Services, Committee for Children

Phone Number:
(800) 634-4449, ext. 200

Address:
568 First Avenue South, Suite 600
Seattle, WA 98104-2804

E-mail:
info@cfchildren.org

Web Address:
http://www.cfchildren.org

Purpose

Second Step is a school-based social skills curriculum for preschool through junior high that teaches children to change the attitudes and behaviors that contribute to violence. These same skills promote social, academic, and lifelong success. Second Step teaches three skill units at each grade level: empathy, impulse control, and anger management. The goals are to reduce aggression and promote social competence.

Program Background

Committee for Children is the developer and sole vendor of Second Step. The organization began in the 1970s as a group of social scientists in Seattle concentrating on the prevention of child abuse. More recently, Committee for Children has focused on breaking the cycle of abuse by addressing a core cause, namely, a lack of social and emotional skills among victimizers. Second Step, a violence prevention curriculum, is the result of this new focus. Second Step has been translated into Norwegian, German, Danish, and Japanese. Second Step has been named an Exemplary program by the U.S. Department of Education's Expert Panel on Safe, Disciplined and Drug-Free Schools; a Model Program by the U.S. Department of Health and Human Services, Substance Abuse and Mental Health Services Administration, Center for Substance Abuse Prevention; and a CASEL Select program by the Collaboration for Academic, Social, and Emotional Learning. Currently, Second Step is being used by approximately 15,000 schools in the United States and Canada.

Scope of Program

Second Step is a universal intervention intended for use with students in pre-kindergarten through ninth grade. The content of the lessons varies according to the grade level, and the skills targeted for practice are designed to be developmentally appropriate. At all grade levels, Second Step provides opportunities for modeling, practice, and reinforcement of skills. The lesson techniques include discussion, teacher modeling of the skills, and role plays.

Specific Problems/Risk Factors Targeted by Second Step

Research reveals a set of social skills commonly lacking in people prone to violent and aggressive behavior: empathy, impulse control, problem solving, and anger management. Research also indicates several reasons children do not use prosocial behavior, including lack of modeling, lack of opportunities to practice behaviors, and inadequate reinforcement. Second Step focuses on training developmentally appropriate manifestations of these specific social skills.

Empathy. Second Step begins with a focus on empathy. Empathy skills provide a foundation on which problem-solving and emotion management skills are built. Second Step uses a broad definition of empathy that includes knowledge about emotions, taking the perspectives of others, and responding with sensitivity to others. Empathy contributes to children's academic gains and to improvements in their social behavior (Fabes et al., 1994; Hastings, Zahn-Waxler, Robinson, Usher, & Bridges, 2000). Children are more likely to offer help and emotional support if they can take another's perspective. Children's understanding of their peers' intentions may also affect their aggressiveness, with more benign attributions leading to less aggressive behavior among some children.

Impulse Control and Problem Solving. The Impulse Control and Problem Solving unit builds on empathy skills. Children are taught that when they are having a problem with peers, it is useful to first calm down and then apply a set of problem-solving steps (Shure & Spivack, 1974). The sequence of problem-solving steps is based on what we know about effective patterns of thinking in social situations. Aggressive children, for example, differ from other children in the ways they think. They offer fewer positive strategies than other children do (Richard & Dodge, 1982). They are more certain that aggressive strategies will work, they judge aggressive

strategies as less likely to cause harm, and they have lower expectations that prosocial strategies will work.

Emotion Management or Anger Management. Effective management of emotions is related to both decreased levels of aggression (Underwood, Coie, & Herbsman, 1992) and increased levels of social-emotional competence (Eisenberg, Fabes, & Losoya, 1997). In the emotion/anger management unit, calming-down strategies are introduced. Children learn to recognize anger triggers and physical signs that they are angry and use the signs as cues that it is time to use the anger management strategies they have learned. They learn to prevent escalation of angry feelings by using strategies to relax, such as counting, taking deep breaths, and making helpful self-statements (such as "I can calm down"). In the grade school programs, children learn to apply the problem-solving steps.

Program Operations

For preschool and elementary students, the main lesson format is the use of an 11-by-17-inch photo lesson card. The teacher shows the photograph to the class and follows the lesson outline on the back of the card. The lesson techniques include discussion, teacher modeling of the skills, and role plays. Classroom kits contain lesson cards, videos, teacher and administrative guides, and other learning aids.

The lessons in the middle school or junior high curriculum are divided into three levels: Level 1, Foundation, and Levels 2 and 3, Skillbuilding. Each includes discussion, overhead transparencies, reproducible homework sheets, and a video. The three levels of lessons provide students with comprehensive multiyear training in prosocial skills.

At each grade level (preschool through ninth grade), the lessons build sequentially and should be taught in the order intended. The lessons vary in length from 20 minutes at the preschool level to 50 minutes in middle school/junior high. There are approximately 20 lessons for each grade level. Researchers have demonstrated the usefulness of the story format for teaching young children about emotions. Each Second Step lesson is based on a story that demonstrates an important peer relations skill. This story format makes it easier for children to discuss feelings and gives them concrete ways to understand complex social skills concepts. These stories are used to teach affective, cognitive, and behavioral social skills in a developmental sequence.

Additionally, Committee for Children has developed *A Family Guide to Second Step*. This is a six-session, facilitator-led program designed specifically for families of children in preschool to fifth grade who are receiving Second Step in their school or youth program. The *Family Guide* offers school and youth agency personnel a systematic way to include families in their violence prevention efforts. The family component familiarizes parents with the Second Step curriculum, assists them in reinforcing the skills at home, and gives families the skills to communicate feelings, solve problems, control anger, and deal with conflict.

Determining Your School's Readiness for Second Step

To determine whether Second Step is right for your school or program, consider the following:

- ▲ **Audience.** Ongoing groups of children, usually school classrooms, participate.
- ▲ **Presenter.** Ideally the same person presents all lessons to a group and has continuing contact to be able to reinforce skills.
- ▲ **Time Commitment.** Ongoing curriculum requires up to 20 lessons.
- ▲ **Resources.** The curriculum requires investment of funds to purchase materials and time to train presenters.

Committee for Children's Client Support Services Department assists schools, districts, and agencies in determining their training needs and developing their implementation plans. Further information is available at (800) 634-4449, ext. 200, or on the Committee's Web site.

Getting Training to Begin Second Step

Training plays a critical role in the success of the program, helping to ensure that classroom teachers or agency staff (the primary curriculum presenters) are not only comfortable and confident in teaching the skills presented, but also are inspired and motivated. Committee for Children offers Second Step Training for Trainers, Second Step Staff Training, and *A Family Guide to Second Step* Facilitator Training. Both regional and on-site training options are available.

Program Costs

Curricula for Second Step are available separately for preschool through grade nine. Prices for these curricula vary from $125 to $295, with $50 Spanish supplements (*Segundo Paso*) available for pre-K through grade five. Many supplementary materials are available for purchase, and discounts are available for combination purchases. Features and pricing for the 2002 third edition *Second Step* can be found at http://www.cfchildren.org/program_ss.shtml.

Other Resources Required to Implement Second Step

Many other resources are available but no research is available to identify those items that are absolutely required for faithful implementation.

Modifying Second Step for Your School/ Classroom Context

n/a

Components That Cannot Be Modified or Excluded From Second Step

n/a

Program Outcomes

Researchers at the University of Washington undertook a one-year evaluation of Second Step for grades 2–3 (Grossman et al., 1997). Funded by the Centers for Disease Control and Prevention, they examined the impact of the program on aggression and positive social behavior. Twelve schools were paired on socioeconomic and ethnic makeup. One school in each pair was randomly assigned to a control group and the other to Second Step. Behavioral observations indicated that physical aggression and hostile and aggressive comments decreased from autumn to spring among students who were in the Second Step classrooms and increased among students in the control classes. Friendly behavior, including prosocial and neutral interactions, increased from autumn to spring in Second Step classrooms but did not change in control classrooms. Six months later, students in the Second Step classes maintained the higher levels of positive interaction and lower levels of aggression.

Investigators at DePaul University conducted an uncontrolled pre-post evaluation of Preschool-Kindergarten Second Step with 109 predominantly African American and Latino three- to seven-year-old children from low-income urban families (McMahon, Washburn, Felix, Yakin, & Childrey, 2000). Following completion of the Second Step lessons, the children demonstrated an increased conceptual knowledge of social skills and a decrease in observed levels of physical aggression, verbal aggression, and disruptive behavior.

Researchers conducted an evaluation of the Second Step Middle School curriculum to examine its effects on adolescents' attitudes about physical and relational aggression. Two-thirds of the study's 714 sixth- through eighth-grade students were taught Second Step lessons; the remaining third were not. After receiving Second Step lessons, students in their first year of middle school endorsed social exclusion less than nonparticipants, and students in their second year of middle school were less likely to endorse social exclusion and physical and verbal aggression.

A three-year longitudinal study is being conducted by the University of Washington and Committee for Children to examine the impact of Second Step implementation on student behavior, teacher attitudes and practices, and student perception of class climate. Control and experimental participants come from 15 elementary schools in five Western Washington school districts. Data collection for the study has been completed and analyses are currently under way.

Possible Negative Outcomes Related to the Implementation of Second Step

None known.

References and Resources

Eisenberg, N., Fabes, R. A., & Losoya, S. (1997). Emotional responding: Regulation, social correlates, and socialization. In P. Salovey & D. J. Slutyer (Eds.), *Emotional development and emotional intelligence: Educational implications* (pp. 129–163). New York: Basic Books.

Fabes, R. A., Eisenberg, N., Karbon, M., Bernzweig, J., Speer, A. L., & Carlo, G. (1994). Socialization of children's vicarious emotional responding and prosocial behavior: Relations with mothers' perceptions of children's emotional reactivity. *Developmental Psychology, 30,* 44–55.

Grossman, D. et al. (1997). The effectiveness of a violence prevention curriculum among children in elementary school. *Journal of the American Medical Association, 277,* 1605–1611.

Hastings, P. D., Zahn-Waxler, C., Robinson, J., Usher, B., & Bridges, D. (2000). The development of concern for others in children with behavior problems. *Developmental Psychology, 36,* 531–546.

Litvack-Miller, W., McDougall, D., & Romney, D. M. (1997). The structure of empathy during middle childhood and its relationship to prosocial behavior. *Genetic, Social, & General Psychology Monographs, 123,* 303–324.

McMahon, S. D., Washburn, J., Felix, E. D., Yakin, J., & Childrey, G. (2000). Violence prevention: Program effects on urban preschool and kindergarten children. *Applied and Preventive Psychology, 9,* 271–281.

Richard, B. A. & Dodge, K. A. (1982). Social maladjustment and problem-solving in school-aged children. *Journal of Consulting and Clinical Psychology, 50,* 226–233.

Shure, M. B. & Spivack, G. (1974). *The Hahnemann Preschool Behavior (HPSB) rating scale.* Philadelphia: Hahnemann University, Department of Mental Health Sciences.

Underwood, M. K., Coie, J. D., & Herbsman, C. R. (1992). Display rules for anger and aggression in school-age children. *Child Development, 63,* 366–380.

U.S. Department of Health and Human Services, Substance Abuse and Mental Health Services Administration, Center for Substance Abuse Prevention. (n.d.). *SAMHSA model programs.* Rockville, MD: Author. Available: http://modelprograms.samhsa.gov

Van Scholack-Edstrom, L., Frey, K. S., & Beland, K. (2002). Changing adolescents' attitudes about relational and physical aggression: An early evaluation of a school-based intervention. *School Psychology Review, 31,* 201–216.

SOAR, The Seattle Social Development Project

Contact:
Sarah Clay

Position/Title:
Program Marketing Specialist

Phone Number:
(877) 896-8532

Address:
Channing Bete Co., Inc.
One Community Place
South Deerfield, MA 01273

E-mail:
PrevSci@channing-bete.com

Web Address:
www.channing-bete.com

Purpose

The purpose of the SOAR program is to promote the healthy development of young people by increasing opportunities for active involvement in family and school, improving skills for successful participation in family, school, peer groups, and community, and providing consistent recognition for effort and improvement.

Program Background

Initiated in 1981, SOAR is implemented in 17 schools in four districts. It is designed for students in kindergarten through sixth grade.

Scope of Program

SOAR is a universal schoolwide program.

Specific Problems/Risk Factors Targeted by SOAR

SOAR targets the reduction of risk factors, including lack of commitment to school, poor family management, family conflict, favorable parental attitudes toward drugs, alienation and rebelliousness, friends who use drugs, favorable attitudes by students toward drug use, early initiation of drug use, and early antisocial behavior. SOAR also seeks to enhance protective factors of bonding to family and school. It provides opportunities for prosocial involvement, recognition for prosocial involvement. It also sets healthy beliefs and standards for behavior, and social and teacher emotional skills.

Program Operations

SOAR has three major components. The school staff development component provides a series of instructional improvement workshops and classroom coaching sessions for teachers. Training enhances academic achievement and bonding to school and reduces classroom behavior problems. The family component offers developmentally sequenced parenting workshops to increase attachment and enhance parents' skills in helping their children succeed academically. Parents help their children develop strong bonds to school. Finally, the project provides social and citizenship skills training for children to learn and practice social and citizenship skills and to learn and practice social and emotional skills in the classroom and in social situations.

Determining Your School's Readiness for SOAR

n/a

Getting Training to Begin SOAR

Teachers at SOAR schools spend five days in training during each of the first two installation years (three days during each summer before classes begin and two days during each school year). The Implementation Team (principal, facilitator, and family support coordinator) attends a three-day training and planning session before each of the first two installation years. In the third installation year, the team attends a SOAR Program Conference that brings together all program users to network, update skills, and exchange expertise on institutionalization of the SOAR program.

Program Costs

The SOAR program is not currently available for purchase because development of the commercial version continues. A SOAR school implements the program over two years. Direct costs from the publisher for program and training materials, as well as principal/facilitator, staff, and parent workshop leader trainings and technical assistance, are estimated at $52,000 in Year 1 and $38,000 in Year 2.

Other Resources Required to Implement SOAR

Schools must support a full-time in-school Facilitator/Coach and a half-time Family Support Coordinator. There are additional costs for teacher inservice days. (The school must base these cost estimates on current salaries and costs.)

Modifying SOAR for Your School/ Classroom Context

Before beginning the formal training events, the SOAR Trainer consults with the school implementation team to assess current needs and identify relevant issues that should be incorporated into training events. In addition, during the Year 1 Implementation Team Training, Implementation Teams (Principal, Facilitator, Family Support Coordinator) develop implementation plans that address the unique needs of the learning community (e.g., integrating SOAR with learning standards, involving hard-to-reach families). During their training, leaders for the SOAR parent workshops learn to adapt the curricula to diverse parent populations.

Components That Cannot Be Modified or Excluded From SOAR

n/a

Program Outcomes

SOAR reports more commitment and attachment to school, better school grades, and less school misbehavior among program participants in grades 1–6 than peers at age 18. Further, at age 18, fewer full-intervention students had engaged in violent delinquent acts, heavy drinking, sexual activity; or had multiple sex partners. By age 18, fewer SOAR students had become pregnant or had caused pregnancies.

By the end of sixth grade, according to SOAR, boys from low-income families in the full intervention condition showed significantly higher scores on standardized achievement tests, higher levels of classroom participation, higher levels of social skills, better work skills, greater attachment and commitment to school, lower levels of interaction with antisocial peers and a trend toward lower levels of initiation of delinquency when compared with controls. Girls from low-income families in the full intervention condition showed significantly higher levels of classroom participation, greater attachment and commitment to school, and a trend toward lower rates of initiation of alcohol, marijuana, and tobacco use compared to controls.

At the end of second grade, teachers reported that boys in the full intervention group were significantly less aggressive and demonstrated significantly less externalizing antisocial behavior than control boys. Teachers reported that girls in the full intervention group were significantly less self-destructive than control girls at the end of second grade.

Direct effects of the intervention were found on alcohol initiation and on delinquency initiation by fifth grade, with intervention students reporting significantly less initiation for both behaviors than control students.

The only negative effects occurred in the evaluation of students entering fifth grade. Control students scored significantly higher than intervention students on the California Achievement Test. According to SOAR, this effect was no longer in evidence at sixth and seventh grades.

Possible Negative Outcomes Related to the Implementation of SOAR

None known.

Resources

Hawkins, J. D., Catalano, R. F., Kosterman, R., Abbott, R., & Hill, K. G. (1999). Preventing adolescent health-risk behaviors by strengthening protection during childhood. *Archives of Pediatric Adolescent Medicine*, *153*(3), 226–234.

Hawkins, J. D., Catalano, R. F., Morrison, D., O'Donnell, J., Abbott, R., & Day, E. (1992). The Seattle Social Development Project: Effects of the first four years on protective factors and problem behaviors. In J. McCord & R. E. Tremblay (Eds.), *Preventing antisocial behavior: Interventions from birth through adolescence*. New York: The Guilford Press.

Hawkins, J. D., Doueck, H. J., & Lishner, D. M. (1988). Changing teacher practices in mainstream classrooms to improve bonding and behavior of low achievers. *American Educational Research Journal*, *25*, 31–50.

Hawkins, J. D., Von Cleve, E., & Catalano, R. F. (1991). Reducing early childhood aggression: Results of a primary prevention program. *Journal of American Academy Child Adolescent Psychiatry*, *30*, 208–217.

O'Donnell, J., Hawkins, J. D., Catalano, R. F., Abbott, R. D., & Day, E. (1995). Preventing school failure, drug use, and delinquency among low-income children: Long-term intervention in elementary schools. *American Journal of Orthopsychiatry*, *65*, 87–100.

Social Decision Making/ Problem Solving Program (SDM/PS)

Contact:
Maurice Elias, Ph.D. and
Linda Bruene Butler, M.Ed.

Position/Title:

Elias: Professor, Department of Psychology, Rutgers University

Butler: Clinician Administrator, Behavioral Research and Training Institute, University of Medicine and Dentistry of New Jersey, University Behavioral HealthCare

Phone Number:
(732) 235–9280

Address:

Elias:
Department of Psychology, Rutgers University
53 Avenue E
Livingston Campus
Piscataway, NJ 08854–8040

Butler:
151 Centennial Ave., Ste. 1140
Piscataway, NJ 08854

E-mail:
EQ@Eqparenting.com and
spsweb@umdnj.edu

Web Address:
http://www.umdnj.edu/spsweb and
http://www.Eqparenting.com

Purpose

The Social Decision Making/Problem Solving program (SDM/PS) is intended to teach children to think clearly and make emotionally intelligent decisions in academic situations and in complex and emotional real-life situations.

Program Background

SDM/PS has been available since 1979. It originally served grades K–8, and middle school. High school materials were developed later. The program has been implemented in more than 200 schools nationally and internationally.

Scope of Program

The program is designed to build a schoolwide foundation, but its methods fortify and are integrated into early and intensive interventions.

Specific Problems/Risk Factors Targeted by SDM/PS

▲ Poor self-management, self-awareness, self-control, and emotional recognition skills

▲ Poor interpersonal relationships, inability to work in groups, intolerance of difference

▲ Inadequate skills for problem solving, decision making, and nonviolent conflict resolution

A developmentally sequenced curriculum with reinforcement in academics and in situations throughout the school day, for the entire school year, provides the potency needed to produce attitudinal and behavioral skills change. It is only when skills are overlearned (with multiyear repeated and varied practice) that skills are accessible under stress and can generalize and transfer to complex and emotional real-life situations. This is true for all children but especially for children at risk.

Program Operations

The Social Decision Making/Problem Solving program is composed of curriculum-based lessons, teaching skills, and skill prompts. Lessons are taught weekly and combined with ongoing infused opportunities to prompt skill practice within existing academic curriculum, discipline and classroom management practices, classroom procedures/policy, and everyday life problem solving and conflict resolution. Skill prompting and practice are also infused within individual/group counseling and before/after school programs (at some sites), and shared with support staff and parents.

A Leadership and Management Team is highly recommended to coordinate activities needed to institutionalize programming (such as designing plans for expansion, monitoring implementation and technical assistance, parent awareness/involvement/training, and program evaluation.

Determining Your School's Readiness for SDM/PS

Consultation during needs and resources assessment early in the process allows tailoring to local needs and circumstances. Further, action research efforts are strongly recommended to foster ongoing adaptation.

Getting Training to Begin SDM/PS

Recommended training is as follows:

▲ Teacher training (and follow-up)

▲ Training of a Leadership and Management Team

▲ Training of all school support staff and parents in methods for prompting ongoing practice of skills in real-life situations (Books and computer software for parents are also recommended.)

Training duration for SDM/PS varies. A full-day format with follow-up consultation is available. However, the program developers prefer a two-day training for implementers (scheduled a month or two apart if possible to allow for skill practice by teachers) and a day of training for the Leadership and Management Team (highly recommended). The training gives an overview of the program, a description and overlearning of the instructional

design by modeling and participation in systematic skill-building activities, hands-on practice, and time for planning.

Social Decision Making/Problem Solving has versions of the manual for elementary and secondary education, an overview book (Elias & Tobias, 1996, *Social Problem Solving: Interventions in the Schools*), and books for parents (e.g., Elias, Tobias, & Friedlander, 2000, *Emotionally Intelligent Parenting* and *Raising Emotionally Intelligent Teenagers*).

Program Costs

A minimum of three hours of pre-implementation consultation is highly recommended. On-site training costs begin at $800 per day per trainer, plus expenses. A Master Curriculum costs $75, and teacher training packages that include introductory curriculum packets, posters, and training handouts cost $57 per copy. Ongoing support and consultation is available for $90 per hour. An 800 number, e-mail, and a Web site also provide resources for technical assistance.

Other Resources Required to Implement SDM/PS

The program does not require new staff. It includes existing staff and parents in awareness, involvement, and training regarding methods for promoting skill practice outside the classroom.

Modifying SDM/PS for Your School/ Classroom Context

Due to the sound theoretical foundation and instructional design, this model has been adapted and modified by a wide variety of school districts, including special services systems. The goal is to provide school districts with a research-based model and framework for organizing and developing comprehensive and integrated programming for social and emotional learning.

Components That Cannot Be Modified or Excluded From SDM/PS

Curriculum-based instruction in the Social Decision Making/Problem Solving skills must coincide with and be combined with ongoing and infused opportunities to practice the skills in academic and real-life situations.

Program Outcomes

The SDM/PS research–validated model and methods are intended to be used by school districts as a framework for organizing programming to promote social and emotional learning in students K–12.

Elementary school children of varying demographics (urban and suburban populations) who received SDM/PS training significantly improved their social decision-making and problem-solving skills relative to controls. Specifically, children who received the program were more sensitive to others' feelings, had a better understanding of consequences, showed an increased ability to analyze interpersonal situations and plan appropriate actions, were more socially appropriate and realistic in the way they coped with problems and obstacles, and used what they had learned in SDM/PS lessons in situations occurring both inside and outside the classroom.

Students who received the training in elementary school showed more prosocial behavior in school and a greater ability to cope with stressors (e.g., conflicts with authority and older students, peer relationships, academic pressure, and substance abuse) upon transition to middle school as compared to controls. High school students trained in elementary school also showed higher levels of positive behavior and decreased antisocial, self-destructive, and socially disordered behavior.

Teachers trained in SDM/PS improved in the ability to teach and facilitate children's social decision making and problem-solving skills. Positive effects on school attendance, discipline referrals, parent satisfaction, academic grades, and standardized test scores have been shown. There is evidence that the program is effective for white, black, Hispanic and Asian students.

Elements of the program have been translated into Hebrew, Spanish, German, Dutch, Italian, Polish, Indonesian, and Portuguese, with Korean and Chinese translations under way. There are also U.K. and Australian editions. Implementation is under way in Israel, Mexico, Belgium, and Switzerland.

Possible Negative Outcomes Related to the Implementation of SDM/PS

None known.

References and Resources

Clabby, J. F. & Elias, M. J. (1987). Your child can learn to make decisions. *PTA Today*, December 1987–January 1988, 14–15.

Elias, M. J. (1990). *Problem solving/decision making for social and academic success*. Washington, DC: National Education Association.

Elias, M. J. & Clabby, J. F. (1988). Teaching social decision making. *Educational Leadership, 45*(6), 52–55. Elias, M.J., Gara, M.A., Schuyler, T.F., Braden-Muller, L.R., Sayette, M.A. (1991). The promotion of social competence: Longitudinal study of a preventive school-based program. American Journal of Orthopsychiatry, 61(3), 409–417.

Elias, M. J. & Tobias, S. E. (1996). *Social problem solving: Interventions in the schools*. New York: Guilford Press.

Elias, M. J., Tobias, S. E., & Friedlander, B. S. (1994). Enhancing skills for everyday problem solving, decision making, and conflict resolution in special needs students with the support of computer-based technology. *Special Services in the Schools, 8*(2), 33–52.

Elias, M. J., Tobias, S. E., & Friedlander, B. S. (2000a). *Emotionally intelligent parenting: How to raise a self-disciplined, responsible, and socially skilled child*. New York: Crown Publishing Group.

Elias, M. J., Tobias, S. E., & Friedlander, B. S. (2000b). *Raising emotionally intelligent teenagers: Parenting with love, laughter, and limits*. New York: Crown Publishing Group.

Strengthening Families Program: For Parents and Youth 10–14 (SFP 10–14) (Iowa Strengthening Families Program [ISFP])

Contact:
Virginia Molgaard, Ph.D.

Position/Title:
Program Developer/Researcher

Phone Number:
(515) 294–8762

Address:
Institute for Social and Behavioral Research
2625 N. Loop, Suite 500
Iowa State University
Ames, IA 50010

E-mail:
vmolgaar@iastate.edu

Web Address:
http://www.extension.iastate.edu/sfp

Purpose

The Strengthening Families Program: For Parents and Youth 10–14 (SFP 10–14) is designed to bring parents together with their children with the goal of reducing substance abuse and other problem behaviors in youth.

Program Background

SFP 10–14 has been in use for eight years. It is designed for grades 5–8 and has been implemented in 500 school districts.

Scope of Program

SFP 10–14 is specifically designed to address the following risk factors:

- ▲ Demanding/rejecting behavior of parents
- ▲ Poor communication skills (parent and youth)
- ▲ Harsh and inappropriate parental discipline
- ▲ Poor child-parent relationship
- ▲ Aggressive or withdrawn behavior of youth
- ▲ Poor parental monitoring
- ▲ Negative peer influence
- ▲ Poor school performance
- ▲ Poor social skills of youth
- ▲ Ineffective conflict management skills

Program Operations

- ▲ A seven-week (plus four optional booster sessions) curriculum for parents and youth is typically held in the evening; 10–12 families are in each group.
- ▲ Booster sessions are optional.

Determining Your School's Readiness for SFP (10–14)

Resources needed for SFP 10–14 are three facilitators per group and two classrooms (one for the parent group and one for the youth and family group), for seven weeks (plus four booster session weeks) two hours per evening, room for childcare (can be a classroom), TV, VCR, and flip chart.

Getting Training to Begin SFP 10–14

There is no formal network, but the program developer has records of contact people for groups who have received training and implemented the program. A training manual and program session videotapes are required. Training is available and is strongly recommended. Most trainings are two days, 16 hours total. A three-day training is available for groups who plan to make adaptations for non-English-speaking parents or ethnic groups not represented in program videotapes. A train-the-trainer program is available.

Program Costs

▲ Two-day training is $2,500 plus travel and per diem for two trainers.

▲ Three-day training is $3,500 plus travel and per diem for two trainers.

▲ Manual is $175 (one per facilitator). The set of nine videotapes is $250.

▲ Total cost for all materials for Sessions 1 through 7 is $775.

▲ Booster manual is $50 (one per facilitator), and a set of two additional videos is $60.

▲ Total cost for all materials for Booster Sessions 1–4 is $210.

▲ Technical assistance by phone is available without cost after training. On-site consultation post-training is $800 per day plus travel and per diem for two trainers.

▲ Cost for materials per family is $15 ($150 for a group of 10 families).

▲ Facilitators: Sessions 1 through 7: $30 per hour. The cost for 21 hours of teaching is $630 times three facilitators, or $1,890.

▲ Facilitators: Booster Sessions 1 through 4: $30 per hour. The cost for 12 hours of teaching is $360 times three facilitators, or $1,080.

▲ Childcare (includes one adult and two teen helpers per group): The cost is $50 per night times seven nights, or $350.

▲ The cost for four booster nights at $50 per night is $200.

▲ Secretarial help: Assembling program handouts and game cards per group; lining up rooms, TV, and VCR; providing flip charts; and lining up child-care workers. The cost for 20 hours at $10 per hour is $200.

▲ Administrative time: Recruiting facilitators, arranging training, recruiting families. Cost for 15 hours at $30 per hour is $450. This cost may be covered by salaried school staff or by paying individuals who also serve as facilitators.

Based on the figures above, the total expense (after materials and training) for a group of ten families is $3,040. If salaried school staff help with facilitation and administration, the cost is considerably lower.

Other Resources Required to Implement SFP 10–14

n/a

Modifying SFP 10–14 for Your School/Classroom Context

SFP 10–14 has been modified to be appropriate for African American and Hispanic families, as well as white families. A nonvideo version is available for use with non-English-speaking parents. The seven sessions may be divided into two program segments: three weeks, break, four weeks. With slight modifications, the program has been successfully implemented with high school youth, but it has not yet been scientifically evaluated with this age group.

Components That Cannot Be Modified or Excluded From SFP 10–14

SFP 10–14 must include parent, youth, and family sessions; all seven sessions must be provided.

Program Outcomes

Youth who attended the program have significantly lower rates of substance initiation and use. These positive results continue through four years post-baseline (tenth grade).

Youth attending the program have significantly less aggressive and hostile behavior. These positive results are in evidence four years post-baseline (tenth grade). Parents attending the program have significantly higher scores on specific parenting skills taught in the program designed to lower risk factors and raise protective factors.

Possible Negative Outcomes Related to the Implementation of SFP 10–14

None known.

Resources

Molgaard, V. M. & Spoth, R. (2001). Strengthening Families Program for young adolescents: Overview and outcomes. In S. Pfeiffer & L. Reddy (Eds.), *Innovative mental health programs for children*. Binghamton, NY: The Haworth Press.

Molgaard, V. M., Spoth, R., & Redmond, C. (2000). Competency training: The Strengthening Families Program for Parents and Youth 10–14. *Juvenile Justice Bulletin* (NCJ 182208). Washington, DC: U.S. Department of Justice, Office of Juvenile Justice and Delinquency Prevention.

Redmond, C., Spoth, R., Shin, C., & Lepper, H. (1999). Modeling long-term parent outcomes of two universal family focused preventive interventions: One year follow-up results. *Journal of Consulting and Clinical Psychology*, 67(6), 975–984.

Spoth, R., Goldberg, C., & Redmond, C. (1999). Engaging families in longitudinal preventive intervention research: Discrete-time survival analysis of socioeconomic and social-emotional risk factors. *Journal of Consulting and Clinical Psychology*, 67(1), 157–163.

U.S. Department of Health and Human Services, Substance Abuse and Mental Health Services Administration, Center for Substance Abuse Prevention. (n.d.). *SAMHSA model programs*. Rockville, MD: Author. Available: http://modelprograms.samhsa.gov

Syracuse Family Development Research Program (FDRP)

Contact:
Alice S. Honig

Position/Title:
Program Director

Phone Number:
(315) 443-4296 or (315) 472-1234

Address:
201 Slocum Hall
Syracuse University
Syracuse, NY 13244

E-mail:
ahonig@mailbox.syr.edu

Purpose

The Syracuse Family Development Research Program (FDRP) is intended to support and nurture low-income, low-education families from the last trimester of the teenage mother's pregnancy until the child reaches five years of age.

Program Background

The program began under Dr. Bettye Caldwell as the Children's Center, which initially served low-income families with infants and then served the children as they grew older. Dr. J. R. Lally became Project Director (with Dr. A. S. Honig as Program Director) and expanded the program to include services to families and pregnant teens, beginning before the birth of the child. Under Dr. Caldwell, the program served infants, toddlers, and preschoolers to age five. Under Dr. Lally, the program expanded intensively to become an omnibus intervention program to serve the parents and families of the children from before birth to the end of preschool and eligibility for kindergarten. The program was implemented in Syracuse (NY) with federal grant support administered through Syracuse University.

Scope of Program

FDRP is a family-focused program for children placed at risk by poverty and other factors.

Specific Problems/Risk Factors Targeted by FDRP

The program targets single mothers, mothers and fathers who have dropped out of high school, and families who are in poverty and have little education.

Program Operations

The Infant Fold component serves babies (from six months of age to about 15–18 months) with individualized care, language-enriching experiences, and developmentally appropriate toys to stimulate sensorimotor competencies.

The curriculum was embedded as much as possible during routine childcare, such as diapering, bathing, feeding, carrying, and soothing. A transition group for young toddlers was available for more advanced sensorimotor activities. Older toddlers and preschoolers were in mixed age groups. Piagetian preoperational games and activities were carefully planned to include all the toddlers and preschoolers in enriched activities to encourage learning categorization, serration, role playing, prosocial peer interactions, fine and gross motor dexterity, and language facility.

Families were served by a cadre of Home Visitors. During weekly home visits they provided young pregnant mothers, and later the mothers of the enrolled children, with information about nutrition, child development (both emotional and cognitive), and language milestones. They modeled how to carry out Piagetian sensorimotor activities and later, preoperation learning games. They encouraged mothers actively to create learning games for their children. They provided a book and toy-lending library for the family to use with the children. They provided transportation to the Children's Center for the children by bus (with trained bus staff to sing and talk with the children during travel time) as well as transportation for the mothers to group meetings at the Center. The FDRP Child Development Trainers (CDTs) had weekly case conferences and meeting times for support and education of the staff. The CDTs were advocates for the families. They carried out varying tasks, such as finding housing and medical care, and provided supports for families with urgent needs.

Determining Your School's Readiness for FDRP

n/a

Getting Training to Begin FDRP

The training is a one-week workshop offered annually in mid-June (eight hours a day for five days) at Syracuse University. Taught by Dr. Honig, the workshop provides intensive training in infant/toddler development and working with families. The title is *National Quality Infant/Toddler Caregiving Workshop*. For information, call Continuing Education at Syracuse, (315) 443-3299.

The training covers a variety of theories regarding child development (e.g., those of Mahler, Piaget, Vygotsky, Eriksons, Freud, Bandura). Topics include books and songs for babies, pediatric difficulties, legal aspects of childcare, working with parents, cost budgeting for childcare for infants and toddlers; massage for infants and toddlers, cognitive milestones and how to stimulate early learning; creating prosocial curricular opportunities, creating secure attachments; choosing developmentally appropriate toys, games, and activities; and assessments of caregivers and of young children.

The preferred manual for trainers is *Infant Caregiving: A Design for Training* by A. S. Honig and J. R. Lally (Syracuse University Press, $17). Tips for training are explicit; the manual is written at a tenth grade reading level.

Other training resources include *Talking With Your Baby: Family as the First School* by A. S. Honig and H. Brophy (Syracuse University Press, $16). Specific language interaction games are offered for parents and family child-care workers as well as for center personnel working with infants, toddlers, and preschoolers.

Behavior Guidance for Infants and Toddlers by A. S. Honig (Southern Early Childhood Association, $6, (800) 305-7322) offers clear suggestions for positive discipline techniques for educators of zero to three-year-olds.

Playtime Learning Games for Young Children, by A. S. Honig, is written at a fifth-grade reading level. Simple and easy to play in a home setting, a family daycare setting, or a center, the learning games are geared to children from about one to six years of age. The games are intended to enhance cognitive skills and language development.

Secure Relationships: Nurturing Infant/Toddler Attachment in Early Care Settings by A. S. Honig (2002), published by NAEYC.

Program Costs

The Syracuse workshop is offered at 60 percent of the customary price per credit for graduate students, undergraduates, and nonstudents at Syracuse who want to audit the sessions.

Modifying FDRP for Your School/ Classroom Context

With good will, intensive training, high morale, and motivation to help low-income, low-education families help their children become emotionally expressive, loving persons who are well prepared to succeed in school, any community could implement this program.

Components That Cannot Be Modified or Excluded From FDRP

Recent research has confirmed that starting during pregnancy; meeting the family's needs rather than just the child's needs; and working toward tender, individualized care as well as cognitive, language, and gross and fine motor curriculum goals are essential for optimal programming. Home visits need to be frequent in order to address crises and special family needs.

Program Outcomes

The fifteen-year follow-up found that females who had been in the program were far less likely to cut school. They attended more frequently, had better teacher ratings of interpersonal behaviors, and were far less likely than contrast youth to receive grades lower than C.

Male youth did not perform statistically better in school than contrast males who had not attended the program, but juvenile delinquency was much less frequent among the FDRP graduates when they became teenagers. They committed far fewer crimes overall. The contrast youth were more likely to commit more serious crimes, such as burglary and rape, and they were significantly more likely to be recidivists. The data in this follow-up study is on African American children who had been in FDRP.

Possible Negative Outcomes Related to the Implementation of FDRP

None known.

References and Resources

Honig, A. S. (1982). *Playtime learning games for young children*. Syracuse, NY: Syracuse University Press.

Honig, A. S. (1996). *Behavior guidance for infants and toddlers*. Little Rock, AK: Southern Early Childhood Association.

Honig, A. S. (2002). *Secure relationships: Nurturing infant/toddler attachment in early care settings*. Washington, DC: National Association for the Education of Young Children.

Honig, A. S. & Brophy, H. (1996). *Talking with your baby: Family as the first school*. Syracuse, NY: Syracuse University Press.

Honig, A. S. & Lally, J. R. (1981). *Infant caregiving: A design for training* (2nd ed.). Syracuse, NY: Syracuse University Press.

Honig, A. S. & Lally, J. R. (1982). The Family Development Research Program: Retrospective review. *Early Child Development and Care, 10*, 41–62.

Honig, A. S. & Lally, J. R. (1988). Behavior profiles of experienced teachers of infants and toddlers. In A. S. Honig (Ed.), Optimizing early child care and education (Special Issue). *Early Child Development and Care, 33*, 181–199.

Honig, A. S., Lally, J. R., & Mathieson, D. H. (1982). Personal and social adjustment of school children after five years in the Family Development Research Program. *ChildCare Quarterly, 11*(2), 138–146.

Lally, J. R. & Honig, A. S. (1975). Education of infants and toddlers from low income and low educational backgrounds: Support for the family's role and identity. In B. Friedlander, G. Kirk, & G. Sterritt (Eds.), *Exceptional infant: Assessment and observation* (Vol. 3, pp. 285–303). New York: Brunner-Mazel.

Lally, J. R., Mangione, P. L., & Honig, A. S. (1989). The Syracuse University Family Development Research Program: Long-range impact of an early intervention with low income children and their families. In D. Powell (Ed.), *Parent education as early childhood intervention: Emerging directions in theory, research, and practice* (pp. 79–104). Norwood, NJ: Ablex.

U.S. Department of Health and Human Services, Substance Abuse and Mental Health Services Administration, Center for Substance Abuse Prevention. (n.d.). *SAMHSA model programs*. Rockville, MD: Author. Available: http://modelprograms.samhsa.gov

The Think Time® Strategy

Contact:
J. Ron Nelson

Position/Title:
Associate Research Professor,
Center for At-Risk Children's Services

Telephone:
(402) 472-0283

Address:
202 Barkley Center
University of Nebraska—Lincoln
Lincoln, NE 68583

E-mail:
rnelson8@unl.edu

Web Address:
www.sopriswest.com

For more information regarding program
materials, contact:

Sopris West Educational Services
4093 Specialty Place
Longmont, CO 80504
Phone: (800) 547-6747
www.sopriswest.com

Purpose

Think Time is designed to accomplish the following:

▲ Reduce the intra- and interpersonal effects of child-teacher interactions.

▲ Deliver a stable response to problem behaviors across all staff.

▲ Provide the student an antiseptic bounding condition (quiet period to enable the child to save face and regain control).

▲ Provide the child with feedback and an opportunity to plan for subsequent performance.

▲ Enable the teacher and student to cut off a negative social exchange and initiate a positive one.

Program Background

The Think Time Strategy for grades K–9 has been used extensively in schools since 1994. The program is implemented by means of video-based training and through direct staff development, making it difficult to determine how many schools have implemented Think Time. Based on the 40–50 workshops that the program designers conduct annually, they estimate that 300–400 schools, including urban, rural, and Title I schools, have implemented Think Time.

Scope of Program

The Think Time Strategy has been used as a schoolwide program and as an early intervention. It can also be part of an intensive intervention.

Specific Problems/Risk Factors Targeted by Think Time Strategy

Think Time is used as a response to challenging behavior and disruptive behavior.

Program Operations

The Think Time Strategy includes three interventions common to schools:

- An effective request (i.e., elimination of threats, ultimatums, warnings, or repeated requests)
- An antiseptic bounding condition (quiet reflective period in which everyone disengages from the student)
- A behavioral debriefing process

The five interrelated steps listed below are crucial to the effectiveness of the strategy:

- Catching problem behavior early
- Moving to and entering the designated Think Time classroom
- Experiencing the Think Time period and debriefing process
- Checking the student's debriefing responses
- Rejoining the classroom

Some of these steps are restatements of the Think Time Strategy presented earlier, but the steps are crucial to the effectiveness of the Strategy.

The Think Time Strategy is used in combination with other interventions and approaches. Throughout Think Time, teachers are not drawn into a discussion with students. All interactions are limited, unemotional, and matter-of-fact. There is no set time limit on when the cooperating teacher approaches the student to complete the debriefing process. The time required for the Think Time Strategy depends upon the student (how long it takes to calm down and be responsive to positive adult-student interactions) and upon when the cooperating teacher has a moment to conduct the debriefing (waiting for an appropriate moment when interacting with the student will be least disruptive to the class).

Determining Your School's Readiness for Think Time Strategy

Think Time requires teamwork between two or more teachers (i.e., the homeroom teacher and a cooperating teacher who provides the designated Think Time area).

The four steps in preparing to implement the Think Time Strategy are relatively simple and straightforward: (1) identify a cooperating teacher, (2) physically prepare the classroom, (3) inform parents, and (4) teach students how the Think Time Strategy works in the classroom.

First, identify a cooperating teacher or set of teachers. The cooperating teacher's room (the Think Time classroom) should be located in close proximity to a second classroom in order to reduce the amount of travel time and the potential for problems when a student is moving to the Think Time classroom.

Second, physically prepare the room. Typically, teachers place two or three desks in a designated Think Time area. The area should be free of visual distractions such as posters or students walking back and forth. It should be situated in a low-use part of the room some distance from where the other students in the classroom are working.

Third, tell parents how the Strategy will be used in the classroom. Teachers should develop and send home a parent information letter and discuss the Think Time Strategy with parents during conference time or at other informational meetings.

Fourth, familiarize the students with Think Time, both the Strategy and the classroom.

Getting Training to Begin Think Time Strategy

The ideal implementation training includes attendance at a two-hour workshop. The Think Time Strategy can then be maintained easily using the video-based training program. However, many schools have implemented the Strategy using video training alone. The video training program with implementation manual is available through Sopris West Educational Services at http://www.sopriswest.com or (800) 547-6747.

Program Costs

The video-based training program is $49. The two-hour workshop is $1,000 plus travel expenses.

Other Resources Required to Implement Think Time Strategy

n/a

Modifying Think Time Strategy for Your School/Classroom Context

The Think Time Strategy can easily be modified to fit the structures and practices of individual schools and teachers. Natural modifications do not decrease the effectiveness of the Strategy if the general principles and steps are followed.

Components That Cannot Be Modified or Excluded From Think Time Strategy

It is critical that staff do not use warnings, threats, or ultimatums. It is also important that staff do not treat the children coldly when reengaging them after the Think Time period.

Think Time Strategy should be founded on an underlying understanding of "with-itness," defined as the teacher's ability to communicate an overall awareness of the classroom to the students. Students' tendency to exhibit problem behaviors is directly linked to the level of teacher awareness of what is occurring in the classroom. A with-it teacher shows an awareness of times of high probability for problem behaviors, increases monitoring, and takes preventive steps. A with-it teacher also shows an awareness of whether the student complies with teacher attempts to redirect behavior. For example, the teacher who tells a student to stop disturbing his classmate and then ignores the fact that the child failed to comply is inviting challenges and is reducing credibility. The elimination of threats and warnings in the Think Time Strategy increases the with-itness of teachers, but it is critical that teachers demonstrate that they are with-it in a variety of ways.

Program Outcomes

Nelson (1996) examined the effects of setting clear limits in combination with the Think Time Strategy on the school survival skills, social adjustment, and academic performance of a group of diffi-cult-to-teach students. Comparisons between target students (i.e., those with or at risk for emotional and behavioral disorders), and criterion students (i.e., those without and not at risk for emotional and behavioral disorders) indicated statistically significant effects on the social adjustment, academic performance, and school survival skills of the target students.

Building on this work, Nelson, Martella, and Galand (1998) conducted a component analysis to provide more conclusive information regarding the effects of the Think Time Strategy on severe challenging behaviors that require an administrative intervention (e.g., suspension). The results indicated that the strategy alone resulted in a 70 percent decrease in such behaviors. Think Time Strategy validation studies have included diverse groups of elementary-aged students. The Strategy appears to be effective with diverse groups of students, including students with disabilities.

Possible Negative Outcomes Related to the Implementation of Think Time Strategy

The Think Time Strategy would be inappropriate with children who are socially withdrawn (e.g., autistic children) or who have significant developmental disabilities.

References and Resources

Nelson, J. R. (1996). Designing schools to meet the needs of students who exhibit disruptive behavior. *Journal of Emotional and Behavioral Disorders, 4,* 147–161.

Nelson, J. R., Martella, R., & Galand, B. (1998). The effects of teaching school expectations and establishing consistent consequences on formal office disciplinary actions. *Journal of Emotional and Behavioral Disorders, 6,* 153–161.

Nelson, J. R. & Carr, B. A. (1999). *Think Time Strategy for schools.* Longmont, CO: Sopris West Educational Services.

Checklists, Surveys, and Tools

Schoolwide Team Checklist

Name: _____   Date: _____

Positive Traits Our Schoolwide Team . . .	What Is in Place	Rating		Needs to Be Developed	Actions to Be Taken
		+	–		
Expresses a shared vision for an improved school.					
Has identified existing resources that are available to support our vision.					
Has identified additional resources necessary in order to further shape our vision.					
Has identified the schoolwide team leaders.					
Has distributed planning and development responsibilities among all school-community stakeholders.					
Has made plans to sustain stakeholder involvement over the reform period.					
Has established group norms and strategies to ensure mutual trust and respect among team members.					
Has identified mechanisms to share critical information among stakeholders.					
Has a plan to publicize and share the decision-making process among stakeholder groups.					
Has strategies to ensure consensus decisions.					

→

Schoolwide Team Checklist (continued)

Positive Traits Our Schoolwide Team . . .	What Is in Place	Rating		Needs to Be Developed	Actions to Be Taken
		+	–		
Has distributed planning and development responsibilities among all school-community stakeholders.					
Has included the individuals and groups (i.e., parents, teachers, students, community members, etc.) whose behavior we hope to change.					
Has developed the specific behavioral changes we expect to see.					
Has developed the appropriate measures of these behaviors.					
Has identified the existing sources of information to track behavior change.					
Has identified the additional information we need to collect.					
Has developed data collection strategies.					
Has identified systems that are currently in place to address these problems.					
Has identified the individuals responsible for these systems and how they can be involved in the school improvement effort.					
Has developed the appropriate performance measures for individuals responsible for these systems.					

Community Linkages Assessment Form

Name: _____ Date: _____

Community Partner	Nature of Partnership	Who Is Served	Goodness of Fit With School/ District	Memorandum of Agreement	Length of Commitment/ Partnership
Youth centers					
County recreation programs					
Community-based organizations					
Universities and colleges					
Businesses					
Faith community					
Community mental health agencies and community health agencies					
Social service agencies					
Community police, juvenile justice, and the courts					
Parent groups, including PTAs and PTOs, and special groups					
Civil rights and advocacy organizations					
Foundations					

Vision Statement Checklist

Name: _____   Date: _____

Positive Traits Our School's Vision Statement Is . . .	What Is in Place	Rating		Needs to Be Developed	Actions to Be Taken
		+	−		
Concise (fewer than 100 words).					
Powerful enough to enable stakeholders to look beyond barriers and focus their thoughts on the benefits of their efforts.					
Written in ambitious but meaningful terms, and explicitly complements the school's overall vision statement (if one exists).					
Able to establish a relationship between school-community members' activities (in carrying out a schoolwide plan) and the vision.					
Consistent with district-level mandates.					

Needs Assessment Checklist

Name: _____   Date: _____

Positive Traits **Our Schoolwide Team Has Identified . . .**	What Is in Place	Rating		Needs to Be Developed	Actions to Be Taken
		+	−		
The individuals and groups (i.e., parents, teachers, students, community members, etc.) whose behavior we hope to change.					
The specific behavioral changes we expect to see.					
Appropriate measures of these behaviors.					
Existing sources of information to track behavior change.					
Additional information we need to collect.					
Data collection strategies.					
Systems currently in place to address these problems.					
Individuals responsible for these systems and how they can be involved in the school improvement effort.					
Appropriate measures of these behaviors.					

Adapted from the National Resource Center for Safe Schools.

California School Climate and Safety Survey
Elementary Version

Directions for Students—We want to hear from you about safety, school work, and other school issues. Answer these questions by the circling number that goes with your answer. Please mark only one number for each question.

Part I: How often do these things happen at your school?

	Not At All	A Little	Some	Quite a Bit	Very Much
1. Students using drugs (alcohol, marijuana).	1	2	3	4	5
2. Students destroying things (vandalism).	1	2	3	4	5
3. Students getting into fights.	1	2	3	4	5
4. Students stealing things.	1	2	3	4	5
5. Students threatening or bullying other students.	1	2	3	4	5
6. Students carrying weapons.	1	2	3	4	5

Part II: What is your school like? When you answer, think about the way your school is most of the time. Please circle one answer.

	Strongly Disagree	Disagree	Agree	Strongly Agree
7. I feel very safe at this school.	1	2	3	4
8. I really want my school to be "the best."	1	2	3	4
9. There are gangs at this school.	1	2	3	4
10. When there is an emergency, someone is there to help.	1	2	3	4
11. Teachers here are nice to the students.	1	2	3	4
12. I really belong at this school.	1	2	3	4
13. I work very hard on my school assignments.	1	2	3	4
14. When students break rules, they are all treated fairly.	1	2	3	4
15. The campus is very neat and clean.	1	2	3	4
16. Most people at this school can be trusted.	1	2	3	4
17. Everyone is expected to do their best at this school.	1	2	3	4
18. Students really want to learn.	1	2	3	4
19. Teachers let me know I am doing a good job.	1	2	3	4
20. My parents get involved in school activities.	1	2	3	4
21. Students of all racial and ethnic groups are respected.	1	2	3	4
22. I am a success in school.	1	2	3	4
23. My classrooms look very nice.	1	2	3	4
24. People at this school really care for each other.	1	2	3	4
25. The rules at my school are fair.	1	2	3	4
26. My school is a very safe place.	1	2	3	4
27. Teachers do a good job of looking out for troublemakers.	1	2	3	4
28. I learn a lot about myself at this school.	1	2	3	4
29. I have a lot of friends at this school.	1	2	3	4
30. I am comfortable talking to teachers about my problems.	1	2	3	4

Used with permission from the University of California, Santa Barbara Gevirtz Graduate School of Education.

Safe, Supportive, and Successful Schools Step by Step

California School Climate and Safety Survey
Elementary Version (continued)

Part III: This part asks about the things that have recently happened to you at school. Answer by circling "YES" or "NO" for each item. Which of these things happened to you at school in the PAST MONTH? (We mean things that have actually happened to you, not things you have just heard about.)

Have any of these things happened to you AT SCHOOL during the past MONTH?

31. You were grabbed or shoved by someone being mean . . . . NO . . . . YES
32. You were punched or kicked by someone trying to hurt you . . . . NO . . . . YES
33. You personally saw another student on campus with a gun . . . . NO . . . . YES
34. Someone hit you with a rock or another object . . . . NO . . . . YES
35. You took ten field trips . . . . NO . . . . YES
36. You went to a school office because you were hurt in a fight . . . . NO . . . . YES
37. You had something stolen . . . . NO . . . . YES
38. You saw another student on campus with a knife or razor . . . . NO . . . . YES
39. Someone said they were going hurt you or beat you up . . . . NO . . . . YES
40. You bought three brand new bicycles at school . . . . NO . . . . YES
41. Someone yelled bad words . . . . NO . . . . YES
42. Someone threatened you going to school in the morning . . . . NO . . . . YES
43. Someone threatened you going home after school . . . . NO . . . . YES
44. Someone made fun of you, put you down . . . . NO . . . . YES
45. A student threatened you with a knife and you saw the knife . . . . NO . . . . YES
46. You were pushed around by gang members . . . . NO . . . . YES

Part IV: Questions

47. How many good friends do you have at school?
    1. One student
    2. Two students
    3. Three students
    4. Four or more students
    5. No students

48. How many teachers are you able to talk to about any problems you might have?
    1. One teacher
    2. Two teachers
    3. Three teachers
    4. Four or more
    5. No teachers

49. Which one of the following are you MOST worried about? (Choose ONLY one.)
    1. Getting good grades
    2. Violence in your school
    3. Being liked by other students
    4. Violence in your neighborhood
    5. Getting along with your parents and other family members

50. How do you feel about going to this school?
    1. I like school very much.
    2. I like school a lot.
    3. I like school.
    4. I don't like school very much.
    5. I hate school.

51. What is your racial/ethnic background?
    1. White, European American
    2. Black, African American
    3. Latina(o), Chicano(a), Mexican, Hispanic
    4. Native American (American Indian)
    5. Asian American (Japanese, Chinese, Filipino, Vietnamese, Laotian, Pacific Islander)

Prides: (Please describe what you like best about your school.) _____

_____

_____

_____

Needs: (Please describe positive ways your school could improve.) _____

_____

_____

_____

Used with permission from the University of California, Santa Barbara Gevirtz Graduate School of Education.

California School Climate and Safety Survey
Secondary Version

Directions for Students—We want to hear from you about safety, school work, and other school issues. Answer these questions by circling the number that goes with your answer. Please mark only one number for each question.

Part I: How often do these things happen at your school?

	Not At All	A Little	Some	Quite a Bit	Very Much
1. Students using drugs (marijuana, coke, crack).	1	2	3	4	5
2. Students destroying things (vandalism).	1	2	3	4	5
3. Students drinking beer/wine/liquor.	1	2	3	4	5
4. Students getting into fights.	1	2	3	4	5
5. Students stealing things.	1	2	3	4	5
6. Students threatening or bullying.	1	2	3	4	5
6. Students carrying weapons.	1	2	3	4	5

Part II: This section asks about what your school is like. When you answer, think about the way your school is most of the time. Please circle your answer.

	Strongly Disagree	Disagree	Agree	Strongly Agree
8. I feel very safe at this school.	1	2	3	4
9. They take good care of the school grounds.	1	2	3	4
10. I like everyone I meet.	1	2	3	4
11. This school is being ruined by youth gang activity.	1	2	3	4
12. Teachers here are nice people.	1	2	3	4
13. I always think before I act.	1	2	3	4
14. This school is badly affected by crime and violence in the community.	1	2	3	4
15. My teachers respect me.	1	2	3	4
16. When students break rules, they are treated firmly but fairly.	1	2	3	4
17. I tell the truth every single time.	1	2	3	4
18. Gang members make this school dangerous.	1	2	3	4
19. They keep the campus well maintained and clean.	1	2	3	4
20. My teachers are fair.	1	2	3	4
21. You can trust most people at this school.	1	2	3	4
22. At this school, the students are really motivated to learn.	1	2	3	4
23. Crime and violence is a major concern on this campus.	1	2	3	4
24. My classrooms look very nice.	1	2	3	4
25. Most students here get involved in sports, clubs, and other school activities.	1	2	3	4
26. At this school, students and teachers really care for each other.	1	2	3	4
27. The rules at my school are fair.	1	2	3	4
28. I do not feel safe at this school.	1	2	3	4
29. I learn a lot about myself at this school.	1	2	3	4
30. I have many friends at this school.	1	2	3	4

Used with permission from the University of California, Santa Barbara Gevirtz Graduate School of Education.

California School Climate and Safety Survey
Secondary Version (continued)

Part III: What Happens to Me at My School. This section asks about the things that have recently happened to you at school. Answer by circling "YES" or "NO" for each item. Which of these things happened to you at school in the PAST MONTH? (We mean things that have actually happened to you, not things you have just heard about.)

Have any of these things happened to you AT SCHOOL during the past MONTH?

31. You were grabbed or shoved by someone being mean . . . . NO . . . . . YES
32. You were punched or kicked by someone trying to hurt you . . . . NO . . . . . YES
33. You personally saw another student on campus with a gun . . . . NO . . . . . YES
34. Someone hit you with a rock or another object trying to hurt you . . . . NO . . . . . YES
35. You took ten field trips . . . . NO . . . . . YES
36. You had personal property stolen . . . . NO . . . . . YES
37. You personally saw another student on campus with a knife or razor . . . . NO . . . . . YES
38. Another student threatened to hurt you . . . . NO . . . . . YES
39. You were voted student of the week four times . . . . NO . . . . . YES
40. Someone yelled bad words, cursed at you . . . . NO . . . . . YES
41. You were threatened by a student with a gun and you saw the gun . . . . NO . . . . . YES
42. Someone made unwanted physical sexual advances toward you . . . . NO . . . . . YES
43. Someone sexually harassed you (made unwanted sexual comments to you) . . . . NO . . . . . YES
44. You were threatened by a student with a knife and you saw the knife . . . . NO . . . . . YES
45. You were bullied, threatened, or pushed around by gang members . . . . NO . . . . . YES
46. Someone tried to scare you by the way they looked at you . . . . NO . . . . . YES

Part IV: Questions

47. How many good friends do you have at school?

    1. One student
    2. Two students
    3. Three students
    4. Four or more students
    5. No students

48. How many teachers or other adults (principal, counselor, nurse, etc.) are you able to talk to about problems you might have?

    1. One
    2. Two
    3. Three
    4. Four or more
    5. None

49. Which one of the following are you MOST worried about?

    1. Getting good grades
    2. Violence in your school

50. In general, what are your grades this school year?

    1. Mostly A grades
    2. Mostly B grades
    3. Mostly C grades
    4. Mostly D grades
    5. Mostly F grades

Part IV: Questions

51. Who is at home when you get home from school in the afternoon?

    1. No one
    2. Father or mother
    3. Friends
    4. Brother or sister
    5. Other relative

52. How do you feel about going to school?

    1. I like school very much.
    2. I like school quite a bit.
    3. I like school.
    4. I don't like school very much.
    5. I hate school.

53. What is your racial/ethnic background?

    1. White, European American
    2. Black, African American
    3. Latina(o), Chicano(a), Mexican, Hispanic
    4. Native American (American Indian)
    5. Asian American (Japanese, Chinese, Filipino, Vietnamese, Laotian, Pacific Islander)
    6. Multi-ethnic/racial
    7. Other (specify) _____

54. What is the highest grade in school which your father/stepfather/male guardian has completed? **(Mark only one answer.)**

    1. I do not live with my father or have a stepfather/male guardian.
    2. He did not finish high school.
    3. He finished high school.
    4. He took some college or trade school.
    5. He finished college.

55. What is the highest grade in school which your mother/stepmother/female guardian has completed? **(Mark only one answer.)**

    1. I do not live with my mother or have a stepmother/female guardian.
    2. She did not finish high school.
    3. She finished high school.
    4. She took some college or trade school.
    5. She finished college.

Areas of Pride and Strength: (Please describe what you like best about your school.)_____

_____

_____

_____

_____

_____

_____

Concerns and Needs: (Please describe positive ways your school could improve.)_____

_____

_____

_____

_____

_____

_____

Used with permission from the University of California, Santa Barbara Gevirtz Graduate School of Education.

Goals and Objectives Checklist

Name: _____   Date: _____

Our Schoolwide Team Has Identified . . .	What Is in Place	Rating		Needs to Be Developed	Actions to Be Taken
		+	–		
Are measurable and achievable within a reasonable time frame.					
Include at least one short-term objective that will mark progress toward achieving goals.					
Are supported by the entire schoolwide team.					
Are sufficient so that the vision can be achieved, but small enough in number to keep track of and work on.					
Have been assigned to one or more school-community members for oversight and coordination.					
Are monitored in a systematic way so that periodic progress reports can be made to the schoolwide team and district leadership.					
Are consistent with district-level protocols or expectations regarding these problems.					

Financial Planning Checklist

Name: _____   Date: _____

Our School Is Being Efficient by . . .	What Is in Place	Rating		Needs to Be Developed	Actions to Be Taken
		+	–		
Looking at the entire school budget and working with the schoolwide team to identify funds that could be reallocated. These are funds that are being used ineffectively or are redundant with school improvement efforts and so need to be realigned with the schoolwide team's program.					
Investigating the availability of public funds for reform, including flow-through State Improvement Grants under IDEA, Federal ESEA, Safe and Drug-Free School allocations, Improving America's Schools Fund, Comprehensive School Reform Design funds, Federal and State Vocational Rehabilitation funds, Medicaid planning funds, and Supplementary Security Insurance (SSI).					
Organizing for and identifying local funding sources to support reform efforts.					
Talking with program sponsors and other school reform organizations about finding resources to support the reform. This may include working directly with district, state, and national organizations that will help locate funds for reform.					
Assigning school-community members the responsibility of publicizing the school's efforts and improving community perception of the school.					

→

Safe, Supportive, and Successful Schools Step by Step ▲

Financial Planning Checklist (continued)

Our School Is Being Efficient by . . .	What Is in Place	Rating +	Rating –	Needs to Be Developed	Actions to Be Taken
Publicizing the good things that happen at the school.					
Inviting public officials and members of the business community to participate in special events, take leadership roles within the schoolwide team, and hold meetings on campus.					
Having interagency funding agreements in place.					
Having a manual that describes resources already available to parents, students, and teachers.					
Assigning school-community members responsibility for exploring local and national foundations, philanthropies, businesses (including the local chamber of commerce), and individuals that may be interested in supporting one or more elements of our reform.					
Including trained volunteers in school activities.					

Schoolwide Prevention Program Checklist

Name: _____ Date: _____

Our School Has . . .	What Is in Place	Rating +	Rating −	Needs to Be Developed	Actions to Be Taken
A Focus on Academic Achievement					
Clearly stated goals for student academic achievement.					
Academic goals that are linked with systemwide and community academic expectations.					
Means of ensuring that students know what the academic expectations are.					
Faculty and staff who understand and support these expectations.					
Ongoing training resources for faculty and staff that are aligned with academic expectations.					
Academic goals coordinated across grade levels and subject areas.					
Instructional opportunities aligned for ALL students to achieve academic goals.					
Meaningful and reliable ways to assess students' progress on these academic goals.					
Tutorial and remediation programs for students with learning difficulties.					

→

Safe, Supportive, and Successful Schools Step by Step ▲

Schoolwide Prevention Program Checklist (continued)

Our School Has . . .	What Is in Place	Rating +	Rating –	Needs to Be Developed	Actions to Be Taken
Meaningful Ways of Involving Families					
A school-family liaison.					
Invitations presented in families' native languages.					
Data collection strategies that are manageable and nondisruptive.					
Clear problem-solving processes used by schoolwide and student support teams.					
Strategies to Address the Transition Needs of All Students					
Procedures and practices to address all (or appropriate) developmental transitions, including preschool to primary, primary to middle, and middle to high school.					
Activities that will systematically expose all students to a wide variety of post-school employment and higher education opportunities, and mentors from the business and academic communities.					
Policies that give school staff access to formal reporting procedures and adequate professional consultation regarding their concerns.					
Extended Day Programs for Children					
Before- and after-school activities, available to and accessible by all students, which take into account different student strengths and interests.					

→

Schoolwide Prevention Program Checklist (continued)

Our School Has . . .	What Is in Place	Rating +	Rating −	Needs to Be Developed	Actions to Be Taken
Ways to Promote Good Citizenship and Character					
Instruction in and support for social skills development and problem solving.					
Visual displays that promote citizenship values.					
Systematic instruction for children about responsibility for their actions—that the choices they make have consequences for which they will be held accountable.					
Activities that encourage citizenship, including clubs and service groups.					
Ways to Identify Problems and Assess Progress Toward Solutions					
Carefully defined problem definitions.					
Ways that staff and students can help identify problems and solutions.					
Opportunities for Students to Learn How to Express Safety Issues and Concerns Openly					
Formal training sessions and discussions where students hear from school-community members about safety issues and have the opportunity to share their own ideas.					
Support personnel (school psychologists, counselors, etc.) available for students when they need help.					

Schoolwide Prevention Program Checklist (continued)

Our School Has . . .	What Is in Place	Rating +	Rating −	Needs to Be Developed	Actions to Be Taken
Ways for Students to Feel Safe Expressing Their Feelings					
Regularly scheduled individual and small-group activities that elicit student feedback and deepen connections between students and staff.					
Easy ways for students to access counselors and other support personnel in a confidential manner.					
A System in Place for Referring Children Who Are Suspected of Being Abused or Neglected					
Legal policies and procedures regarding children who are suspected of being abused or neglected, and school personnel who understand these policies.					
School staff trained to recognize the signs and symptoms of physical and sexual abuse.					
Readiness and capacity to be responsive to parental concerns about academic behavior and psychosocial needs of children.					
Parent volunteer opportunities.					
Links to the Community					
Links with the faith-based community and other community-based organizations.					
Partnerships with community organizations such as county recreation programs, universities and colleges, businesses, civil rights and advocacy organizations, and foundations.					

➝

Schoolwide Prevention Program Checklist (continued)

Our School Has ..	What Is in Place	Rating +	Rating –	Needs to Be Developed	Actions to Be Taken
Positive Relationships Among Students and Staff					
Staff in the school-community that are expected to listen to students and are supported in doing so.					
Regularly scheduled opportunities for students and staff to interact in informal ways.					
Equal Respect for All Students					
Programs that are inclusive of all students.					
Staff trained to be responsive in a timely and sensitive manner to the psychosocial needs children and youth express.					
Discipline policies that do not single out students from particular racial or cultural groups.					

Checklist of Students' Social
Problem-Solving Strengths Across Situations

Child:_____ Date:_____

Directions—Record situations by entering the numbers of those in which particular skills appear to be demonstrated, using the following codes:

1 = with peers in classroom

2 = with peers in other situations in school

3 = with teachers

4 = with other adults in school

5 = with parents

6 = with siblings or other relatives

7 = with peers outside of school

8 = when under academic stress or pressure

9 = when under social or peer-related stress or pressure

10 = when under family-related stress or pressure

11 = other: _____

In what situations is this child able to: **Situations**

A. **Self-control skills**

   1. Listen carefully and accurately   _____

   2. Remember and follow directions   _____

   3. Concentrate and follow through on tasks   _____

   4. Calm him- or herself down   _____

   5. Carry on a conversation without upsetting or provoking others   _____

B. **Social awareness and group-participation skills**

   6. Accept praise or approval   _____

   7. Choose praiseworthy and caring friends   _____

   8. Know when help is needed   _____

   9. Ask for help when needed   _____

  10. Work as part of a problem-solving team   _____

C. **Social problem-solving and decision-making skills**

  11. Recognize signs of feelings in self   _____

  12. Recognize signs of feelings in others   _____

  13. Describe accurately a range of feelings   _____

  14. Put problems into words clearly   _____

  15. State realistic interpersonal goals   _____

  16. Think of several ways to solve a problem or reach a goal   _____

  17. Think of different types of solutions   _____

  18. Do (16) and (17) for different types of problems   _____

  19. Differentiate short- and long-term consequences   _____

  20. Look at effects of choices on self and others   _____

  21. Keep positive and negative possibilities in mind   _____

  22. Select solutions that can reach goals   _____

  23. Make choices that do not harm self, others   _____

  24. Consider details before carrying out a solution (who, when, where, with whom, etc.)   _____

  25. Anticipate obstacles to plans   _____

  26. Respond appropriately when plans are thwarted   _____

  27. Try out his or her ideas   _____

  28. Learn from experiences or from seeking input from adults, friends   _____

  29. Use previous experience to help "next time"   _____

Adapted from *Social Problem Solving*, by Maurice J. Elias and Steven E. Tobias. © The Guilford Press.

Assessing Behavioral Support in Your School: Features

SYSTEM	FEATURES OF THE SYSTEM

Schoolwide

1. A small number (e.g., 3–5) of positively and clearly stated student expectations or rules are defined.
2. Expected student behaviors are taught directly.
3. Expected student behaviors are rewarded regularly.
4. Problem behaviors (failure to meet expected student behaviors) are defined clearly.
5. Consequences for problem behaviors are defined clearly.
6. Distinctions between office vs. classroom-managed problem behaviors are clear.
7. Options exist to allow classroom instruction to continue when problem behavior occurs.
8. Procedures are in place to address emergency/dangerous situations.
9. A team exists for behavior support planning and problem solving.
10. School administrator is an active participant on the behavior support team.
11. Staff receive regular (monthly/quarterly) feedback on behavior patterns.
12. School includes formal strategies for informing families about expected student behaviors at school.
13. Booster training activities for students are developed, modified, and conducted based on school data.
14. Schoolwide behavior support team has a budget for (a) teaching students, (b) ongoing rewards, (c) annual staff planning.
15. All staff are involved directly and/or indirectly in schoolwide interventions.

Specific Settings

1. Schoolwide-expected student behaviors apply to nonclassroom settings.
2. Schoolwide-expected student behaviors are taught in nonclassroom settings.
3. Supervisors actively supervise (move, scan, and interact) students in nonclassroom settings.
4. Rewards exist for meeting expected student behaviors in nonclassroom settings.
5. Physical/architectural features are modified to limit (a) unsupervised settings, (b) unclear traffic patterns, and (c) inappropriate access to and exit from school grounds.
6. Scheduling of student movement ensures appropriate numbers of students in nonclassroom spaces.
7. Staff receive regular opportunities for developing and improving active supervision skills.
8. Status of student behavior and management practices are evaluated quarterly from data.
9. All staff are involved directly or indirectly in management of nonclassroom settings.

Classrooms

1. Expected student behavior routines in classrooms are stated positively and defined clearly.
2. Problem behaviors are defined clearly.
3. Expected student behavior and routines in classrooms are taught directly.
4. Expected student behaviors are acknowledged regularly (positively reinforced) (more than four positives to one negative).
5. Problem behaviors receive consistent consequences.
6. Procedures for expected and problem behaviors are consistent with schoolwide procedures.
7. Options exist to allow classroom instruction to continue when problem behavior occurs.
8. Instruction and curriculum materials are matched to student ability (math, reading, language).
9. Students experience high rates of academic success (more than 75% correct).
10. Teachers have regular opportunities for access to assistance and recommendations (observation, instruction, and coaching).
11. Transitions between instructional and noninstructional activities are efficient and orderly.

Individual Settings

1. Assessments are conducted regularly to identify students with chronic problem behaviors.
2. A simple process exists for teachers to request assistance.
3. A behavior support team responds promptly (within two working days) to students who present chronic problem behaviors.
4. The behavioral support team includes an individual skilled at conducting functional behavioral assessment.
5. Local resources are used to conduct functional assessment-based behavior support planning (~ten hours/week/student).
6. Significant family and/or community members are involved when possible and appropriate.
7. School includes formal opportunities for families to receive training on behavioral support and positive parenting strategies.
8. Behavior is monitored and feedback provided regularly to the behavior support team and relevant staff.

Adapted from *Effective School Practices, 17*(4), Spring 1999.

Safe, Supportive, and Successful Schools Step by Step

Assessing Behavioral Support in Your School: A Survey

Name: _____   Date: _____

Schoolwide Systems—For each statement, rate the level of implementation that you believe occurs at your school AND rate your priority level for improvement or maintenance for this school year.

Feature	Priority Level for Improvement/Maintenance			Level of Implementation		
Schoolwide is defined as involving all students, all staff, and all settings.	High	Medium	Low	In Place	Partially in Place	Not in Place
1. Expectations for student behavior are defined.						
2. Discipline procedures are implemented consistently by staff and administration.						
3. Appropriate student behavior is taught.						
4. Student behavior is monitored and staff receive regular (monthly/quarterly) feedback on behavioral outcomes.						
5. Problem behaviors have clear consequences.						
6. Positive behaviors are publicly acknowledged.						
7. Rapid response procedures are in place to address dangerous situations.						
8. Teachers have clear options that allow classroom instruction to continue.						
9. A team is responsible for addressing behavior support problems.						
10. An office referral process is operational and functional.						

Adapted from U.S. Department of Education, Office of Special Education Programs Evaluator's Briefing Book: *Technical Assistance Center on Positive Behavioral Intervention and Support*, 2000.

Responding to Early Warning Signs Checklist

Name: _____ Date: _____

Positive Traits Our School Has . . .	What Is in Place	Rating		Needs to Be Developed	Actions to Be Taken
		+	–		
A plan in place to evaluate staff responses to early warning signs and other problem behaviors.					
Staff that understand the principles underlying the identification of early warning signs.					
All staff trained about the early warning signs of behavior and academic problems and how to respond appropriately.					
All staff trained to identify and respond to imminent warning signs.					
Quick access to a student support team for staff consultation.					
A referral process that has a simple procedure for responding to requests for urgent assistance, gives scheduling preference to urgent referrals, encourages informal consultation, and is responsive to and inclusive of parents.					
A referral process that provides interventions as soon as possible after the referral is made.					
A referral process that maintains confidentiality and parents' rights to privacy.					
A referral process that includes a way to circumvent the referral process in cases of imminent warning signs.					
A student support team that is trained in comprehensive problem solving and that takes time to identify and measure the problem behavior(s), using functional behavior assessment methods when appropriate.					

⟶

Safe, Supportive, and Successful Schools Step by Step ▲

Responding to Early Warning Signs Checklist (continued)

Positive Traits Our School Has ...	What Is in Place	Rating +	Rating –	Needs to Be Developed	Actions to Be Taken
A student support team with knowledge of interventions (including family and community supports) appropriate for a variety of behavioral problems and a team-based decision-making strategy to select the appropriate response.					
A way for the student support team to systematically monitor the problem concerns and behaviors once they have been identified and discussed.					
Policies and procedures in place that support quick and effective responses to early warning and imminent warning signs.					
Training and support for staff, students, and families in understanding factors that can set off and/or exacerbate aggressive outbursts.					
Skill training, therapeutic assistance, and other supports for the family through school and community-based services.					
Strategies to encourage families to make sure that firearms are out of children's immediate reach.					
A simple mechanism for the student support team to use when referring children at risk for serious behavior problems for more comprehensive early intervention support. A memorandum of understanding between school and community agencies should support the availability of intensive services and interventions.					

Providing Intensive Interventions Checklist

Name: _____ Date: _____

Positive Traits Our School Has . . .	What Is in Place	Rating		Needs to Be Developed	Actions to Be Taken
		+	–		
Consultation for helping teaching staff support high behavioral and academic standards.					
Effective anger and impulse control training, psychological counseling, academic and remedial instruction, and vocational training as appropriate.					
School-based support and clinical services that are available to all students needing services, their families, teachers, and administrators.					
Learning and behavior supported by school-based and school-focused wraparound supports.					
School-based case management.					
Evidence-based schoolwide prevention and early intervention programs that address academic and behavioral risks.					
Evidence-based interventions and services within the school that support children and youth with emotional and behavioral needs, as well as their families.					

→

Safe, Supportive, and Successful Schools Step by Step ▲

Providing Intensive Interventions Checklist (continued)

Positive Traits Our School Has . . .	What Is in Place	Rating		Needs to Be Developed	Actions to Be Taken
		+	−		
Links to a system of care, if it exists in the community, or links to all relevant agencies if it does not.					
Family liaisons or advocates to support and strengthen the role of family members in the school and in their children's education and care.					
Staff who understand the availability of school-based resources, including mental health programs, special education and related services, alternative programs and schools, and other components of the continuum of care.					
Opportunities for staff to continually develop and improve their skills and knowledge related to schoolwide prevention programs, early and intensive interventions, positive behavioral support, functional behavior assessment, and other proven interventions.					
Opportunities for the student, his or her family, and appropriate school staff to be involved in developing and monitoring interventions.					
Partnerships with community-based service providers and teams or committees to foster collaboration and delivery of services.					

Program and Provider Checklist

Program: _____

Contact person: _____ Date: _____

School visited where design is used: _____

	Performance Indicators			
	A Priority Identified in Your School's Needs Assessment	**Provides or Demonstrates STRONG Evidence (for Which Types of Students/Schools)**	**Provides or Demonstrates SOME Evidence (for Which Types of Students/Schools)**	**Provides or Demonstrates LITTLE or NO Evidence (for Which Types of Students/Schools)**
RESEARCH BASE				
An approach that is theory-based and supported by research.				
Evidence that the program or intervention has demonstrated effectiveness using a research model having a control group or comparison group.				
Published in a peer-reviewed professional journal.				
PERFORMANCE OF PROGRAM (The provider/program ensures the following:)				
A direct relationship between program components and raising achievement across grade levels and content areas for all students within three to five years.				
Gains in student achievement sustained for more than five years.				
Improved student attendance.				
Reduction in the number of discipline referrals and dropouts.				
Reduction in school violence.				
Improved school climate.				
Improved staff, students, and community relations.				
Implementation in multiple sites for multiple years.				

→

Program and Provider Checklist (continued)

	Performance Indicators			
	A Priority Identified in Your School's Needs Assessment	Provides or Demonstrates STRONG Evidence (for Which Types of Students/Schools)	Provides or Demonstrates SOME Evidence (for Which Types of Students/Schools)	Provides or Demonstrates LITTLE or NO Evidence (for Which Types of Students/Schools)
PROGRAM FIT (The provider/program ensures the following:)				
A commitment to address school- or district-specific goals.				
Implementation in schools with characteristics and demographics similar to yours, such as size, languages spoken, and racial and ethnic composition.				
Broad stakeholder involvement.				
A strategy for continuous improvement that includes the use of standardized tests results and other important measures of performance to drive the annual school improvement plan.				
A strategy to transfer ownership of the project to school-community members (e.g., training-of-trainers program).				
A detailed process for faculty, administrators, parents, and community members to actively participate in choosing a program.				
Specifications of any necessary changes in curriculum, instructional practices, scheduling, and class structure to implement the program.				
QUALITY OF ASSISTANCE (The provider/program ensures the following:)				
A review of the school's needs assessment, showing how the program/approach will help meet your goals.				
A description of how the program will be implemented and a specific explanation of the human resources, facilities, and funds needed for implementation.				
A contract that specifies the roles and responsibilities of the program provider.				
A contract that describes the roles and responsibilities of the school.				

→

Program and Provider Checklist (continued)

	Performance Indicators			
	A Priority Identified in Your School's Needs Assessment	**Provides or Demonstrates STRONG Evidence (for Which Types of Students/Schools)**	**Provides or Demonstrates SOME Evidence (for Which Types of Students/Schools)**	**Provides or Demonstrates LITTLE or NO Evidence (for Which Types of Students/Schools)**
QUALITY OF ASSISTANCE (continued) (The provider/program ensures the following:)				
A contract that describes the roles and responsibilities for shared data collection and dissemination.				
A contract that itemizes the costs of implementation and specifies whether the cost of materials, staff development, and additional personnel are included in the price.				
A contract that lists all services to be provided, and by whom.				
A contract that specifies the amount of on-site services.				
A contract that specifies time lines, milestones, and performance targets for key program dimensions for each phase of implementation.				
Specification of the time to be devoted to professional development, customized to your school's needs.				
Specifications of the kind of ongoing communication opportunities among schools using the program.				
Specification of how often the provider will communicate information about implementation progress and results to school staff and parents.				
Feedback to teachers or designated staff trainees on their progress in implementing the design components.				
A system for resolving problems and complaints, and procedures for providing remedies.				
Interviews and/or surveys of school staff to monitor the progress of the school in implementing elements of the program.				
Specification of how the provider will help sustain the program.				

→

Program and Provider Checklist (continued)

	Performance Indicators			
	A Priority Identified in Your School's Needs Assessment	**Provides or Demonstrates STRONG Evidence (for Which Types of Students/Schools)**	**Provides or Demonstrates SOME Evidence (for Which Types of Students/Schools)**	**Provides or Demonstrates LITTLE or NO Evidence (for Which Types of Students/Schools)**
CAPACITY OF PROGRAM AND PROVIDER (The provider/program supplies the following:)				
Identification of provider resources needed to sustain and support program-related efforts.				
Information on the credentials and experience of the team that will be working with your school.				
Evidence demonstrating that the provider has the capacity and expertise to implement the program in your school.				
Audited financial statements.				
A credit rating for the provider from an independent rating agency.				
A business plan or profile.				

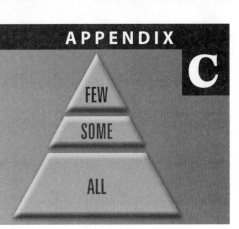

Acknowledgments

Howard Adelman
University of California, Los Angeles

George Batsche
University of South Florida

Barbara Bazron
Institute for Research, Education, and Training in Addictions

Betty Chemers
U.S. Department of Justice

Lucy Davidson
Center for Child Well-Being

Celene Domitrovich
Penn State University

Kellie Dressler-Tetrick
Office of Juvenile Justice and Delinquency Prevention, U.S. Department of Justice

Theodore Feinberg
National Association of School Psychologists

Ken Feske
Salinas, California, Safe Schools/Healthy Students Initiative

Michael J. Furlong
University of California, Santa Barbara

Susan Gorin
National Association of School Psychologists

Pat Graczyk
University of Illinois, Chicago

Pat Guthrie
Council for Administrators of Special Education

Tom Hanley
Office of Special Education and Rehabilitative Services, U.S. Department of Education

Norris Haynes
Southern Connecticut State University

Shep Kellam
American Institutes for Research

Denise Middlebrook
Substance Abuse and Mental Health Services Administration

John Mitchell
American Federation of Teachers

William Modzeleski
U.S. Department of Education

Eve Moscicki
National Institute for Mental Health

Ron Palomares
American Psychological Association

John Reid
Oregon Social Learning Center

Peter Sheras
University of Virginia

Russell Skiba
Indiana University

George Sugai
University of Oregon

Carlos Sundermann
National Resource Center for Safe Schools

Linda Taylor
University of California, Los Angeles

Richard Verdugo
National Education Association

Darren Woodruff
American Institutes for Research

Anne Matthews-Younes
Substance Abuse and Mental Health Services Administration

The Center for Effective Collaboration and Practice

Principal Investigator: David Osher
Co-Project Director: Mary Quinn
Co-Project Director: David Osher
Research Team: Huda Aden, Kevin Dwyer, Stephanie Jackson, Cameron Nelson, David Osher, Chad Rodi, Lauren Stevenson
Editing/Formatting Team: Holly Baker, Eric Spears, DeWan Lee, Tony Johnson

Expert Panel Members for the *Early Warning Guide*

The expert panel included national experts from a variety of disciplines, as well as principals, teachers, pupil personnel staff, families, and youth.

J. Randy Alton, Teacher
Montgomery County, MD

George Batsche, Professor
University of South Florida

George Bear, Professor
University of Delaware

Renee Brimfield, Principal
Montgomery County, MD

Michael Bullis, Professor
University of Oregon

Andrea Canter,
Lead School Psychologist
Minneapolis, MN

Gregory Carter, Teacher
Richmond, VA

Deborah Crockett,
School Psychologist
Atlanta, GA

Scott Decker, Professor
University of Missouri
St. Louis

Maurice Elias, Professor
Rutgers University, NJ

Michael J. Furlong,
Associate Professor
University of CA
Santa Barbara

Susan Gorin, Executive Director
National Association of
School Psychologists
Bethesda, MD

Denise Gottfredson, Director
National Center for Justice
University of Maryland

Beatrix Hamburg, Professor
Cornell Medical Center, NY

Norris Haynes, Director
Center for School Action Research and
Improvement, Southern Connecticut
State University
Professor of Child and Adolescent
Psychiatry, Yale University Child
Study Center

DJ Ida, Director
Asian Pacific Development Center
Denver, CO

Yvonne Johnson, Parent
Washington, DC

Gil Kerlikowske,
Former Police Commissioner
Buffalo, NY

Paul Kingery, Director
Hamilton Fish National Institute on
School and Community Violence
Arlington, VA

Howard Knoff, Professor
University of South Florida

Judith Lee Ladd, President
American School Counselors
Association
Arlington, VA

Brenda Muhammad, Founder
Mothers of Murdered Sons &
Daughters
Vice Chair, Atlanta, GA School Board

J. Ron Nelson, Associate Professor
Arizona State University

Dennis Nowicki, Police Chief
Charlotte, NC

Scott Poland, Director
Psychological Services
Cyprus-Fairbanks ISD
Houston, TX

Gale Porter
American Institutes for Research

Elsa Quiroga, Student
University of California,
Berkeley
Graduate of Mount Eden High School

Michael Rosenberg, Professor
Johns Hopkins University

Mary Schwab-Stone, Associate
Professor
Yale University Child Study Center

Peter Sheras, Associate Director
Virginia Youth Violence Project
University of Virginia

Russell Skiba, Professor
Indiana University

Leslie Skinner, Assistant Professor
Temple University

Jeff Sprague, Co-Director
Institute on Violence and Destructive
Behavior
University of Oregon

Betty Stockton, School Psychologist
Jonesboro, AR

Richard Verdugo, Senior Policy
Analyst
National Education Association
Washington, DC

Hill Walker, Co-Director
Institute on Violence and Destructive
Behavior
University of Oregon

Index

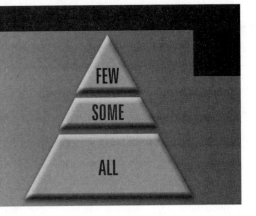

The letter "a" proceeding a page number indicates the material is located in the *Action Guide* on the accompanying CD-ROM.

G

gangs, 92

goals
  of action plans, 28
  checklist, 252
  counteracting resistance, 35
  defined, 21
  evaluating results, 37–38
  long-term focus, 6, 7

The Good Behavior Game, 155–157
  adapting, 156–157
  background, 155
  contact information, 155
  costs, 156
  features comparison, 132
  operations, 156
  outcomes, 157
  purpose, 155
  references/resources, 157
  required components, 157
  scope, 155
  targeted problems/risk factors, 155–156
  training, 156

grants. *See* federal funds

GrantsWeb, 58

Gun-Free Schools Act, a19

guns, 92

H

health education, 108

health services, 108

High/Scope Preschool Curriculum Framework, 158–161
  adapting, 159
  background, 158
  contact information, 158
  costs, 159
  features comparison, 132
  operations, 158
  outcomes, 159–160
  purpose, 158
  readiness determination, 159
  references/resources, 160–161
  required components, 159
  scope, 158
  targeted problems/risk factors, 158
  training, 159

hitting, chronic, 91

I

I Can Problem Solve (ICPS), 162–164
  adapting, 163
  background, 162
  contact information, 162
  costs, 163
  features comparison, 132
  operations, 163
  outcomes, 164
  purpose, 162
  readiness determination, 163
  references/resources, 164
  required components, 163
  scope, 162
  targeted problems/risk factors, 162
  training, 163

idea champions, 14

identification, a18–a19, a24

IEPs. *See* Individualized Education Programs (IEPs)

immediate interventions, a13, a20

imminent warning signs, a19–a20

indicators
  behavior (state-defined) example, 30
  defined, 21
  examples, 30, 31
  selecting data for, 29
  using, 29

Individualized Education Programs (IEPs), 84–85

individualized mental health services, a35–a36

Individuals with Disabilities Education Act (IDEA), a6, a24–a25, a32

instructional techniques, 85

intensive interventions, 7, 8, 101–120. *See also Appendix A; specific program names;* mental health services
  alternative programs/schools, 116–118
  barriers, overcoming, 102–105
  checklist, 265–266
  clinical mental health service needs, 101
  community-based, 118
  community schools and, 102, 110–111
  competing priorities and, 103
  coordinated school health model, 108–109
  culturally competent, 106
  defined, 9
  emotional disturbances and, 111–113